The Gold Star Mother
Pilgrimages of the 1930s

The Gold Star Mother Pilgrimages of the 1930s

Overseas Grave Visitations by Mothers and Widows of Fallen U.S. World War I Soldiers

John W. Graham

McFarland & Company, Inc., Publishers
Jefferson, North Carolina, and London

Quotations from Grace Ziegler's stories in the *Rockford Star* are copyright 2004 *Rockford Register Star*. Used with permission.

LIBRARY OF CONGRESS CATALOGUING-IN-PUBLICATION DATA

Graham, John W., 1961–
　　The Gold Star Mother pilgrimages of the 1930s : overseas grave visitations by mothers and widows of fallen U.S. World War I soldiers / John W. Graham.
　　　　p.　　cm.
　　Includes bibliographical references and index.

　　　　ISBN 0-7864-2138-X (softcover : 50# alkaline paper)

　　　1. World War, 1914–1918 — Women — United States.　2. World War, 1914–1918 — Psychological aspects.　3. Mothers of war casualties — Travel — France.　4. Grief.　I. Title.
D639.W7G55　2005
940.4'6'086540973 — dc22　　　　　　　　　　　　　2005007320

British Library cataloguing data are available

©2005 John W. Graham. All rights reserved

No part of this book may be reproduced or transmitted in any form or by any means, electronic or mechanical, including photocopying or recording, or by any information storage and retrieval system, without permission in writing from the publisher.

On the front cover: Maude Betterton at the grave of her son, Cherrill, at Meuse-Argonne American Cemetery in France *(National Archives and Records Administration)*

Manufactured in the United States of America

McFarland & Company, Inc., Publishers
　Box 611, Jefferson, North Carolina 28640
　　www.mcfarlandpub.com

To my mother, the memory of my father,
the soldiers who die in war,
and the mothers who mourn them.

Acknowledgments

I am most grateful to acknowledge the help of dozens of individuals in the researching and writing of this book. All of these people have contributed to whatever value the book has, yet I remain solely responsible for any mistakes, errors, or oversights.

First and foremost, I thank Alison Davis Wood. Alison produced, directed, and edited the documentary *Gold Star Mothers: Pilgrimage of Remembrance* for WILL-TV in Urbana, Illinois. She included me in every step of the film's production. I accompanied her on interviews from Washington, DC, to the Oregon high desert. She was good-natured, productive, and positive all through the process, and the final product is due far more to her efforts than my relatively minor contribution. My thanks also go to Tim Hartin from WILL-TV. Tim served as director of photography and accompanied Alison on all the shoots nationwide.

I would also like to thank all those at WILL-TV at the University of Illinois at Urbana-Champaign for making *Gold Star Mothers: Pilgrimage of Remembrance* a reality. Special thanks are due to Henry Frayne, at WILL, who introduced me to Alison back in 1999.

Holly Fenelon (Estes Park, Colorado), who has collaborated with the American Gold Star Mothers in writing a history of the organization, has been very helpful in sharing her expertise and research.

Descendants of several World War I figures were gracious enough to share their recollections with me. They include Elnora Davis McLendon, daughter of General Benjamin O. Davis Sr.; Anne Wolf, daughter of Captain Robert Ginsburgh; Mrs. Jane Wooten, Louis Gjosund, Janet Payne, Margaret Ramsey, Barbara Lepley, Frank Luke Jr., and several descendants of Joyce Kilmer.

I most especially thank Ed and Fred Bliss of Durand, Illinois, for sharing their stories of Grace and Louise Ziegler. The Ziegler family occupies a chapter of this book and is featured in the documentary. Ed Bliss shared his aunt Louise's scrapbook and other family photos very willingly.

William Stevens Prince of Bend, Oregon, wrote the first book on the pilgrimages, *Crusade and Pilgrimage*. He graciously shared his recollections and family mementoes at his home in Oregon in 1999.

At the National Archives, I want to thank Mitch Yockelson and Connie Potter. Both have published articles in the journal *Prologue* that aided my research. Mitch Yockelson was especially helpful with records at the archives, and both were interviewed for the documentary.

I would also like to thank all who shared their time and talents with the *Gold Star Mothers: Pilgrimage of Remembrance* production. I wish to thank Marvin Fletcher, professor of history at Ohio University in Athens, Ohio, for sharing his insights on the pilgrimages in general and on Gen. Benjamin O. Davis in particular. Edward "Mac" Coffman shared his time at his Lexington, Kentucky, home and provided a World War I education to all present. Rebecca Jo Plant, formerly of Vanderbilt University, Barbara Ransby, University of Illinois Chicago, and Lisa Budreau, Oxford College, all shared their expertise.

G. Kurt Piehler of the University of Tennessee deserves special thanks. He was interviewed for the documentary and arranged for its premiere at the Society of Military Historians' annual conference at Knoxville, Tennessee in May 2003.

I am especially grateful for the Gold Star mothers who agreed to share their experiences for the documentary. They include Theresa Davis, Winifred Lancy, Valerie May, Iris Walden, and Mary Wheeler. I have come to admire all the Gold Star mothers I've been fortunate enough to meet.

Staff at the following facilities aided my research: Herbert Hoover Presidential Library, West Branch, Iowa; National Archives in College Park, Maryland; Sagamore Hill National Historic Site, Long Island, New York; and the Military History Institute, Carlisle Barracks, Pennsylvania.

Steve Ruffin, Bob Kasprzak, and Jim Streckfus from the aviation journal *Over the Front* have provided valuable assistance. My article on Quentin Roosevelt's impact on the pilgrimages was published in the fall, 2004 issue.

I would like to thank Col. Anthony Corea and the staff at the American Battle Monuments Commission. Thanks also to Craig Buthod, mentor and director of the Louisville Free Public Library, for his encouragement. Several individuals in Cincinnati provided support and encouragement. They include Connie Menefee, Genevieve Pennington, and Jane Alden Stevens, a photography professor at the University of Cincinnati. I also thank Sandy Duwel and Janice Walton-Williams in the Document Delivery Department of the Public Library of Cincinnati and Hamilton County for their assistance. Thanks to Becky Kennedy, manager of my neighborhood Mariemont branch library, who invited me to speak on the pilgrimages not once but twice. I am grateful to everyone on my staff at the Public Library of Cincinnati and Hamilton County's Public Documents and Patents Department for listening to me talk about this project for several years.

Finally, thanks to my aunt Judy Murphy of Orlando, Florida, for reviewing the manuscript, and to my wife, Wendy Havlick, for her support and keen editorial assistance.

Contents

Acknowledgments	vii
Preface	1
Pilgrimage Chronology	5
1. What Were the Gold Star Pilgrimages?	11
2. The Great War	26
3. Pilgrimage Legislation: A Decade in the Making	50
4. Do-It-Yourself Pilgrimages	75
5. The Quartermaster Corps in Peace and War	95
6. Black Stars and Gold	116
7. Pilgrim Profile: Louise and Grace Ziegler	139
8. Party A	159
9. The Pilgrimage Experience	178
10. Conclusion	202
Notes	207
Bibliography	217
Index	223

Preface

I first learned of the Gold Star mothers and widows pilgrimages by accident. On the job as manager of the Public Library of Cincinnati and Hamilton County's Public Documents and Patents Department in 1998, I was scanning through an index to Congressional documents to answer a library patron's question. The index made reference to "Pilgrimage of Mothers and Widows." I had never heard of this event before, so I retrieved one of the documents referenced in the index. *Pilgrimage for the Mothers and Widows of Soldiers, Sailors, and Marine Forces now Interred in the Cemeteries in Europe*, issued as House of Representatives Document H. Doc. 71-1404. I was amazed. Published in 1930 by Congress, the document was a list of several thousand mothers of deceased World War I soldiers. The soldiers were all buried in Europe. The book listed the mother's name, home address, soldier's name, cemetery in which he was buried, and a simple yes-or-no column indicating if the mother wished a pilgrimage. I was instantly intrigued because I had never heard of such an event in American history.

I undertook a personal research journey, not with a book in mind at first, but with questions to answer. First, who were these women and what was a Gold Star mother? I learned that during the war, families used a red and white flag, with a blue star in the center, to indicate they had a son in the service. They replaced the blue star with a gold star if the soldier died in the war. This led to the name Gold Star mothers.

What were the pilgrimages? Who organized and paid for them? I learned that the Gold Star mother pilgrimages took place between 1930 and 1933. During those four years, the U.S. government funded, organized, and conducted trips for over 6,500 mothers and widows to American cemeteries in Belgium, England, and France.

Some questions were easy to answer with enough digging. I learned also that no amount of research can answer the most personal, final question: What was it like to stand at the grave of a son, buried far away in another country, and say goodbye?

The story of the Gold Star pilgrimages is full of individual grief and loss against a background of national issues and figures. Teddy Roosevelt, Fiorello LaGuardia, and Joyce Kilmer are as much a part of the pilgrimages as are average citizens Fred Ziegler and Laura Stevens. My book tries to balance the sphere of personal loss with the public sphere of politics and battles.

My research into this fascinating subject inspired me to write this book. There could well be 6,500 books, one for each pilgrim, but my goal was to write a book to capture both the public and the personal. I shared each step along with way with a friend, Henry Frayne, of Champaign, Illinois. Henry works for WILL, the PBS affiliate at the University of Illinois. He suggested this topic would make an engaging documentary. I agreed, and he introduced me to Alison Davis Wood at WILL-TV. Alison is an experienced, Emmy-Award–winning producer. She and WILL-TV agreed to make the documentary.

Making the *Gold Star Mothers: Pilgrimage of Remembrance* documentary was a joy. Alison and her colleagues were delightful to work with. Despite funding cuts and uncertainty, she coaxed the project along to completion. The final product, I must say, is terrific, and it is all due to Alison's efforts and the resources at WILL-TV. I was lucky enough to accompany Alison and Tim Hartin, director of photography, on several shoots across the country. I quickly learned what a grip does: serve as a glorified caddy. But I was happy to help lug camera equipment for the crew. The interviews with World War I experts and family members of Gold Star pilgrims helped with both the big picture and the smaller details.

The documentary premiered in Urbana-Champaign on Memorial Day 2003 and received nationwide PBS distribution in spring 2004. This book is an outgrowth of the documentary, yet it stands alone with plenty of original material and background information.

The pilgrimages remain for me a fascinating topic. They may be approached from any point of the political spectrum. Everyone seems to find that some aspect of the pilgrimages rings true in his or her own life. However, I don't attempt to overload the pilgrimage movement with an exhaustive search for meaning. Not only is that task better left to capable scholars, it will always miss the mark. The pilgrims themselves, by and large, sought personal solace and individual meaning. My aim is to let them tell their own stories wherever possible, through diaries, letters, newspaper accounts, and personal recollections. The Gold Star mothers and widows were strong, capable women. I've come to admire them, and their sons and husbands, during the past five years. I think readers will, too.

Pilgrimage Chronology

This selective chronology lists significant dates in the Gold Star pilgrimage movement. Newspaper clippings, army records, and published accounts furnished the information for the chronology.

1917

6 April	Congress declares war and the United States enters World War I.
13 June	Maj. Gen. John Pershing arrives in France.
14 July	First American casualty.
4 September	First American battle deaths.
6 November	Captain Robert L. Quiesser, an Ohio officer with two sons in the war, receives a design patent for the Blue Star service flag.

1918

5 February	Private Percy Stevens dies when his troopship, the *Tuscania*, is torpedoed off the Irish coast.
16 May	President Woodrow Wilson proposes the notion of the Gold Star in a letter to Dr. Anna Howard Shaw, chairperson of the Women's Committee of the Council of National Defense. The council agrees and publicizes later in May the wearing of the Gold Star to commemorate the loss of a family member in the war.
14 July	Quentin Roosevelt shot down and killed.
30 July	Joyce Kilmer killed in battle.

6 October	Second Lt. Erwin Bleckley killed on a mission to locate the "Lost Battalion." Bleckley posthumously received the Congressional Medal of Honor for his efforts.
11 October	Fred M. Ziegler killed in the Meuse-Argonne offensive.
13 October	Alexander Norris killed in battle.
10 November	Corporal Oscar Haug is wounded, later dies.
11 November	Armistice ends the war.

1919

6 January	Theodore Roosevelt dies.
19 February	Edith Roosevelt and her son Theodore Jr. visit Quentin's grave in France.
19 May	Fiorello La Guardia introduces first pilgrimage bill in Congress. It does not pass.

1920

5 September	Joyce Kilmer's parents visit his grave in France.

1921

Summer	King George V of England makes a pilgrimage to the battlefields and cemeteries of the war.

1923

4 March	The American Battle Monuments Commission is created by act of Congress.
Summer	30,000 people make a pilgrimage to the grave of British nurse Edith Cavell.

1924

19 February	The U.S. House of Representatives holds the first hearing on pilgrimage legislation. The bill in question does not become law.

1925

May and June	Gold Star mothers sail on a privately funded pilgrimage aboard United States Lines ships.

1927

September	20,000 Americans, including Gold Star Mothers, visit France as part of the American Legion's 2nd AEF.

1928

4 June	25 Gold Star mothers gather in Washington, DC, to plan a national Gold Star mothers association.
August	The British Legion organizes a pilgrimage of 11,000 members to cemeteries and battlefields in France and Belgium.

1929

5 January	American Gold Star Mothers, Inc., chartered in Washington, DC.
2 March	Pilgrimage legislation signed, Public Law 70-952.
July and August	First Australian War Graves pilgrimage to Europe.

1930

21 January	The House of Representatives holds a hearing to discuss appropriations to cover the pilgrimages.
5 February	The House of Representatives appropriates $5.3 million for Gold Star pilgrimages.
6 February	Senate passes pilgrimage legislation.
7 February	Mrs. Herbert Hoover draws lots to determine state order of pilgrimages.
16 April	Pilgrimage escort officers leave for Europe.
25 April	Army officers arrive in Europe for pilgrimage duty.
6 May	Party A is welcomed in New York City.
7 May	Party A sails for Europe.
16 May	Paris welcomes Party A.
18 May	First pilgrims visit graves at Suresnes Cemetery outside Paris.
22 May	German officers salute pilgrims at St. Mihiel.
23 May	Party B arrives in France.
30 May	Party A sails for America.
23 June	Pilgrim dies in Pullman railroad car on the way to New York City, first fatality.
1 July	Laura Stevens, with Party H, visits the grave of her son, Percy Stevens, in Brookwood American Cemetery, England.

7 July	First African American party of pilgrims gathers in New York City.
12 July	First black party, Party L, sails for Europe.
22 July	French welcome first party of African American pilgrims
3 August	Party L leaves France.
12 August	First black party returns to the United States.
14 August	First Gold Star mother dies in Europe, Mrs. Harriet Bates, Portage, Pennsylvania.
25 August	Noble Sissle greets second African American party in Paris, Party Q.
7 September	Second and final African American party leaves Europe.
12 September	Party T, final party of 1930, visits Paris.
16 September	Party Q arrives reaches America.
22 September	Party T leaves France. 3,653 Gold Star mothers and widows traveled to Europe in 1930, the first year of the pilgrimages.

1931

11 April	Pilgrimage officers sail for France.
20 April	Escort officers arrive in Paris.
8 May	Party A, 1931, leaves New York City.
17 May	Party A, 1931, spends its first day at the cemeteries.
27 May	Party A returns to Paris, while Party B prepares to leave the French capital.
5 June	Party A arrives back in New York City.
7 June	First African American party of 1931, Party E, arrives in Paris.
20 June	Party E leaves France.
21 June	Four French farmers die in a crash with a bus carrying Gold Star pilgrims.
10 July	The second African American group of 1931, Party K, sails for Europe.
17 August	Erwin Bleckley's mother visits the grave of her son, Lt. Erwin Bleckley.

	Pilgrimage Chronology
19 August	The final party of 1931, Party Q, sails for Europe.
6 September	The final party departs Paris for London, then returns to the United States. A total of 1,766 pilgrims sailed in 1931.

1932

17 May	Party A, the first group of 1932, sails for Europe.
24 May	First group arrives in France.
19 June	First African American group of the year arrives in Paris.
6 July	Louise and Grace Ziegler leave New York City for Europe with Party E.
19 July	The Zieglers visit Fred Ziegler's grave in the Meuse-Argonne cemetery.
5 August	Party E arrives back in the United States.
16 September	Last group of the year, Party E, returns to the United States. 566 women made their pilgrimages during 1932, the lowest number of any of the four years.

1933

18 January	Press accounts report five trips planned for 1933.
17 May	Party A sails with 130 aboard.
26 July	The last party of pilgrims leaves New York Harbor for Europe.
July	*Pilgrimage* film directed by John Ford premieres.
17 August	Party E, the last pilgrim party sails back to the United States with 169 aboard. A total of 669 pilgrims sailed in 1933, bringing the total number of pilgrims to 6,654.
24 August	Party E arrives back home in the United States.

1934

26 February	President Franklin Roosevelt signs Executive Order 6614 to transfer control of America's World War cemeteries from the War Department to the American Battle Monuments Commission later in 1934.

1935

3 January	Congressman John Dingell, Michigan, introduces a bill

	to pay Gold Star mothers who did not travel on a pilgrimage the amount it would have cost to send them to Europe. The bill failed to gain support and did not pass.
January	Philip Stevenson publishes "Gold Star Mother" in *Esquire* magazine.

1936

July	8,000 Canadians make the pilgrimage to Vimy Ridge, France, for unveiling of a memorial.
27 September	President Franklin Roosevelt establishes the last Sunday in September as Gold Star Mother's Day.

1941

Gold Star mother Henrietta Haug solicits letters from other Gold Star mothers and publishes them in her book, *Gold Star Mothers of Illinois: A Collection of Notes Recording the Personal Histories of the Gold Star Mothers of Illinois*. Mrs. Haug's son Oscar was killed in battle.

1958

21 July	Mathilda Burling, leader of the pilgrimage movement, dies at age 78.

1986

Crusade and Pilgrimage by William Stevens Prince is published. Mr. Prince is the grandson of pilgrim Laura Stevens of Bend, Oregon. It is the first book published on the pilgrimages.

2002

July	The Dusters, Quads, and Searchlights veterans group takes Gold Star mothers to Vietnam as part of its Operation Gold Star.

2003

26 May	The documentary *Gold Star Mothers: Pilgrimage of Remembrance* makes its broadcast premiere on WILL-TV in Urbana, Illinois, on Memorial Day.

1

What Were the Gold Star Pilgrimages?

The story of the Gold Star mothers and widows pilgrimages of the 1930s is as moving, and as important to American history, as when the pilgrimages first took place over 70 years ago. The Great War pilgrimage movement was both patriotic and profound. Yet the movement was also very personal. A mother mourned her son at his graveside half a world away from home.

The pilgrimages saw the expenditure of public funds for the relief of private grief. They also turned veteran army officers, for a few years, into tour guides for women the age of their own mothers or grandmothers. The officers did their jobs well; the pilgrimages worked. They succeeded not simply by moving a number of citizens from point A to point B and back again. Rather, they achieved the important personal goal of helping grieving mothers and widows come to terms with their losses and move on with their lives.

For 6,654 women, Gold Star mothers and widows pilgrimages were the answer to grief and loss. That figure is the total number of women who went on a pilgrimage. The Army's Quartermaster Corps organized and conducted the trips, which took place in the months from May through September, during the four-year period 1930 through 1933. Over half of the total, 3,653, sailed during the first year in one of 20 groups or parties. In 1931, another 1,766 had sailed. The smallest number of pilgrims, 566, sailed in 1932. By the start of 1933, 90 percent of these women who were going to Europe had already done so; just five parties of pilgrimages, 669 strong, decorated their loved ones' graves during the 1933 pilgrimage season.[1]

The government extended thousands more invitations to eligible women. Many, however, declined the offer. A total of 9,812 said "thanks but no thanks" to the chance to go on a pilgrimage. Old age and poor health probably accounted for the majority of this total.

The Gold Star

The story of the pilgrimages began with the Gold Star mothers, and their story began with the symbol of the gold star itself. The symbol originated during World War I as a uniquely American way to commemorate loss. (It should be noted World War I was not called World War I until World War II came along. It was called the Great War or the World War by many participants, terms that will often be used throughout this book.) The exact origin of the Gold Star symbol is open to debate. In late 1917, a group of Illinois families found a solution to the dark clothes of mourning adopted by many families, especially in Europe, when a soldier in the family had died in battle. A news story with a dateline of Chicago, November 12, 1917, was one of the earliest published accounts about the usage of the gold star for a symbol of mourning:

> A movement was begun here today for the substitution for the black garb of mourning, such as a Gold Star in memory of American soldier dead. The glory of death should be emphasized rather than its sadness. "The psychological effect of multitudes in mourning [clothes] is not good. Soldiers do not like it, and Germany forbids it."[2]

President Woodrow Wilson had much the same idea. He disliked the prospect of thousands or tens of thousands of black-clad relatives dotting the landscape. In a letter to Dr. Anna Howard Shaw dated May 16, 1918, Wilson outlined his ideas. Dr. Howard was chairperson of the Council of National Defense's Women's Committee.

"It has occurred to me," Wilson wrote,

> therefore that your own committee might think it timely and wise to give some advice to the women of the country with regard to mourning. My own judgment is that the English are treating it more wisely than the French. It may be that service badges, upon which the white stars might upon the occurrence of a death be changed into stars of gold, would be a very beautiful and significant substitute for mourning. What do you think? Can your committee wisely act in the matter?[3]

Wilson further added he felt it unwise for him to intercede personally in this issue.

1. What Were the Gold Star Pilgrimages?

Gold Star mothers, Grant Park, Chicago, 1918. President Woodrow Wilson advocated the gold star, worn as an armband, as a symbol of mourning. The public adopted the gold star rapidly, and these Chicago mothers wore the symbol in public even before World War I ended. (*Chicago Daily News* negatives collection, DN-0070373. Chicago Historical Society.)

Some view Wilson's efforts with a bit of cynicism. His behind-the-scenes approach strikes many as a bit too calculated. Professor Kurt Piehler from the University of Tennessee is a pilgrimage expert who sees Wilson's attempt as "... a very deliberate conscious effort to change mourning practices."[4] Women adopted the gold star so readily and universally, however, that the country was probably ready for such an alternative to traditional black dress.

The meaning of the symbol was clear during the war and remains so today. "The idea of the Gold Star was that of honor and glory accorded the person for his supreme sacrifice, rather than the sense of personal loss which would be represented by mourning symbols," the American Gold Star Mothers proclaimed.⁵

Regardless of the exact origin of the gold star, the service flag's origins are clearer. The flag was commonly flown by family members who had men in the armed forces. The flag had a red border with a blue star in the center of a white field. A silver star could be placed over the blue star to indicate a wounded soldier, the familiar gold one to take place of a blue star to indicate the serviceman had died. The army attributed the flag's original design to Capt. Robert L. Queisser of Cleveland, Ohio, who received a design patent for his creation on November 6, 1917. It was an instant success. The flag "has, however, taken such firm root in popular sentiment and has been of such beneficial influence that it is officially recognized, and everyone who is entitled to fly it is encouraged to do so."⁶

A brief look at a few wartime songs reveals not only the quick adoption of the gold star symbol but also how the focus on loss shifted from the family in general to the mother in particular.

A 1917 song, "There's a Service Flag Flying at Our House," is the earliest of three samples. With music by Al Brown and words by Thomas Hoier and Bernie Grossman, the song told the story of a proud family flying their service flag. The "our" in

Americans adopted the Blue Star service flag during World War I. Families displayed the flag to show a member of the household served in the armed forces. It quickly became the custom to replace the blue star with a gold one when the soldier died in the war. The Gold Star mothers derived their name from this widely accepted symbol of mourning. (American Legion and the U.S. Institute of Heraldry, Ft. Belvoir, Virginia.)

the song's title was significant. The service flag belonged to the family, not just to the mother. The song's chorus ran: "There's a service flag flying at our house / A blue star in a field of red and white / Father is so proud of what his boy has done / There's a tear in Mother's smile as she murmurs 'my son' / Perhaps he may return with fame and glory / But if by chance we lose him in the fight / There'll be a service flag flying at our home / And a new star in Heaven that night, that night."⁷ The cover to the sheet music showed a parade of confident doughboys marching down a broad boulevard, with three large service flags over the street.

The second example of the service flag song was "When a Blue Star Turns to Gold," written in 1918. It featured words and music by Theodore Morse and Casper Nathan. The song's chorus addressed loss. The image of the gold star is clearly accepted and established. Although the mother was the chief focus of the song, she is not the only one experiencing a loss; a girlfriend is mentioned. The song asked the listener to "picture a mother or a sweetheart, Proud tho' the worst has been told / Picture that scene, what it must mean / When a blue service star turns to gold." The chorus of the song explained its full meaning: "When a blue service star turns to gold / What a tale of affection is told! / Duty to country has cost one his all/While others, at home, are bowed down with the call / In their sorrow, the ones left behind/Voice a pray'r that is e'er borne in mind / Till souls meet on high, they must whisper 'goodbye' / When a blue service star turns to gold."⁸

A final song, "The Heavens Are a Mother's Service Flag," was published after the war ended in 1919. The song has words by Nathan A. Conney and music by J. Edward Woolley, with revisions by Paul L. Specht. In just two years' time from "There's a Service Flag Flying at Our House," several things had changed. First, the mother is now the sole focus of loss; she is even featured in the song's title. The song mentioned no other family members, and certainly no sweetheart. The attention is on loss, not simply on service. The song also repeated the idea of a star in heaven representing a dead soldier, whose blue star has been replaced by a gold one on the now-familiar service flag. The song's chorus illustrated these changes: "Each little mother who gave up a boy / Is a 'hero' as brave as can be / Though she never fought with sword or gun / Her deeds are greater when the battle is done / The stars above shine for heroes so brave / Unrewarded their burdens they drag / But God up on high, keeps a mark in the sky / For the Heavens are a mother's service flag."⁹

This trio of popular tunes captured the spirit of the era. Americans were, by and large, eager to fight in the Great War. Families knew loss was inevitable, but their faith was ready to sustain them. For the mothers, however, flags and symbols were not enough to help cope with their loss.

Mothers who had experienced the loss of a son in battle began to seek solace in each other. One gets the impression Gold Star mother groups began to spring up in an organic, unplanned fashion throughout the country during and after the war. The American Gold Star Mothers was organized by a group of 25 mothers from the Washington, DC, area in 1928. The organization was incorporated under the laws of the District of Columbia. Most of the smaller, local chapters affiliated themselves with this national organization soon after its founding.[10]

The organization still exists today, based in Washington, DC, and still carries out its mission of comfort to its members and service to the community. Admission as a member of the organization could not come at a higher price. The full membership requirement according to the association's website reads as follows:

> Natural mothers, who are citizens of the United States of America or of the Territorial or Insular Possessions of the United States of America, whose sons or daughters served and died in the line of duty in the Armed Forces of the United States of America or its Allies, or died as a result of injuries sustained in such service, are eligible for membership in American Gold Star Mothers, Inc. Adoptive or Stepmothers who reared the child from the age of five years, whose natural mother is deceased, are also eligible under the above conditions.

It should be noted any mother who lost a child in the military may be considered a Gold Star mother, even if she does not formally join the organization.

The members hold an annual convention where, during official ceremonies, all the women dress in white. Several of the mothers sat down for an interview during their annual convention in Knoxville, Tennessee, in June 2001. All but one was a Vietnam Gold Star mother, but their interviews for *Gold Star Mothers: Pilgrimage of Remembrance* showed how much they had in common with their World War I–era counterparts. Valerie May lost her son in Vietnam. She finds comfort in their group's annual meetings. "The love and friendship are just unreal," she said.[11] "It's just that there's a closeness here that until you experience it, you really can't know what it is," she added.[12]

Her fellow Gold Star mother Theresa Davis agreed. The Massachusetts mother spoke of the bond among all the mothers who had lost children in war. Some mothers choose not to join. She joined the group "because it's very comforting to be around people who are in the same position as you are. They all lost a child in the war. And a lot of people you can't talk to them about it. The Gold Star mothers you can."[13]

The Gold Star mothers have always been more concerned about easing the suffering of others than about helping themselves, however. Nevertheless, the mothers found in lobbying Congress for pilgrimages during the 1920s, they needed all their individual and collective efforts to make the trips a reality.

A Decade in the Making

Hundreds of families visited their loved ones' graves at their own expense almost as soon as the armistice was signed. Two of America's most prominent families were included: the parents of poet Joyce Kilmer and Edith Roosevelt, mother of Lt. Quentin Roosevelt and wife of the late President Theodore Roosevelt. These "do-it-yourself" pilgrimages are a fascinating topic in their own right and are the subject of Chapter 4.

However, most Americans were neither Roosevelts nor Kilmers. They needed assistance to make a pilgrimage to Europe. The Gold Star mothers and their supporters turned their attention toward Congress. New York Congressman Fiorello La Guardia introduced the first bill in Congress to sponsor a pilgrimage to Europe. La Guardia's 1919 bill called for free trips for mothers and fathers to France to visit their sons' graves. (The vast majority of American dead were buried in France.) La Guardia was a decorated war hero who would go from his service in Congress to become the colorful Depression-era mayor of New York City.

La Guardia's bill was noteworthy for two reasons. First, it included the fathers, not just the mothers, among the pilgrims. Second, it went absolutely nowhere in Congress. La Guardia's measure had little support and was also premature, something he himself acknowledged later in his career. In 1919, not all the soldiers' bodies had been permanently buried. After some substantial and acrimonious debate, the government gave the next-of-kin a choice: leave the body overseas for permanent burial in an American cemetery or have the body brought back to the family for burial. About one-third of the families, or around 30,000, chose permanent burial in Europe.

Congress was not finished with the pilgrimage issue. It considered pilgrimages in a series of hearings in 1924 and again in 1928. The measure was approved in 1929 but only after a decade of debate.

Eligibility was the key issue in later bills. Fathers were out, but soldiers' widows who had not remarried were in. Stepmothers and adoptive mothers were included under some very narrow circumstances. Logistics were another big concern. The military at first did not want the job of tour guide. The Red Cross was suggested, but it was lukewarm on the issue.

The Army's Quartermaster Corps ended up with the job, and ended up doing it superbly. Even a decade in Congress was not enough to resolve all the issues. Congress amended the original pilgrimage act at least three different times, the last one coming after the first group of pilgrims had already sailed for France. The cost of the trips, however, was never really at issue. The government was running a surplus and had very few qualms about appropriating money for the pilgrimages once they were approved. Professor Kurt Piehler in his interview for *Gold Star Mothers: Pilgrimage of Remembrance* realized "the government did not try to be cheap about this."[14]

Pilgrimage A to Z

President Calvin Coolidge signed the pilgrimage bill into law in March 1929, shortly before his term of office ended and 10 years after La Guardia first introduced it. The army immediately began its plans to organize and conduct the pilgrimages. However, among the many good decisions was one bad one. The War Department declared black pilgrims would be segregated from the white ones.

No amount of protest from the black pilgrims themselves or from the NAACP could change the decision. Many black mothers and widows canceled their trips. The army and the bulk of American society was segregated at the time. In 1930 Americans did not fight together in the segregated armed forces, and the mothers of the fallen soldiers were not allowed to mourn together either.

Although the pilgrimage parties were segregated, that did not necessarily mean they were homogenous groups of women. They came from all walks of life and from all sets of circumstances. Many were immigrants from the same European shores to which they now returned. Others were from small towns who had never been outside the county where they were born or raised. "There were college-trained mothers and widows who often helped their conducting officers translate a rapid flow of French words from the mouth of a harassed traffic officer, and others who had difficulty comprehending even the simplest English," observed one of these conducting officers.[15] In the world of 1930, in fact, the pilgrim parties, although segregated by race, would have been viewed as diverse and multicultural.

What took place on a pilgrimage? What did the mothers see and do? What type of food did they eat, and in what hotels did they stay? Those answers started in the offices of the Quartermaster Corps, an organization accustomed to moving troops and supplies great distances. Before the pilgrimages began, the Corps hired dozens of additional staff to handle correspondence with tens of thousands of family members. Invitations were extended, tickets supplied, and arrangements finalized for some 6,000 pilgrims.

After accepting her invitation, each woman received a comprehensive packet from the government. It contained a check to cover meals and incidentals on her trip to New York City, a train ticket, and a unique Gold Star Mothers and Widows badge. Each pilgrim wore her badge, which was a small gold medallion suspended from a red, white, and blue ribbon, from the time she left home until she returned. All arrangements were designed not only to make the pilgrimage as easy as possible but also to ensure no out-of-pocket expense was necessary. The army realized it had to

> provide custom fees, tips for bell-boys and maids at hotels and on the boat, tips for porters, waiters, stewards on the steamer, bath and laundry, steamer chairs and rugs, drugs and medicines, to say nothing of interpreters and guides, all the railroad and steamship fares, all the automobile and bus transportation, and many other incidentals too numerous to mention.[16]

Once the trips began, officers met each woman at the train station as she arrived in Manhattan and escorted her to her hotel. All baggage was checked and checked again, not only to make sure no item was left behind but also to make sure no woman took more than she was allotted to bring.

North Dakota pilgrim Eva Trowbridge recalled:

> All our baggage was tagged for the hotel in New York City and we were taken such good care of that we were sure to be all right and land safe and when we went on the ship our baggage was tagged again. We never had to look after our luggage or anything, army officers took care of that.[17]

Parties often received an official welcome ceremony at City Hall in New York. From there, the women were taken to Hoboken Harbor in New Jersey, where they boarded one of the luxury ships of United States Lines. United States Lines, an American-flag carrier, transported all pilgrim parties during their trips. The pilgrims traveled in cabin class, the first-class accommodations of the day. Service was lavish on the voyage, which lasted about one week. The liner often had teas or special dinners in each group's honor. The daily printed menu from one 1932 voyage included several kinds of roasts, fish, salads, and even a dessert called bombe St. Honore.[18]

Most ships docked at Cherbourg, on a peninsula of land on the northwest corner of France. Parties boarded small boats to take them to land, and French officials cleared each party through customs quickly. Parties boarded special "boat trains" for the four-hour trip to Paris. Paris was the base of operations for each party. Important ceremonies were planned in the French capital city, and the army had already established the Graves Registration Headquarters there, too.

Pilgrims arrived by train in Paris at the Gare des Invalides, a station generally reserved for VIP travelers. There the party boarded waiting buses for a night or two in a first-class Paris hotel. Parties were separated based on what cemeteries the women were to visit. (There are eight permanent American World War I cemeteries in Europe.) In some instances, women bound for specific cemeteries stayed in different hotels for ease of logistics. Mrs. Trowbridge recalled how members of her party were given different color badges while still on the Paris boat-train to indicate which cemetery each would visit. "Mine was blue, some had pink, some lavender, in fact every color. The blue were all to go in the same bus to the same hotel" for travel to the designated cemetery.[19]

On the morning of their first full day in Paris, the women attended an orientation meeting with one of their escort officers. Depending on the day of the week, each party paid a ceremonial visit to the Arc de Triomphe. The party chose one of its own as the honor pilgrim, who was responsible for laying a wreath on France's Tomb of the Unknown Soldier.

The whole concept of a tomb to honor an unknown warrior was uniquely a Great War development. With millions of unidentified war dead in all nations, each country had no choice but to build a monument to honor one of the fallen to represent the many.

After this brief ceremony, the party left for a tea in its honor, usually at the nearby Restaurant Laurent. French and American dignitaries were often on hand at this and other welcoming ceremonies. Gen. John Pershing, America's Great War hero, spoke at a number of these gatherings. He told a group of mothers in 1930, "I greet with reverence these mothers of the brave who sleep here. They inspired their sons with courage and fortitude."[20] Following their tea, the mothers did a bit of sight-seeing before returning to their hotels for dinner. Schedule permitting, more sight-seeing followed the next day, including sights such as the Eiffel Tower, the palace at Versailles, or Napoleon's Tomb.

Following these preliminaries, each group prepared to leave Paris for its cemetery. Each group traveled by bus. Along with the pilgrims, an escort officer, driver, interpreter, and one or more nurses accompanied each group. These groups averaged around 30 women but ranged from fewer than a dozen to 75 or more. The bus took a leisurely route from Paris, often making a stop for lunch and tea. The final destination was a hotel nearby the cemetery, which the women could use as a base of operations for several days' worth of visits.

"After a good night's sleep, each group of mothers and widows, in charge of an officer of the Regular Army," an officer wrote about this phase of the pilgrimages,

> will proceed, by motor bus, to a small town in the vicinity of the cemetery to be visited, the establishing of this town as a temporary headquarters making it possible for the pilgrims to visit the final objective of their trip with as little difficulty and fatigue, and as much comfort, as possible, for the period of time to be spent in the immediate vicinity will be about seven days.[21]

Whether the women felt either fatigue or comfort is open to speculation. Very few kept written accounts, and even fewer have been published. The published ones refrain from sharing the emotions and feelings of the graveside visit. That the pilgrims felt a mix of gratitude, pride, and relief is beyond question. Perhaps anything more would be impossible to share, if it could or even should be shared at all.

Each group of pilgrims visited its cemetery for several days in a row. The pilgrims had approximately one hour per day for a graveside visit, as well as time to tour nearby historic and wartime sites. The pilgrims who shared their feelings, if they shared them at all, described these visits in a very matter-of-fact style. "We put flowers on our loved ones' graves three different days, and the fourth day we paid our last visit to the Somme Cemetery on the way back to Paris. The cemetery is such a beautiful place and so well kept," one Illinois pilgrim remembered.[22]

The army overlooked no detail in these visits. Escort officers and nurses stood by, if needed. An official photographer took each mother's photo at her son's grave and gave her a copy of the picture. "We found our government had a fresh wreath of flowers for us to place on the graves," recalled a pilgrim, "a camp chair at each grave and a flag on the grave of each mother's son, who was in the group."[23] The larger cemeteries, especially the Meuse-Argonne, had rest facilities built for the parties.

Mothers expressed serious concern over the condition of the cemeteries. Would they be in good condition? Were the markers in disrepair? Some had been frightened by reports on the makeshift postwar cemeteries. These were just temporary burial grounds, but fresh mounds of earth and wooden crosses appalled some early pilgrims shortly after the war.

An army officer summarized the experience all pilgrims probably shared through the eyes of a fictionalized Mrs. Brown.

> And as she looks around [the cemetery] to drink in the beauty of the scene as a whole, Mrs. Brown sees the unfurled Stars and Stripes of Old Glory, floating in the breeze and symbolizing our nation's tender and protective care for this bivouac of its soldier dead, an interest that will continue in its zeal through all the coming years.[24]

Perhaps something else was at work here, too. Many people saw the pilgrimages in a different light. The most basic thesis was an attempt to attach a larger, nationalistic meaning to America's involvement in the war. Many did wish to remember the soldier dead in heroic light, and the dead doughboys certainly deserved this honor.

> So, by sending these mothers on pilgrimages, I think that the government was in fact trying to restore valor to what had become widely regarded as a war that just seemed in many ways futile.... By celebrating the sacrifices in that kind of fashion, I think there was an attempt to restore a sense of integrity, of honor, of valor, to the war effort,[25]

observed Rebecca Jo Plant, formerly of Vanderbilt University, in her interview for *Gold Star Mothers: Pilgrimage of Remembrance*. The mothers and widows, for their part, would have agreed wholeheartedly.

With their sense of valor restored, if indeed it had ever left them, the mothers began to make their way back to Paris. Parties again took time for sight-seeing and took a day or two to arrive back in the French capital. Battlefields were a common stop. In many places, nature had begun to reclaim these damaged areas. In other locations, however, they found trenches and other wartime areas virtually unaltered since the armistice. "As we were taken over much of the ground where our boys fought," recollected Mrs. J. L. Davis, "we realized to a small extent the awfulness of war. Beyond Verdun there were still traces of the shell holes, a few tanks and devastated towns."[26]

The pilgrims developed a close bond with each other on the trips. Battlefield visits probably enhanced this closeness. They understood the loss each other suffered, and they spent many weeks in each others company. The parties developed a sort of cohesion not unlike that which characterized the units in which their sons fought and died. Many developed lifelong friendships. Agnes Joos and Mrs. Kendall were roommates on a pilgrimage. "We became good friends and saw each other several times before she passed away," Mrs. Joos remembered.[27]

Once the parties arrived back in Paris, they checked into the same hotels they had stayed in during their first stop. Time was available for a little more sight-seeing and shopping before the parties made their way to

Cherbourg for the trip back to America. These side trips and diversions were carefully planned. Stops at museums, battlefields, and department stores in no way diminished the true meaning of the pilgrimages. The army and mothers who had already made personal pilgrimages to Europe quickly realized trips focused solely on grief and loss would defeat the purpose of hope and uplift for the pilgrims, especially when the women would be away from home for over a month.

Diversions were necessary, and sight-seeing and shopping served a purpose.

> One is full of attention for these venerable Mothers, and in order that their journey would not leave them only sad memories, one shows them the treasures of France; the Louvre, Versailles, Fountainbleu; sights of Art and Beauty, which will leave a luminous trace in their modest existence, observed one French newspaper.[28]

There was also, schedule permitting, time to meet some of the Americans in Paris.

Thelma "Tommie" Edwards, a popular singer and dancer, entertained a group of mothers from her hometown of Buffalo, New York, at her Paris apartment on July 7, 1930. Edwards was an internationally known performer who left Paris shortly after the gathering for a leading role in the Broadway production of *The Desert Song*. In what was reported as "the only social function by a private individual for Gold Star Mothers permitted by the Government," Edwards hosted 18 women for donuts and coffee. At the small party, Tommie's manager suggested she sing a song, and Edwards complied. In what must have been a delight for the Buffalo women, "the Broadway favorite turned bashful, closed the shutters to her flat to keep out the noise, switched out the lights, and leaned her chestnut brown head against the green door of the modern parlor and sang the "Pagan Love Song.'"[29]

Even with this unique entertainment, the pilgrims were on a tight schedule. They weren't allowed to linger in Tommie's modern parlor for long. "Lt. William J. Moroney pulled his watch on the party in the midst of their *degustation* and bustled them back to their hotels for dinner."[30]

All pilgrims, not just Tommie Edwards's Buffalo guests, took the train to Cherbourg from Paris for their trip home. The voyage home took a little longer, perhaps seven or eight days, than the trip to Europe. They stayed a night or two in New York City before catching trains for their final, separate trips back home.

The women could not have been more pleased and comforted. "It was all a glorious trip from start to finish; everything was planned so well by the government as to care and courteous treatment. We were looked after all the time to see that we were comfortable, to see we were provided for, and taken care of," Mrs. Trowbridge wrote in her hometown newspaper when she returned.[31]

Other Stories

Each pilgrimage party was unique, and each pilgrim had a personal story to tell. A Winnebago Indian woman, Kate Mike, visited France to decorate her son's grave. Mrs. Mike dressed in her tribe's native garb and caught the eye of several reporters, both for her clothing and for her limited knowledge of English.

A Florida woman, Anna Platt, suffered a heart attack at her son's grave. She survived and recuperated sufficiently to make the journey back home. (The army was especially worried about this type of incident, but it was extremely rare.)

Two members of the first group of pilgrims, Party A in 1930, could not have been more different from each other. Sarah Thompson was the wife of a powerful Manhattan businessman and the mother of an officer. Minnie Throckmorton from a Nebraska hamlet was widowed, and her son had been an enlisted man. Yet both were united by the confusion surrounding hasty wartime burials. Each woman's son's remains were misidentified and both were in fact buried in graves with the wrong names. The army resolved each of these mistakes well before the pilgrims sailed, but the experiences underscore how so many uncommon experiences were common for this group of women.

The Gold Star mothers also numbered among them the story of America's best-loved poet of the day, Joyce Kilmer. (Kilmer's "Trees," "I think that I shall never see / A poem lovely as a tree," is still recited today.) Kilmer cheerfully volunteered for duty overseas. Sgt. Kilmer was a real soldier, not a pretend one, and he died fighting shoulder to shoulder with an officer who emerged as one of the central figures in World War II intelligence circles. Although his mother was a Gold Star mother, she chose not to take part in the organized pilgrimages. She and Sgt. Kilmer's father had already visited their son's grave.

Finally, the pilgrimages included many stories of women who were born in Germany and lost their sons in a fight against their former homeland. Louise Ziegler was one such German-born woman. She lost her son, Fred, during the heaviest fighting of the Meuse-Argonne campaign. Her daughter Grace accompanied Louise on her own pilgrimage (at family expense, since the organized pilgrimages provided funds only for the mother or widow).

The story of each Gold Star mother is both intensely personal and tragically universal. The women on the pilgrimages were a distinct group with a unique experience, yet it was the common human experiences of love and loss that brought them together and awarded them their place in history.

2

The Great War

The story of the Gold Star mother pilgrimages begins with the story of World War I. It is more than merely a recount of major battles, famous generals, and important treaties. It is equally the story of individual sacrifice and loss, of dying alone but never being forgotten, and of personal choices with national consequences.

Before there could be a pilgrimage of any kind, there had to be American graves in foreign lands. Before these burials, tens of thousands of Americans would lose their lives in France, Belgium, Russia, and the dangerous waters of the North Atlantic. A European war raged for almost three full years even before the United States sent its troops overseas. This chapter tells several separate but closely related stories. There is no need to retell the story of America's participation in World War I in great detail. However, a mother's pilgrimage finds its roots in a son's death, and the deaths of several doughboys are worth full attention. (*Doughboy* was the generic American word for a Great War soldier.) Wartime burial of the dead was both an immediate concern and an issue that stirred an intense national debate. Finally, the cemeteries where the troops were buried and which the pilgrims visited merit a closer examination.

War 101

America declared war on Germany and its allies on April 6, 1917. President Wilson asked Congress for a declaration of war just six months after winning his second term in office. One of his campaign slogans was "he kept us out of war." No-holds-barred German submarine warfare was the chief reason Wilson and Congress had no choice but to join the Great War. The Germans had hoped to sink enough Allied ships, including American merchant ships, to win the war outright before America could turn the tide.

The Germans were very aware of bringing the United States into the war. "We had to keep the prospects of American intervention steadily before our eyes," German Field Marshal Paul von Hindenburg said.[1] Hindenburg's remarks were prophetic, but Germany and its enemies had no way of knowing what the war held when America entered it.

The war the United States joined in spring 1917 had started in a lightning manner but had hardened into the muddy, brutal stalemate of trench warfare. After the assassination of Austria-Hungary's Archduke Ferdinand in 1914, European alliances precipitated a continental crisis. Germany felt a quickly mobilized attack through neutral Belgium could knock the French out of the war in short order. With France subdued, the German goal was to mobilize against France's ally Russia and defeat it in a war on the eastern front.

Neither plan worked. The German advance almost succeeded but became bogged down in northern and eastern France. Both sides held fast, digging a virtually continuous series of trenches from the English Channel to the Swiss border. Germany did eventually defeat Russia, which collapsed under the weight of war and revolution in 1917. While revolutionaries fought for control in Russia, Germany was free to direct its troops against France on the western front. Germany hoped its final push in the west, coupled with its submarine attacks at sea, would enable it to win the war. This was the conflict the United States joined in 1917.

What exactly America had to offer was unclear when Wilson received his declaration of war. "Many assumed that the United States would simply offer naval help, financial support, and war supplies," observed leading World War I historian David F. Trask.[2] The American military in 1917 was small and somewhat backward. The Regular Army had approximately 108,000 men in uniform, and many of them were busy chasing Pancho Villa through Mexico. In terms of manpower, America offered its allies what was then only the 17th largest military in the world.[3]

War matériel did not greatly improve America's position. When war began, the United States had just a few dozen aircraft in service, and all were classified as obsolete or obsolescent.[4] Airplanes were just one part of the picture, however.

World War I featured new and deadly weapons trained against troops in unprecedented lethality and effectiveness. Men died in ways they had never died before, in numbers greater than any contemporary participants could imagine. High-explosive artillery blew soldiers to bits. German U-boats torpedoed ships, sending men to their deaths in the frigid North

Atlantic waters. Poison gas stung their eyes, burned their throats, and, after hours or days of agony, stopped their lungs from working. Tens of thousands of men simply sank in the mud in Belgium and France, and their bodies have still never been found.

The Germans pioneered the use of the portable flamethrower, a truly evil weapon capable of dousing enemy troops with a shower of burning oil in close combat. A weapon as common as the machine gun killed men in record numbers. Machine guns killed hundreds of thousands of men on both sides as troops went "over the top" to attack fortified defensive positions. (The phrase "over the top" is a World War I invention. It meant troops left the relative safety of their muddy trenches and climbed over the top to charge the enemy in its equally fortified position.)

All these weapons, and the mass slaughter they created, made the war unprecedented in its day. "The machine gun alone makes it so special and unexampled that it simply can't be talked about as if it were another one of the conventional wars of history," noted Paul Fussell in his landmark book, *The Great War and Modern Memory*.[5]

It is no wonder most Americans had little idea what they were facing as they prepared to sail over there. The combination of a small military force and new weapons meant the war was a very dangerous place indeed. In other words, the United States "found itself on a futuristic battlefield it had not prepared for, one that it did not anticipate, and that the Marines [and other troops] who were there paid the price in blood."[6]

The men of the World War I generation, with some exceptions, responded enthusiastically to America's entry into the war. The Wilson administration decided American troops overseas, rather than simply naval or financial support, was the best way to win the war. Men enlisted readily in most areas. A draft was initiated to meet manpower quotas. Although it met with some resistance, the efforts were largely successful.

The military was generally satisfied with the caliber of men it received. However, one report noted after the war a number of less than desirable specimens came from states such as Arizona and California, states that had become noted as health resorts.[7] Overall, however, the quality and quantity of troops was enough to fill the bill.

"No one wanted to be termed a slacker, so men joined up to fight," William Stevens Prince observed in his interview for *Gold Star Mothers: Pilgrimage of Remembrance*.[8] Self-styled patriots held "slacker raids" in major cities to round up any draft-age men who did not appear to being doing their share.

The post–Vietnam War generations simply find it hard to imagine the patriotism and war fever World War I generated. Only the patriotism unleashed after the terrorist events of September 11, 2001, offers any glimpse into this lost nationalistic fervor. America was on crusade, most people believed, and the ready assumption was every red-blooded man wanted to see part of the action. Religious leaders and members of the most prominent families stood ready to reinforce this mindset. "Every man ... would be saying he wished he were here, and every man worth his salt would mean it," Father Francis Duffy of the 27th Division told his men during services in France on St. Patrick's Day, 1918.

> The leading men of our country had called us to fight for human liberty and the rights of small nations, and if we rallied to that noble cause we would establish on our own country and on humanity in favor of the dear land from which so many of us had sprung, and which all of us loved.[9]

The notion of being called by the "leading men" to take any course of action seems positively antiquated today; however, it was precisely the leading men of the day who readily joined the war effort.

One such leading man was Lt. Quentin Roosevelt, the youngest son of former president Teddy Roosevelt. The young Roosevelt enthusiastically joined the service and became a pilot. He pulled as many strings as possible, not to avoid combat but rather to get into battle. His story illustrated the combative spirit and bravery that many Americans brought to World War I.

In a letter home to his family, Quentin described his first encounter with German anti-aircraft fire after his assignment to the 95th Aero Squadron. "It is really exciting at first when you see the stuff bursting in great black puffs around you," Quentin wrote, "but you get used to it after fifteen minutes."[10]

To get Quentin Roosevelt, Father Duffy, and the rest of these troops overseas, the United States created the American Expeditionary Force, the AEF, as the military establishment to fight the war. Gen. John J. "Black Jack" Pershing was placed in charge of the AEF, and he arrived in France with a small staff in June 1917.

Once the volunteers and draftees were formed into units in the United States, the task ahead was getting these men to France in one piece. The Allies developed an oceangoing convoy system to escort the troopships to Europe through U-boat-infested waters. By and large, this mission was a resounding success.

At least 370 Americans, however, were killed in six separate attacks on Allied shipping. Two attacks were especially deadly. The *Ticonderoga* was sunk, and 101 doughboys lost their lives. The *Tuscania* attack was far more serious, with over 200 officers and men killed. A German U-boat torpedoed the liner between the coasts of Scotland and Ireland on February 5, 1918. The *Tuscania* was a British oceanliner leased by Cunard for use as a troopship. The ship carried over 2,000 men, and most survived the attack. Some survivors were picked up by escort destroyers, while hundreds of men not only made their way to lifeboats but also survived the rugged shores and violent waves to reach land. Although the *Tuscania* carried men from many units, both British and American, troops from the 20th Engineers predominated. Most were loggers from the Pacific Northwest, sent to Europe to cut timber for the war effort.

One boy who didn't reach shore alive was Percy Stevens from Bend, Oregon. Stevens's body eventually washed up on the Scottish coast. People from nearby Port Charlotte held services for many of the dead. The Scottish townspeople had no American flag, so they made their own out of red, white, and blue strips of cloth. Stevens was buried on February 13 in a village cemetery overlooking Kilnaughton Bay, alongside 78 of his fellow soldiers.

Percy Stevens's death and his mother's subsequent pilgrimage are perhaps the most well-documented Gold Star mother story. William Stevens Prince's 1986 *Crusade and Pilgrimage* was the first published, book-length account of the pilgrimages. Equal parts personal narrative and legislative history, *Crusade and Pilgrimage* is a readable, well-illustrated look at the pilgrimage movement.

Prince was the nephew of Percy and Laura Stevens's grandson. Prince's book is both a personal narrative and professional study. He retraced Percy's final days, photographing the cemetery where his uncle was first buried. From his book, he tells of his grandmother's silence on the matter. Prince recalled how his grandmother, whom he called "Grannie," rarely spoke to him about her experiences, and he is able to devote just one sentence of his book about her reactions at the cemetery. (Laura Stevens, like most pilgrims, left no written account, letters, or diaries about her trip.)

For every boy like Percy who did not reach Europe, tens of thousands of men did. By the end of 1917, 183,000 Americans had joined Gen. Pershing "over there." By summer 1918, troops were arriving at a tide-turning pace. Over 313,000 safely reached Europe in July 1918 alone, and over 2 million Americans were in France by the end of the war. Men, not matériel, were America's primary contribution to the war effort. "But the most valuable resource we had were the soldiers we sent," observed Edward "Mac" Coffman, a leading World War I historian.[11] The basic unit these arrivals joined was the combat division. American divisions, at full strength, numbered some 28,000 troops. Huge by European standards, each American division also carried impressive firepower, including 24

155mm howitzers, 48 75mm guns, 260 machine guns, and some 17,000 rifles. The AEF had 42 such divisions at war's end. Plans called for up to 80 divisions in 1919, and an even 100 in place by January 1920. (In some ways, the Allies were surprised when the war ended in late 1918, given their preparations for a longer conflict.)

Regardless of the numbers, the European Allies were delighted to see American troops flooding European shores. "They were fresh bodies," our Allies observed. "The French were very enthusiastic, and so were the English, when the Americans came in," Mac Coffman noted.[12]

America's war involvement was more than the number of divisions in place or the number of armies formed. It is the story of individuals. It is the stories of men like Quentin Roosevelt and Percy Stevens, and any story of the Great War must also include stories of men like Erwin Bleckley, Alexander Norris, Earl Miller, and Edward Pennington. All died in battle, under different conditions but in service to a common mission.

Perhaps the most well-known of the four was Erwin Bleckley. Nowhere was the American fighting spirit better demonstrated than in the story of the Lost Battalion. The so-called Lost Battalion was neither a full battalion, nor was it ever really lost. Elements of the 77th Division jumped off in an assault in the Argonne Forest on October 2, 1918. Approximately 700 men became cut off from flanking units, and German defenders quickly surrounded them. Germans used mortars, machine guns, and even newly developed flamethrowers against the isolated Americans. The Americans fought off numerous counterattacks and refused to surrender. They were eventually rescued five days later, on October 7. The 194 survivors were tired, hungry, thirsty, and out of ammunition.

If the Lost Battalion wasn't exactly lost, it did prove rather difficult to locate. American pilots flew a number of sorties to locate and resupply the men. The flyers not only hoped to pinpoint the men but also attempted to drop rations and supplies on their position. Two such pilots were Lt. Herman Goettler and his observer, Lt. Erwin Bleckley. Flying their two-seater DeHavilland DH-4, the noted "Flying Coffin" due to its tendency to burst into flames when hit by gunfire, the men crisscrossed the countryside trying to locate the Lost Battalion. When their first mission failed, the two volunteered for a second sortie. The men returned to the battlefield, flying so low through a valley that German gunners actually fired down on their aircraft. The German fire was too intense, and the DH-4 was shot down.

Neither man survived the crash, but Bleckley's notes were sufficient to allow fellow American troops to locate the Lost Battalion. Both Goettler and Bleckley received the Congressional Medal of Honor posthumously. Goettler's body was returned to the United States; Bleckley's was buried in the Meuse-Argonne American Cemetery.

Fliers like Goettler and Bleckley drew the public's imagination during the war. However, it was accurate and deadly field artillery that probably killed more troops (on both sides) than any other weapon. A trio of cases proves the point. Earl Miller of Raymond, Illinois, was one fatality of German artillery. "A shrapnel hit my son. He died at first aid. They all ducked, but alas it took him," his mother, Sophia Miller, wrote in 1941.[13]

Mrs. Miller's laconic view of her son's death, over 20 years after the fact, contained a valuable insight. Earl's wounds were not so severe that he couldn't be removed to a first aid station. Many victims of artillery fire were not so lucky. The barrages were so heavy, with so many shells, that thousands of men were blown to bits. The Great War generation never demanded, nor did they receive, an accounting of every last body on the battlefield. In many cases, there was just nothing left.

Private Alexander Norris, 127th Infantry, 32nd Division, was one man who was not lucky enough to make it to first aid. One of his comrades in arms saw the whole episode, and his account is preserved in the National Archives in Private Norris's burial file. "I, Louis Hein, Sgt. Co. H 127th Infantry was with Pvt. Norris when he was decapitated by an enemy shell in the Bois de Bantheville, France, on October 13th, 1918. He was buried in the same place."[14]

Edward Pennington was a bugler from Cincinnati serving with the 4th Infantry, 3rd Division. He was digging trenches with his unit on the night of July 14, 1918. An artillery barrage surprised Pennington and his buddies. Corporal Thomas Kane recalled how

> the sky was beginning to light up for the guns of the Germans had begun to open up. We had expected this to happen. The shells began to fall around the hill where we were digging and before Bugler Pennington could get to a safe place, and he was hit by flying fragments of a shell. He was carried to a place that was thought to be safe in the trenches we had dug, and the first aid men bandaged him up. He could not be moved to the hospital right away for the shells were falling too thick, and it was sure death for anyone to try to get to the rear. Early on the morning of July 15th, 1918, we took Pvt. Pennington to the hospital, but he died in a short while.

"He didn't have anything to say," Kane recalled, adding the young bugler had no valuables in his pockets.[15]

Miller, Bleckley, Norris, and Pennington joined a total of 53,313 Americans who were killed in battle or died of their wounds in the war. Battle deaths came in very large numbers. At the height of the Meuse-

Argonne offensive in 1918, the AEF suffered about 1,000 battle deaths per day. In a staggering loss, the only kind that the war seemed to provide, the U.S. Marine Corps lost more men in one day of the battle of Belleau Wood than it had during its previous 142 years combined.

Gunshot accounted for over half of all battle deaths and injuries. Artillery shells and shrapnel claimed another quarter. Mustard, phosgene, and other gas attacks killed almost 10 percent of the doughboy army. Yet at the same time, saber blows killed three men during the war. Another 63,195 died of disease, accident, or other cause.[16] The Worldwide Spanish influenza epidemic is responsible for most of this last total, and the figure includes soldiers who died in Europe, at sea, or even in the United States during training. For the purposes of the pilgrimages, however, a mother would become eligible for a trip to Europe to visit her son's grave no matter if he died in battle or from injury, illness, or accident.

Wartime involvement for the United States lead to the deaths of over 100,000 Americans, both overseas and at home. America's contribution of some 2 million troops helped win the war for the Allies. Historians, for the most part, believe "the American intervention was crucial for the Allied victory. Without Americans, the most the Allies could have hoped for was a stalemate," argued Coffman.[17]

A stalemate looked like something of a sure bet. American troops were green and looked to be too late to slow the Germans in early 1918. Furthermore, the war was fought entirely outside of German territory. Nevertheless, Germany collapsed from the inside and began sending peace feelers to Wilson in mid–1918. The war ended not in 1919 or even 1920, but with an armistice on November 11, 1918. (The armistice dictated a ceasefire at precisely 11:11 A.M. on November 11.)

America, at the end of this World War, found itself in unprecedented territory. It was a truly global world power, and it had tens of thousands of its war dead lying overseas in temporary graves.

Removal of the Dead

After the war started and as American battle deaths began to increase, the AEF realized it would be impractical, if not practically impossible, to return the bodies of our war dead until the war had ceased. As early as May 31, 1917, the Army's Quartermaster General recommended "the bodies of our soldiers who die in Europe be interred there and no attempt to bring them back until after close of hostilities."[18]

This pronouncement was anything but premature. The first Americans were wounded in battle on July 14, 1917, in an artillery barrage. The first Americans to die in battle fell on September 4, 1917, again in an artillery shelling of a British unit to which they were assigned. First Lt. William Fitzsimmons and three enlisted men lost their lives in that first attack.

Wartime burial of the dead was not a new problem for the United States. Organized burial parties had existed as far back as the Civil War. After America first entered World War I, the army had plans to organize a civilian burial corps to bury the war dead. It was not until August 7, 1917, that the War Department approved plans for graves registration units, made up not of civilians but of units composed of 2 officers and 50 enlisted men each. Major Charles C. Pierce and the First Graves Registration Unit reached Europe two months later.[19] Although the military knew a few understaffed units would never be able to meet the demand, it believed basic graves registration units were the best way to avoid delays and mistakes in hasty combat burials.

Major Pierce's mission was clear. As combat ceased in a sector, his troops registered and verified temporary grave markings, located other bodies that had not been buried or buried improperly, and began to rebury and congregate bodies into makeshift American cemeteries.

> In addition to this basic function, the Graves Registration Service (GRS) also kept accurate and complete records on the location and identification of graves of all officers and soldiers of the AEF and all civilians attached to it: located and acquired all necessary cemeteries for American use; maintained and controlled the cemeteries; and compiled a registry of burials.[20]

Major Pierce began work in March 1918 with four separate units. By the end of the war, 18 such units were in place, with a maximum strength of 921 officers and enlisted men. A large number of laborers and clerical support personnel assisted their efforts. At war's end, there were over 70,000 Americans buried in Europe, with some 15,000 resting in isolated, single graves. There were more than 2,300 American military cemeteries, small and large, in five different nations in Europe when the war ended.

Beginning on November 13, 1918, the GRS began two new tasks. First, the service double-checked all graves and registration records for accuracy. Second, in accord with the wishes of the French government, the service began to concentrate the dead into fewer cemeteries. By the beginning of 1920, there were still at least 55 American cemeteries, which contained 200 or more bodies. Some of these were quite large. Ploisy cemetery held 1,821 graves; Lambezellec cemetery held 1,740.[21] This total of 55 included temporary burial sites that would become permanent American cemeteries, including Suresnes, Flanders Field, St. Mihiel, and Meuse-Argonne.

As the process of checking graves and concentrating the bodies continued, the War Department reached its decision on the final disposition of the Great War dead. On October 6, 1919, the War Department announced its policy, one that gave families and next-of-kin a comforting measure of autonomy.

All remains in Great Britain, Italy, and Belgium were to be returned to the United States unless the nearest relative requested overseas burial. All bodies in France were to be returned to the United States only at the direct request of the next-of-kin. No graves were to remain in Russia, Germany, or Luxembourg, regardless of family wishes. By way of contrast, other nations' losses were so great as to make the choice of removal impossible. Families of Canadian, British, or Australian soldiers, for example, had no say in the matter. All their dead would remain forever overseas.

Furthermore, the French government did not authorize the removal of any bodies from France until September 15, 1920, almost two years after the war ended. Once the French and American governments had made their decisions, the GRS handled all the arrangements from its temporary headquarters at Hoboken Harbor in New Jersey.

The GRS returned bodies to America with the same painstaking care and respect the Army's Quartermaster Corps showed the pilgrims a decade later. The army was in constant contact with relatives, delivering the body of a loved one to the next-of-kin.

Corporal Oscar Haug was one such case. His parents requested the return of his body to his home in southern Illinois, in compliance with the American policy. His remains, which records indicated were "badly decomposed, recognition impossible," were exhumed from their initial burial spot in Belgium on August 8, 1921. His body was moved to the American cemetery near Romagne, France. On August 22, the body was moved to Antwerp, Belgium, to await transportation to the United States. Haug's body arrived at Hoboken Harbor on September 20. Army escorts stayed with the body on its rail journey back to Illinois, where a relative met the train at the local railway station.[22]

This process was not always foolproof; mistakes were made. However, the GRS did an admirable job under stressful and difficult conditions.

Whose Body Is It?

The decision to remove a soldier's body from the battlefields in Europe or to leave it forever overseas must have been one of the most difficult choices a parent could have faced. Parents were already traumatized enough by the news their sons had died in Europe. As a Gold Star mother from World War II recalls it, the news was a shock. Winifred Lancy lost her son Norman in the war. In her interview for *Gold Star Mothers: Pilgrimage of Remembrance*, Mrs. Lancy recalled how she received the bad news in an impersonal telegram. "Sorry to inform you your son has been killed," she recalled. "And it told the date, and all I could see was in that was the word 'killed.' It looked like the letters in that were in great big letters and all the other stuff you could barely read."[23] In the final analysis, most parents or next-of-kin agreed with Corporal Haug's folks. They wanted their sons and husbands returned home to them. Patriots and even a former president argued both sides of the issue. Each side waged nothing less than a sophisticated, persuasive public relations campaign to champion its own point of view. The issue put America at odds with its allies, too. In the end, the U.S. government maintained a positive middle ground, ready to assist a family like the Haugs with whatever desire it had for its fallen hero.

Those who objected to removal of the American dead wanted the bodies to remain in Europe. Our European allies felt strongly that all the war dead should be buried in Europe and remain together. British writer Stephen Graham was an especially articulate advocate. Graham's 1921 book, *The Challenge of the Dead*, offered his view of a divided Europe struggling to bury, honor, and remember its dead. As Graham viewed American caskets ready for transport back to the United States, he disliked what he saw. "At Calais now the boxes are stacked on the quays with the embalmed dead," he wrote.

> At great cost of time and labour the dead soldiers are being removed from the places where they fell and packed in crates for transport to America. In this way, America's sacrifice is lessened. For while in America this is considered to be America's own concern, it is certain that it is deplored in Europe. The taking away of the American dead has given the impression of a slur on the honor of lying in France. America removes her dead because of a sweet sentiment towards her own. She takes them from a more honourable resting place to a less honourable one. It is said to be due in part to the commercial enterprise of the American undertakers, but it is more due to the sentiment of mothers and wives and provincial pastors in America. That the transference of the dead across the Atlantic is out of keeping with European sentiment she ignores, or fails to understand. America feels she is morally superior to Europe.[24]

Graham attributed America's aims to the defeat of President Wilson's idealistic peace plans. He felt Britain crushed Wilson's spirit and American hopes with it. Graham considered it impossible to imagine America's war dead being returned home had Wilson's idealism won in Europe and survived at home.

He argued, "Had Wilson carried his great program there had been no estrangement [between Europe and America], no exhuming of the American dead."[25] In this sense, Graham is one of the few Europeans to give Wilson's 14 Points any credit. Most of our allies were content to punish Germany as harshly as possible with the Treaty of Versailles.

French sentiment was equally strong against removal of the American dead. The French believed the best way to honor the war dead was to leave them buried in the very land they fought to free. They envisioned large cemeteries throughout the former battlefields. One French writer was "convinced that the dispersal of the bodies of the fallen heroes would forever destroy the actual reminder of their magnificent feat of arms" of the American doughboys.[26] This sentiment, along with real logistical issues, is partly the reason why the French government prohibited the removal of any bodies before 1920.

The French saw potential Allied cemeteries as sacred places, places of interest for generations to come. Family honor, not simply national patriotism, was offered as an argument against removal. Americans were reminded:

> All along the front there will be a zone, not for cultivation, where little trees will spring up, stretching their branches out among the graves. It will become a sacred forest, a place of pilgrimage for the entire world; and the greatest honor that a family can aspire to is to leave their name there graven on a tomb.[27]

The pilgrim aspect was a strong inducement, especially among former American soldiers. Maj. Gen. John O'Ryan, from the AEF's famed 27th Division, agreed with the French view and argued in favor of leaving all bodies overseas. In fact, O'Ryan noted that private pilgrimages had begun as early as 1920. O'Ryan received a letter from the mayor of Bony, France. The mayor told O'Ryan the French townspeople visited the American cemetery in Bony to pay tribute to their American defenders. This visit, O'Ryan believed, "demonstrates conclusively the effect upon the people of France the presence of those white crosses in their midst of the Americans who died for them."[28]

In addition, O'Ryan believed leaving American bodies overseas could lead to American pilgrimages. O'Ryan hoped

> a strong sentiment will develop among the families of the dead protecting against what seems to be almost a sacrilege — the removal of the bodies of our gallant men from those sacred sites in France where they died together, and which will become places of pilgrimage for the honoring of their memory.[29]

Those who argued against removal attached patriotism to pilgrimage. They argued it was a family's duty to leave a soldier overseas, where his grave would continue, in one sense, to do its duty after the man's death. "In a majority of these cases," Bishop Charles Henry Brent wrote of the decision to leave the remains overseas,

> this action on the part of the relatives in itself was an act of patriotism and sacrifice. They felt that by foregoing their right to have the bodies brought back to the United States they were setting their mark and seal on the sacrifice made by sons and husbands and brothers. The Government has thus failed in no detail to pay the honor due to that sacred dust of America which now blends with the soil upon which our best manhood fought and died.[30]

It is unclear how many average Americans read the words of Graham, O'Ryan, and Brent. However, one name arguing against removal was well known to all Americans: Teddy Roosevelt. Quentin Roosevelt was shot down over German lines on Bastille Day, July 14, 1918. The loss crushed the former president, who died just seven months later. In a letter to the War Department published shortly after the war ended, the Roosevelt family made its feelings known: leave Quentin's body buried on the field of battle. "Let the young oak lie where it fell," their letter pleaded. The letter was published in the *New York Times* and other newspapers around the country.[31] The army granted the wish of the former president and first lady. Quentin's body remained right where it fell, in a remote grave in rural France.

Roosevelt's enormous popularity was an important factor for those families who decided to leave their loved ones overseas. Quentin had grown up in the White House in the public eye. He and his siblings were as well known and well liked by the American public as were John and Caroline Kennedy to a later generation. By leaving his body in France, the Roosevelts' decision was a powerful influence on the thousands of families who chose to leave their sons and husbands overseas. Many Gold Star mothers echoed the president's sentiments to explain why they left their boys in France.

Another reason families left soldiers' remains in Europe was the soldiers themselves. Many doughboys' letters back home during the war urged parents to leave the bodies overseas with fallen comrades in the event of death. Each man believed the ground on which he fought was sacred, made so by his blood and that of his comrades. For example, Jennie Walsh, a Gold Star mother from Brooklyn, told Congress in 1924 her son was buried in France according to his own wishes. "My only child, 18 years of age, lies over in Europe by his own will," she testified in Congress in favor of pilgrimage legislation. "When he went over he asked me, if he was killed on the other side, to please leave him there, and let him lie among the boys with whom he fought."[32] Mrs. Walsh's son was a battalion messenger who was killed near the Hindenburg Line. He was buried in Bony, France. At the same congressional hearing, Mrs. Gilbert Manson of Hillsdale, New York, told how she left her son buried overseas, lying next to his wartime buddy, Lt. Scanlon.[33]

A final reason so many bodies remained overseas was probably simple confusion. A number of families were unaware of the option they had to bring the remains of their loved ones back home. Some never received the government's correspondence; others were unable to read the letter if it arrived. It is likely a small number of families who left remains overseas didn't know they had any other choice.

New York Congressman Samuel Dickstein told his fellow members of the House during a 1924 hearing much the same story. Based on his discussions with Gold Star mothers in his district, Dickstein realized "most of them did not understand they could make a request and bring the boy back here."[34] Dickstein lost a brother in the Meuse-Argonne campaign, and he felt his mother was lucky to have him around to fill out the paperwork to bring his brother back home. Dickstein knew of many cases where the women simply did not know how to fill out the forms, or if they did know, they failed to realize this was the one and only chance to bring the doughboy's body back home. "I want to remind you," Dickstein told his law makers, "that the thing just went like a storm; because you had to file your application within a certain time, and when you failed to file your application with that time you were through."[35] Dickstein was a vocal supporter of government-sponsored pilgrimage legislation throughout the 1920s.

Yet not everyone agreed with writers such as Graham and O'Ryan and with families such as Manson and Walsh. Approximately two-thirds of the families who were eligible to bring back their husbands and sons chose to do so. Their reasons were varied. The funeral home industry waged an intense campaign for removal of all bodies and their return to America. Although their campaign contained no small amount of self-interest, the ability to bury a loved one in the hometown cemetery held a strong appeal for many families.

Others rejected the notion of their loved one continuing to serve the country, even in death. The remains belonged to the family, and most families wanted them back home. Another reason was many soldiers wanted their bodies brought back home if they died in battle, and their letters to their families made their wishes quite clear.

The experiences of the Manson and Walsh families were far from unique. Men often expressed their desired place for burial. Some men wanted to return home. Estella Ann Carpenter from Rochelle, Illinois, lost her son Jay. Jay, like Quentin, was a pilot shot down over enemy lines. Mrs. Carpenter received word from the army her son was downed on June 11, 1918. Unless they heard word from him, the government presumed he was killed in action. Final word did not come for five more agonizing months. After the armistice was signed, Mrs. Carpenter received confirmation her son was dead. The date of his death was given as August 19.

One can only speculate on the stress and anxiety in the Carpenter household while the war was fought to a crescendo and then ended without final word on Jay. Mrs. Carpenter was lucky in one sense, however. A French sergeant found Jay's body, and word of his find made it back to Illinois.

> The sergeant found the body of my son ... under his machine and from the position he was in, he could not have suffered. They removed the body as carefully as possible; on his arm they found his identification tag, two letters from me, and a card was written "Notify Mrs. Estella Ann Carpenter, Rochelle, Illinois, USA."[36]

Lt. Carpenter was buried in a temporary grave near a French orphanage, and his body was later removed to a more permanent cemetery some 75 miles east of Paris. Jay Carpenter made his wishes for his final resting place known to his mother. "My son's request was to come back home to his land to rest. He said that so many times in his letters," Mrs. Carpenter recalled. She honored this request and brought her son's body back to the United States. His body arrived home and was buried on his birthday, April 1, 1921.[37]

The U.S. funeral home industry wanted just what Jay Carpenter wanted: funerals on American soil for the Great War dead. Funeral directors waged an active, sophisticated campaign for public opinion, first to have all bodies brought back home and, failing that, to have as many families as possible choose repatriation to the United States. This pressure took the form of ads in trade magazines for industry insiders, as well as ads in national and consumer magazines for the general public. Stephen Graham is correct in citing the undertakers' lobby as a chief reason so many American bodies were returned home. Kurt Piehler is an expert on the pilgrimages and is a professor of history at the University of Tennessee. He feels the funeral home industry exerted substantial influence of many families' decisions. "The funeral directors saw this as a big money-making opportunity," he said of the repatriation movement.[38] Many relatives were convinced, and the undertakers' lobby must be cited as the single largest reason so many families decided not to leave loved ones overseas.

However, it is wrong to view this practice as just a greedy industry endeavor. Parents and spouses realized leaving a body overseas meant no chance for a funeral, no gravestone to visit, no chance to decorate the grave in the hometown cemetery. Funerals bring closure, an end to life. With no such thing as an organized pilgrimage on the horizon, families had but one choice to say good-bye: a funeral in the United States. The funeral directors were selling what many people wanted, and they were only too glad to provide it.

In the final analysis, many families opted for repatriation, not so much because they were in favor of a funeral but because they were opposed to what overseas burial meant. Many of those who favored burial in Europe wanted the bodies to continue to serve their country. Even in death, the bodies were being pressed into service, in a sense, to serve the nation and its aims. In another sense, the decision to bring the bodies back home was not simply a debate over convenience or confusion. It was about the ownership of the remains of the dead. Did the family and next-of-kin own the body, with the rights to do with it as they best saw fit? Or did the nation for whom the soldiers fought and died still have claims to the remains?

Fortunately, for American families at least, they had the chance to make this choice. Kurt Piehler observed "efforts to press the war dead into further national service required or at least the compliance of their parents and widows."[39] Most next-of-kin were more concerned with personal issues such as mourning and loss, but their decisions had larger ramifications. Parents and wives made the best choices they could under difficult and emotional circumstances. The search for meaning, the "big picture" comes much later. Everything about the Gold Star mothers seems to fit the same pattern.

Cemeteries

By the early 1920s, the families had spoken. All told, about 46,000 bodies were returned to the United States. Some 30,000 bodies were to remain in Europe according to the wishes of the next-of-kin. The United States set out to build cemeteries for its overseas war dead. After rejecting a call for one large cemetery, the government decided on eight. Most were located on the sites of the large, if temporary, American graveyards concentrated in the French countryside. The Army's GRS continued its care of the dead and planned, designed, and executed the cemeteries.

Their designs were to be basic, almost elemental in their simplicity. Older portions of the Arlington National Cemetery served as something of a model. Graves, with a couple exceptions, were placed in even, regular rows. Buildings, plantings, and other elements had been all but eliminated.

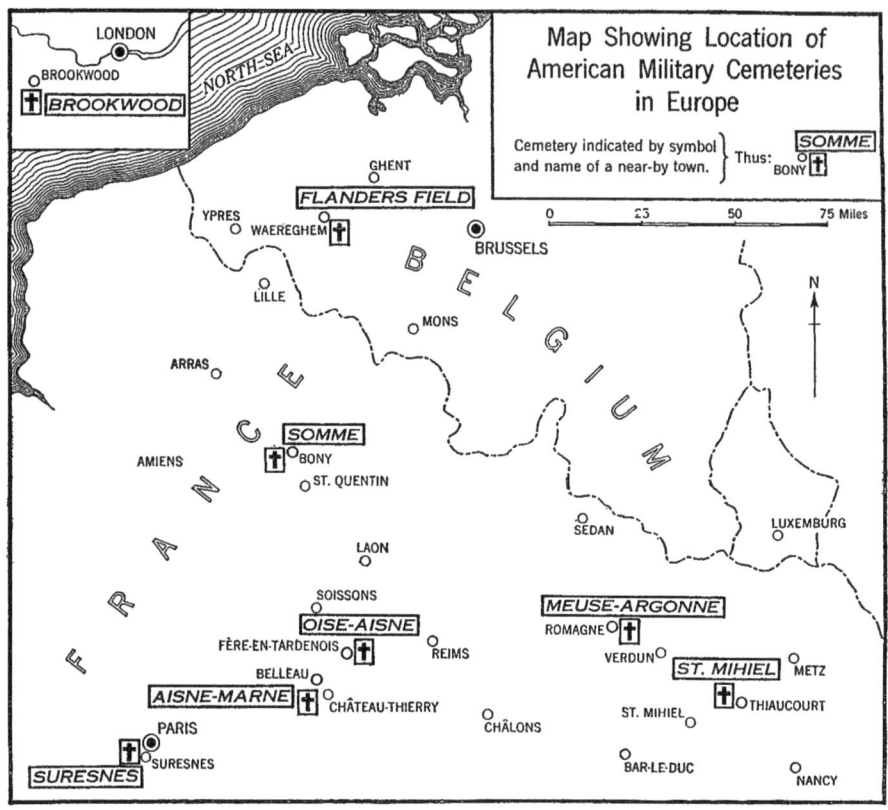

American World War I cemeteries in Europe. The United States built eight permanent cemeteries in Europe after World War I. Six are located in France, and one each in Belgium and England. Gold Star mothers visited these cemeteries during their pilgrimages. Today, the American Battle Monuments Commission operates these and other overseas military cemeteries. (*American Armies and Battlefields in Europe.*)

> The cemeteries have been designed with the idea that trees and shrubs will furnish the main element of beauty. These of course are still in their early stages of growth [in 1925], and the ultimate appearance of the cemeteries can only be visualized in imagination.[40]

Six of the cemeteries were located in France: Aisne-Marne, Meuse-Argonne, Oise-Aisne, Somme, St. Mihiel, and Suresnes. One cemetery was located each in England and Belgium, Brookwood and Flanders Field, respectively. In most cases, the foreign governments granted the land used for the cemeteries to the United States free of charge.

In a separate but related event, Congress created the American Battle Monuments Commission (ABMC) in 1923. It had two important missions. First, the commission oversaw the design, placement, and maintenance of American war memorials overseas. The key was to avoid the practice, already in full swing by that time, for every state, division, and regiment to place its own memorials throughout the French countryside. The ABMC's second mission was to erect memorials, chapels, and other design elements in the permanent American cemeteries in Europe. The commission was composed of eight members. Gen. Pershing was its chairman, and the board included one Gold Star mother, Mrs. Frederic Bentley.

Because the ABMC was separate from the War Department and the GRS, some degree of conflict was inevitable. Each group had separate visions for the memorials and the cemeteries. Members of the ABMC journeyed to Europe and inspected the cemeteries during the summer of 1924. By this time, the cemeteries had a finished look, and the graves were marked with white wooden crosses or stars of David. The ABMC praised the army's work in keeping the cemeteries simple and in maintaining their grounds.

However, the commission members felt much remained to be done. "The gateways and flagpoles are passable, but have not gone beyond that point. In fact, the impression gained in almost every cemetery is that the work has been done with a minimum expenditure of funds," the commission observed in its first annual report, published in 1925.[41]

The army expended few funds because little had been given to it to complete the job. The army felt the ABMC's aims were too costly. "The more economy-minded Graves Registration Service disapproved of the Commission's elaborate plans," an army historian wrote.[42] This divided situation existed all throughout the pilgrimages; the ABMC was finally given sole responsibility over the cemeteries in Europe in 1934.

The Gold Star mothers knew nothing of this controversy, nor did they need to. Both the GRS and the ABMC did their jobs well, and the pilgrims had nothing but universal praise for the cemeteries they visited in Europe. The ABMC still exists today, operating all U.S. military cemeteries abroad. It does its same painstaking, loving job of honoring America's war dead with its cemeteries and memorials.

One of the ABMC's first jobs was to select the permanent headstones. The wood markers, although sturdy, could not be expected to last for decades. The commission first examined other nations' markers, from the stark black crosses used by the Germans to the uniform stone tablets of the Brits. The commission wanted the markers to be the same for both officers and enlisted men. It also wished the markers themselves (and not the buildings or the landscaping) to remain the focus of the cemeteries. Inscriptions were to be kept simple. Markers carried the name, rank, military unit, date of death, and home state of each person. Relatives were permitted to place brief inscriptions on the backs of the markers. Unknown soldiers had this message on their markers: "Here rests in honored glory an American soldier known but to God." Dr. Paul Cret, a Philadelphia architect, submitted the winning design to the commission. His submission was consistent with the temporary wooden markers. His plans called for a large marble cross or star of David. The markers were tall; they reach waist-high on many of the pilgrims. The commission made a concerted, conscious effort to select overtly religious symbols for grave markers. Its members shared the view of many Americans that the nation had fought in something of a crusade and that its troops had died as martyrs in the struggle.

In addition to the grave markers, the commission oversaw the design and construction of a chapel in each cemetery, again with religious symbols and meaning. Kurt Piehler saw these religious symbols as a consistent reflection of society at the time. "I think the cross is an important symbol, and America is much a Protestant nation in this era," he said.[43]

The eight cemeteries

Unknown soldier of World War I grave marker. Grave markers in World War I cemeteries are marble crosses or stars of David. Markers for unidentified bodies read: "Here rests in honored glory an American soldier known but to God." Mothers whose sons' bodies were never identified were allowed to take part in the pilgrimages; they often chose to decorate the grave of one of the unknown troops. (American Battle Monuments Commission, Arlington, VA.)

the pilgrims visited were largely completed by 1933. However, work still continued in some. Flanders Field, for example, was not officially dedicated until 1937. Each one is slightly different from the others. Two are located in the midst of major cities; Brookwood is just outside London, and Suresnes is in suburban Paris.

Although the grave areas and chapels remain the same today, the landscaping has developed. Saplings have grown to leafy maturity. The cemeteries in the early 1930s would have had something of the open, windswept appearance of a new housing development. Nevertheless, the cemeteries do their job. They are places of pilgrimage, and they do represent, for those who care to visit, America's commitment to Europe. There is always a more personal level. The cemeteries remind us for what the soldiers fought and died. "Those people went out and in a sense, they died for us. They died for our future," believes Edward Coffman.[44]

Aisne-Marne American Cemetery is 45 miles northeast of Paris, near the town of Belleau. Aisne-Marne contains the largest number of U.S. Marines of any World War I cemetery. The cemetery contains 2,288 American graves, arranged in a semicircular pattern. The cemetery sits at the bottom of a hill, near the site of the famous battle of Belleau Wood. The firm of Cram & Ferguson of Boston designed the cemetery's tall stone chapel. The chapel's Tablet of the Mission contains 1,060 names. Bugler Edward Pennington from Cincinnati is buried in the Aisne-Marne.

Brookwood Cemetery is the only American World War I cemetery in Britain. It sits within the boundaries of a larger cemetery, the London Necropolis Co., approximately 28 miles southwest of London. Many of the Americans buried here lost their lives at sea. Percy Stevens and many (but not all) of the *Tuscania* dead are buried in Brookwood. Brookwood contains 468 graves in its 4.5 acres. Within the chapel is a Tablet of the Missing, listing 563 names. (Each cemetery has such a tablet in its chapel area.) Brookwood is the only U.S. World War I cemetery that has more missing than actual burials. The graves are arranged in four plots around a central flagpole. A stone chapel sits at the northwest side of the cemetery.

Flanders Field is the only American World War I cemetery in Belgium. It is located 43 miles west of Brussels, near the town of Waregem. One of the smallest in size, it holds just 368 American graves. Most of these men served with the 37th and 91st Divisions, both of which were attached to the French army during the war. The graves are arranged in four rectangular plots around a central memorial designed by Paul Cret. The chapel's Tablet of the Missing contains 43 names.

The name Flanders Field would have been familiar to most of the pilgrims based on the poem of the same name by a Canadian doctor, Lt. Col.

John McCrae. ("In Flanders field, the poppies blow / Between the crosses, row on row.") The poem gained instant popularity when it was published in 1915, two years before the United States entered the war. Charles Lindbergh flew over the cemetery to drop poppies in honor of his fallen countrymen shortly after completing his historic transatlantic flight in 1927. The poppy was adopted by most Allied countries after the war as a symbol of remembrance.

Flanders Field is open to the public but receives very few visitors. A friend of the author visited Flanders Field in January 2002. He reports the caretaker was grateful, if somewhat surprised, to find a visitor to the cemetery that day.[45]

The Meuse-Argonne American Cemetery contains 14,246 graves. This is the largest American military cemetery overseas, including those constructed after World War II. The cemetery is near Romagne-sous-Mont-

Meuse-Argonne Cemetery in the pilgrims' day. This photograph shows the Meuse-Argonne Cemetery during the era of the pilgrimages. Although the American cemeteries were newly constructed, they were well maintained. The manicured cemeteries dispelled the fear some mothers had of unkempt grounds and wooden grave markers. (Courtesy Janet Payne.)

faucon, approximately 18 miles northwest of Verdun. The cemetery sits on a hillside, with a chapel at the top. The chapel's Tablet of the Missing contains an additional 954 names. The graves are arranged in eight rectangular plots. When the cemetery was constructed, small trees had just been planted. Today, these mature trees are lovely, but they obscure the view of the markers. One suspects all 14,000 gravestones made quite a sweeping impression on the pilgrims who saw them in the early 1930s. Most of the men buried here died in the massive Meuse-Argonne offensive, although bodies from all over the war zone were removed here. A reflecting pond, originally stocked with goldfish, occupies the center of the cemetery. A 1.5 mile long fence surrounds the property.

Meuse-Argonne's buildings were not completed until 1931, so pilgrims from the first two years saw the cemetery in somewhat unfinished condition. Lt. Erwin Bleckley of the Lost Battalion fame is among Meuse-Argonne's burials.

Oise-Aisne Cemetery, with its 6,012 graves, is the second largest American World War I Cemetery. The cemetery is 14 miles from Soissons, near the village of Fere-en-Tardenois. The cemetery occupies 36.5 acres on its site near the Ourcq River. The chapel, constructed of pink and gray sandstone, has 241 names on its Tablet of the Missing. Most of the dead lost their lives in action near the Ourcq River, although a number of men who died in and around Paris were moved here at a later date. The graves are arranged in four rectangular plots.

Joyce Kilmer, the AEF's soldier poet, is buried in Oise-Aisne. Kilmer's poem "Trees" is an American classic. When the cemeteries were first built, the trees were sparse and immature. This condition led the American Tree Association to lodge a formal complaint there were no trees near Sgt. Kilmer's grave.

The Somme Cemetery contains the graves of 1,844 war dead. The cemetery is located near the village of Bony, about 13 miles north of St. Quentin. The cemetery's rolling 14 acres is representative of the surrounding Picardy landscape. Most of the dead here lost their lives in fighting while attached to units of the British army or in the battle for the nearby village of Cantigny. The graves are arranged in four plots, with the chapel on the eastern side of the cemetery. Its tablet lists the names of 333 Americans missing and presumed dead. The chapel is a small, blockish stone building unlike that in any other American cemetery. Architect George Howe chose this style partly due to the unique layout of the cemetery. Though some on the ABMC were reported to have been "disturbed" at the plan, the chapel was built as designed. However, "Howe's chapel does not provide a conventional image of spiritual triumph over death," one architectural historian noted.[46]

The ABMC reconciled itself to the design and even found room to praise it in its official tour guide to the battlefields and cemeteries. "Its style of architecture expresses the spirit of rugged determination which inspired the American soldiers in their repeated assaults across neighboring fields while advancing to attack the Hindenburg Line in front of Bony," a contemporary guide stated.[47]

The guide, *American Armies and Battlefields in Europe*, was published in 1938. It was reissued by the Government Printing Office in 1992. It is a fully illustrated tour book, with battlefield maps and numerous photographs. The guide was intended as a handy reference for Americans traveling abroad. The government assumed most Americans visiting Europe would take time to visit the battlefields and cemeteries of World War I. Driving directions were exact. A typical passage read: "Beyond the town, after crossing the railroad, at the first crest where a good view of the hill to the front is obtained, STOP."[48]

The St. Mihiel Cemetery sits on the western edge of Thiacourt, about 190 miles east of Paris. Its 40.5 acres are home to 4,153 American graves. Most of the dead, along with the 284 missing on the chapel's tablet, gave their lives in the St. Mihiel offensive. This battle was the AEF's first major, independent action. Graves are arranged in four rectangular burial areas, surrounded by square-trimmed linden trees. The cemetery features a circular colonnade, with a chapel on one end and a museum at the other. The current site also served as a temporary cemetery during and after the war.

Suresnes cemetery contains the graves of 1,541 American war dead. The cemetery sits on a hillside only four miles from the heart of Paris. The vast majority of burials here are men who died of illness or accident during the war. The chapel's Tablet of the Missing contains 974 names, many of whom were lost or buried at sea. Because of Suresnes's urban location, American officials often us it for ceremonies on Memorial Day and Veterans' Day. Suresnes today most closely resembles any cemetery's appearance during the pilgrimages. Paris and the Eiffel Tower are clearly visibly from the grounds.

Suresnes is the only World War I cemetery to also contain dead from World War II. It should be noted the army adopted the policy after the World War II of keeping graves from each world war separate in their own cemeteries.

Today, few Americans visit the cemeteries of World War I. During the pilgrims' day, they were magnets for tourists and pilgrims alike. Today, the experience of standing in a cemetery is an emotional one. Perhaps it is an intellectual one as well. One is remembering, or learning for the first time, what Americans did in World War I.

If the purpose of a military cemetery is to make sure visitors never forget, then these eight European cemeteries succeed. "When you go to these World War I cemeteries, it is a pilgrimage, and a feeling of awe, of reverence, for those people," Edward Coffman remarked in his "Gold Star Mothers: Pilgrimage of Remembrance."[49] Now that the military had built these cemeteries, it was up to Congress to get the pilgrims to them.

3

Pilgrimage Legislation: A Decade in the Making

Almost as soon as the war ended, a number of legislators began to push for government-funded and organized pilgrimages to the European cemeteries for the Gold Star mothers. The battle lasted four presidential administrations and one full decade. It was a legislative struggle with little overt, vocal opposition but with many hidden enemies. Support was always broadly based. Conservatives such as New York's Hamilton Fish joined forces with a true Pennsylvania Quaker, Samuel Butler, to pass pilgrimage legislation. Money was never the real issue. The U.S. Treasury had large surpluses throughout the 1920s. In the end, however, the world's richest superpower stood alone in footing the bill for war graves pilgrimages.

It is a legislative history complete with surprising drama and famous names cropping up in unexpected places. It is equally the story of concerned legislators crafting and revising bill after bill, even after the first party of pilgrims sailed for France.

To be sure, Americans of the World War I generation did not wait for government handouts. Almost any mother or widow who could afford to visit Europe did so, some as soon as three months after the armistice was signed. Wealthy women and those from prominent families led the way, while women from more modest backgrounds relied on friends, savings, and charity for their own personal pilgrimages. This do-it-yourself phenomenon is perfectly typical of other countries' pilgrimage experiences. No other nation could begin to contemplate a nationally funded effort to take war mothers to visit the battlefields.

La Guardia Leads the Way

Fiorello La Guardia, a New York Congressman and World War I veteran, introduced the very first bill calling for federally funded pilgrimages in 1919. La Guardia, of course, is more well known to most Americans as the flamboyant mayor of New York City, serving 1934–45 and for the New York airport that bears his name.

La Guardia was also a decorated war veteran. After war was declared, La Guardia, a freshman Congressman from New York's 14th district, presented himself at a recruiting station in Washington, DC. He wanted to be a pilot. He neglected to tell the recruiters that he was a Congressman. Instead, he offered his flying credentials; he had taken private lessons in Mineola, New York, before the war broke out. La Guardia was accepted into the service and even managed to retain his seat in Congress once his identity was known. La Guardia was sent to the Italian front to assist the fledgling American aviation effort in this distant corner of the war. He managed to receive his wings, even though a crash during a test flight forced him to spend several days in a hospital.[1] La Guardia not only helped train American fliers for service in Italy but his personality and congressional position also assured that he "virtually took over American policy making in Italy."[2]

La Guardia, however, was not content to make policy; he put himself in harm's way to help win the war. He led 18 of the pilots he trained in a bombing mission on June 20, 1918, against enemy strongholds at Falze di Piave.[3]

La Guardia's bill H.R. 239, remarkably similar to the bill that passed a decade later, was introduced on May 9, 1919. His bill called for visits at government expense for mothers, widows, and fathers to visit graves of sons or husbands in European cemeteries. The bill's second section called for first-class train and steamship travel. He also envisioned special dedicated trains in Europe to meet the family members and carry them directly to their destination cemeteries.

His bill did not pass. In fact, it did not receive a formal hearing or even serious consideration. Nevertheless, May 9, 1919, may be viewed as the start of the organized pilgrimage movement.

In retrospect, the timing was not right for La Guardia's bill. The War Department was still four months away on announcing its policy on repatriation of the war dead. La Guardia acknowledged as much himself during deliberations on a later pilgrimage bill in 1928. Regarding his 1919 bill, he said, "It didn't take hold. It just didn't take hold. Everything was concentrated on getting those bodies back."[4]

The opposition La Guardia faced, in fact, was organized, vehement, and relentless. The funeral home industry was the culprit. The industry fought not so much against the pilgrimages themselves but against any policy that would leave American bodies in Europe.

La Guardia recalled a letter-writing campaign waged against his bill. The campaign produced dozens of identical letters to his office, many of which contained "rather abusive" language. "I was criticized very severely at the time and abused," La Guardia said in 1928.[5] The end result was that La Guardia's early bill was dead and the Gold Star mothers would have to wait a full five years more for the second, serious consideration of the pilgrimage question.

Moving On

By 1924, the issue of overseas burial had been resolved, and eight permanent cemeteries in Europe held American dead. New York Representative Samuel Dickstein introduced his version of a pilgrimage bill, H.R. 4109. Representative Dickstein was an ardent pilgrimage supporter and an intriguing figure in his own right. He was born in Russia in 1885 but moved at age two to the United States with his family. His bill called for pilgrimages for mothers (but not widows or fathers) to be conducted and organized by the War Department. Each woman would receive, in addition to all travel and accommodations, a $100 payment to cover any incidental expenses.

A House of Representatives hearing was held February 19, 1924, to examine Dickstein's bill. This was the first large public forum to explore the pilgrimage issue, and it provided a good opportunity to hear from the Gold Star mothers and their supporters. The New York Congressman predicted 1,500 Gold Star mothers, at most, would wish to go on the trip.

A number of Gold Star mothers were on hand to address the Representatives in support of the bill. Passage, at first, seemed a sure thing. Dickstein stated, "I do not think there will be a Congressman on the floor who will vote against the bill. That is my opinion."

Representative Harry Hull of Iowa agreed. "I know they would not," he added.[6]

When the Gold Star mothers took the floor, sentiments of motherhood and patriotism appeared to carry the day. Mrs. Effie Vedder from New York City, who was introduced as the "mother of this movement," began by telling the all-male committee a thing or two about motherhood.

> I want to begin by telling you that you are all men and you have not and can not feel the way a mother feels. It is part of her body that is lying over there. She

spent 20 years, anyway, in bringing up that boy; she gave her time, both day and night, and none of you can realize what a mother's loss is,

she told the committee.[7] Mrs. Vedder had already made her own private pilgrimage to visit her son's grave in Europe.

Mathilda Burling also testified at this hearing. She reminded the members of the sacred nature of the trips, which were yet to be called pilgrimages in Congress or the press. "We are not asking to be sent across as a pleasure trip. It is a very serious matter," Mrs. Burling stated. "The Government or nobody else asked those Gold Star Mothers what they would have to suffer when they were called upon to have their boys taken away."[8] Mrs. Burling was further identified as a leader of the Gold Star mothers. In fact, she was scheduled to meet the president the next day to discuss the issue.

Mothers tried to convince Congress of the psychological benefits of a gravesite visit. These sentimental pleas were part of every pilgrimage hearing, from 1924 onward. Jennie Walsh told Congress she was so distraught over the death of her son that she lost her hearing and thought she might be losing her mind. She made a private trip at her own expense to kneel at her son's grave in 1921. She testified:

> I think that it helped cure me; it gave me a little solace, and I feel certain if you send over the poor mothers who cannot afford to pay their own way, you will save the minds of a great many of them; because although five years have passed, the mothers' minds are still in some chaos.[9]

Yet despite the impassioned testimony of these mothers and what appeared to be universal support from Congress, Dickstein's bill failed. Two issues killed his measure. One was monetary; the other was logistical. These tough issues indicated the challenges any organized pilgrimage bill faced. Congress supported the notion, beyond a doubt. However, the precise wording of the bills caused contention and ultimately derailed the federally funded pilgrimage movement for several more years.

Financial objections were the first of the two challenges Dickstein's bill faced. His bill called for money to be paid directly to each mother to help her defray the costs of travel and incidentals. Section four of the bill provided "...for the payment to each mother making such a tour, upon request therefore, the sum of $100."[10] Note what became known as a pilgrimage was being called a tour at this time.

This provision bothered some members of Congress, and in fact this should have come as no surprise. Before the New Deal, the idea of direct payments to citizens for any reason was unusual. Most people in and out of Congress would have balked at such a measure.

Legislators raised a number of questions about this part of Dickstein's bill. What about Gold Star mothers who wouldn't be able to make the trip? Would all women be eligible, or would some of them just refund the money? Why was this payment necessary, if the government would provide for all travel, meals, and lodging? "Well, we could not go, we were too old, too sick, and we want our money," Representative John J. McSwain said in his description of mothers unable to make the trip. "We want our money," he could hear them say.[11] McSwain wanted none of it and argued the bill would not pass unless this $100 provision was removed.

Dickstein and his supporters were undeterred. They assumed no self-respecting mother would take the $100 if she could possibly afford the trip herself. Dickstein reassured the committee, "These ladies here, who are the finest type of Americans you have before you, that they are not here in any measure to aid the cause of some who can afford to go there, or who is trying to take advantage of the situation."[12]

Mrs. J. S. Bach agreed. Mrs. Bach was introduced as the Gold Star Mothers' Association executive secretary. She told the committee, "I do not think any woman is going to take advantage of the Government; they have too much pride."[13]

Furthermore, the government could more than afford $100 for each Gold Star mother, Dickstein reminded his colleagues. The federal treasury had a surplus of over $300 million.

Mrs. Walsh, quoted above, chided Congress on how stingy it was when it came to those who fought and lost loved ones in the war. "They have money for everything else — they had money for the war; they had money for the guns; they had money to kill them, and why have they not the money to help these poor mothers, whose hearts are just breaking for a sight of the grave of their boy?" Mrs. Walsh asked Congress.[14]

In addition, each mother who left her son overseas had actually saved the government hundreds of dollars in disinterment and reburial costs. This argument carried some weight with Congress, and it was repeated at all subsequent hearings on the issue. Representative J. Mayhew Wainwright reminded his fellow House members that every mother who left her son in Europe had saved the taxpayers $500 or more per body. "I think we might accord a little privilege," the New York law maker argued, "which will cost us very much less, to those of the mothers who saved the Government that expense."[15]

The issue of what would be called a voucher-style payment did not die with Dickstein's bill. Even after the final pilgrimage bill was signed into law in 1929, some members of Congress still wanted to find ways to provide direct payments to mothers and widows who were unable to make a pilgrimage.

Senator David Walsh from Massachusetts introduced into the *Congressional Record* an editorial from the *Boston Post* April 7, 1930 issue. "What the Government can do, as the 'Post' has urged before, is to give the mothers who are unable to make the trip the actual cost to the Government of the individual passage. This is figured at about $850. This amount would be a blessing to hundreds of them," the 'Post' editorial stated.

> Each gold-star mother whose son is buried in France is entitled to have $850 spent in her behalf by the Government. If she can not go, it is only fair and reasonable to pay her what the trip costs the Government.... Unless this is done the women who benefit from this legislation will be the ones whose circumstances give them the leisure, the money, and the good health to make the pilgrimage, while the others, barred by extreme poverty, household cares, or poor health, will receive no consideration.[16]

By 1930, Senator Walsh's editorial could well have added death to the list. Gold Star mothers by this time had an average age approaching 70 years. However, the direct payment proposal failed in 1930 just as it had in 1924.

The second, and far more troublesome, issue facing Dickstein's bill was the War Department's objection to it. Dickstein's bill directed the War Department to organize and conduct the pilgrimages. The War Department examined the issue and didn't want the job. Perhaps a more accurate way of stating it is It didn't want the job Dickstein's proposal gave it. The War Department's study of the pilgrimage duty is included in the official 1924 hearing publication. The study is remarkably detailed and accurate. For instance, the report estimated 7,600 mothers would actually take part in the pilgrimages, as planned.[17] The actual number turned out to be approximately 6,600.

Secretary of War John Weeks stated several basic objections. First, he pointed out the bill directed the War Department to organize the pilgrimages but gave the agency no money to conduct them. Second, the War Department lacked sufficient troop transport ships to carry the women to Europe and back. Furthermore, these ships would prove too costly to operate if they carried civilian passengers. (Note that this early proposal called for government ships to the do the work. The final pilgrimages used private liners.) Finally, Weeks delivered what was the most serious objection to official military involvement in the pilgrimages. He stated: "The administration of the project would require the assignment of a considerable number of officers and other military personnel, thus necessitating their withdrawal from essential military duties."[18]

This argument had merit, given the greatly reduced nature of the peacetime army. In short, the War Department didn't want the job of tour guide, and its objections were the chief stumbling block until a bill's final passage five years later. Dickstein's bill failed, but it was an important first step. It brought the Gold Star mothers into the public spotlight and helped them identify their supporters in Congress.

Another Try

Congress took four more years to revisit the pilgrimage issue. Supporters crafted an entirely new bill designed to overcome the objections which had swamped the 1924 proposal. The bill, H.R. 5494, was introduced by Representative Thomas Butler. Although this bill led to hearings in the House and Senate that relied heavily on the War Department's 1924 study, the War Department itself was removed from the picture.

As a compromise, the American Red Cross was offered as the ideal tour guide. The Red Cross had credibility and a large organization to attend to the needs of sick or frail pilgrims. In fact, the Red Cross furnished a large number of the nurses to the AEF, and sadly over 100 died in battle.[19] It had already assisted many families to make their own personal — and privately funded — pilgrimages to Europe.

The Red Cross, however, seemed almost as unenthusiastic as the army had in its selection for the job. Its director testified at the hearing but said his organization had "no opinion" about hosting the pilgrims. The measure had support among some Gold Star mothers, however. "I am sure pleased at the idea proposed in the bill to have the arrangements under the auspices of the Red Cross," one said.[20]

At least one member of Congress, Representative Thomas Butler, objected to the military's presence on the pilgrimages. He liked the compromise the Red Cross option offered, and he told his House colleagues that the War Department should have no involvement in the pilgrimages. Butler, identified as a man of Quaker stock, said, "I believe all these [are] missions of mercy, and this is one of them, can be better attended by keeping the soldiery out of it. These people are not to be taken on a parade."[21]

Some of the more vocal Gold Star mothers objected to the Red Cross's involvement, however. Although the mothers had nothing bad to say about the organization, they felt the choice sent the wrong message about the trips. They argued the pilgrimages would then be viewed as a charity operation for an assortment of old and frail women.

Ethel Nock was one of those mothers. She was familiar with the Graves Registration Service and the work it was doing. Only the army escorts could give the trip the dignity they deserved, Mrs. Nock believed. She also felt confident the army could care for any older or ailing war mothers. "We have Army nurses, the mothers are not old, the mothers should go there with a high type of courage because we mothers who gave birth to heroes must have had some courage within us," she stated in her hearing testimony.[22] Mrs. Nock also argued that money was already appropriated for the military's service, whereas choosing the Red Cross would mean additional appropriations for nongovernmental service.

Mrs. Hamilton Bayley told the Senate about her personal pilgrimage to her son's grave. Her contacts with the GRS were very positive. She had no reservations about turning the pilgrimage over to this branch of the army. "I feel that this is something that should be done entirely under the Army," she testified. "I can not say enough in praise of the wonderful service we had in France. I have had experience with the Graves Registration Service in France for the last six years."[23] Mrs. Bayley returned to France yet again in 1931 on her organized pilgrimage with the Gold Star mothers. Mrs. Bayley was quick to say she did not want to criticize the "splendid work" of the Red Cross. Nevertheless, she felt this was clearly a task for the military. "I think that at this time it would be very unwise to not put this matter entirely into the hands of our Quartermaster Service," she stated.[24]

The Red Cross drew praise from all who knew its work, but even those outside of Washington questioned its fitness to conduct the pilgrimages. Meeting at San Antonio for its 10th National Convention, the American Legion adopted a resolution on the pilgrimage question. The resolution read, in part, "We realize that the Red Cross and other similar organizations are good in their field of endeavor but we do not believe they are experienced in European pilgrimages or travel."[25]

The Red Cross question was just one of several issues that presented Congress great difficulty as it wrestled with pilgrimage bills and hearings in 1928. Logistical, financial, and even constitutional challenges lay ahead. The simple question of eligibility — who got to go on a pilgrimage — remained a contentious issue even after the trips had begun. The House Committee on Military Affairs held a hearing on January 27, 1928, and a subcommittee of the Senate Committee on Military Affairs also held a hearing, after the House had passed a bill, on May 14, 1928.

Legislators appeared forcefully in favor of the measures. Objections that had sidetracked or even derailed prior bills were no longer stumbling blocks. Other than the Red Cross issue, the legislation looked to be a sure bet. Because the bill had plenty of momentum, individual legislators even began to speak of the meaning and importance of the trips. Nevertheless, there was much unspoken and invisible opposition to the organized pilgrimage movement, or, more properly, not against the pilgrimages themselves but against the language in specific bills.

Some members of Congress were uncomfortable with the government's role in private pilgrimages. Many in Congress, prior to the New Deal, took an exceptionally narrow view (by today's standards) of the proper role of the federal government. Senator Royal Copeland of New York, a pilgrimage supporter, argued the government had a role to play in citizens' lives.

Copeland stated in the May hearing,

> I resent the idea that the purpose of Government is to protect property. Government has a much wider purpose than that. It is to protect property, but more than that it must serve its citizens. It must do for the citizen the things he can not do for himself"[26]

This was an unusual point of view in 1928, one probably not shared by the majority of Americans.

Yet Copeland himself was quick to draw the line. He wanted no part of a government giveaway for the undeserving. "Under no circumstances would I have Government do for the citizen the things he can do for himself. But there are many times," he reminded his fellow legislators, "when there are things which are beyond the ability of the individual. Here we have one of them. These mothers, most of them, are very poor. They made great sacrifices when they permitted these boys to go abroad."[27]

The only vocal opposition to the pilgrimages came from an unsuspected area. This was not merely opposition to the pilgrimages; it bordered on hostility to the Gold Star mothers themselves. The hostility was unlike the funeral home's lobby. It came from the families of disabled soldiers. Mothers of disabled soldiers received almost nothing from the government; yet the families faced insurmountable medical bills and responsibilities for their sons' care. Mabel Kay wrote Congress from Everett, Washington, to say, "Make life worth living for those that are worse off than dead." She referred to wounded soldiers in hospitals and asylums who had little hope of recovery.[28]

"No gold-star mother lost her son any more than I did mine," Emma Kessler Sweet added from her home in San Francisco. Her letter is bitter, full of the resentment and pain of the mother of a crippled son. She resented the war, the Gold Star mothers, and the pilgrimage bill most specifically. "What did the mothers of the disabled get — what sort of compensation?" she asked Congress. "They had to witness those promising lads, the fruit of their life's work, returned wrecks.... Even after 10 years of hard and devoted work our boys aren't the same and never will be the same." She pulled no punches about mothers whose sons had died either. "Why give it all to the gold-star mothers?"[29]

Who Gets to Go?

Perhaps no pilgrimage issue was as divisive and troubling as the simple question: "Who gets to go on a pilgrimage?" The issue is far more complex than it first appeared. The eligibility requirements for the Gold Star Mothers association should offer some clue of the issues involved. It included natural mothers but excluded most adoptive or stepmothers. Fathers, widows, and other family members each found factions for and against their inclusion. Congress drafted language in the end that turned out to be too restrictive, but the legislative branch deserved credit for trying to make it right.

Perhaps no issue was more divisive than the inclusion of widows. By 1928, some in Congress were willing to consider the notion, but most were less than enthusiastic. Representative Butler was willing to include war widows who had not remarried, but the lack of any specific numbers troubled him. Representatives Hamilton Fish Jr. and Mary Norton both mentioned widows in their remarks on the bill.[30] Others agreed. "Let it be a mothers and widows bill. Do not open it up to anybody else," Representative David Garrett from Texas argued.[31]

Yet Congress heard some very strong sentiment against the inclusion of widows. These objections got downright personal. Mrs. Ethel Nock expressed her resentment toward widows on the pilgrimages. "I fear [the consequences] if these widows go," she told Congress. She reminded the legislators

> You must remember ... that many of the widows are girls whom the boys would never have married had it not been for the contingency of camp life. Many of these girls were married immediately after their departure. Many of these boys would not have been married except under the sympathies of the moment. Many of these widows are not worthy. I can not talk against them, but I do fear that many of the widows are going over with the thought of Paris."[32]

Mrs. Charles Haas, a Gold Star mother from New York, agreed. "We also have a great many mothers who object very much to the widows going over," she testified.[33]

The widows, for their part, did not take an active role in lobbying Congress for pilgrimages. Therefore, we won't know their feelings at being called little better than "camp followers" by some of the Gold Star mothers. Although there was no open animosity, some Gold Star mothers objected to the government benefits the widows receive for which the mothers are ineligible.[34] Widows eventually made it into the pilgrimage legislation with one notable caveat. Only widows who had not remarried were allowed to join the pilgrimages. This distinction is one that illuminated the view society held toward women in the 1920s, especially as this view related to mourning, grief, and sacrifice.

For some, the notion of excluding all widows, then letting only some of them in, holds tremendous significance.

> That really speaks to the role that women had in the culture as being people who carried the emotional burden of loss and suffering and sacrifice. So it was women's role to enact these emotions. And I think that the legislation made it very clear, by refusing to allow women who had remarried to make the trip,

Rebecca Jo Plant said in her interview for *Gold Star Mothers: Pilgrimage of Remembrance*. "What Congress was essentially saying," she continued,

> is that we will honor women's sacrifices to the extent that they have continued to suffer. That they had sacrificed had continued to honor the place of that fallen soldier in their lives. And that at this point in history, to honor the place of the fallen soldier meant to refuse to allow another to take his place.[35]

At the same time, the issue of widows was an important but minor one in the overall debate over the pilgrimages. One should recall the segregation of African American mothers that followed was far more divisive. Kurt Piehler is correct, in other words, when he looked at the broad picture and concluded "the widows hardly enter into the debate at all."[36]

Eligibility issues for a pilgrimage extended beyond widows to the mothers themselves. The bills in question provided for pilgrimages only to those mothers of members of the U.S. armed forces who were buried in identified graves in one of the eight permanent U.S. cemeteries. Mothers of missing soldiers and sailors lost at sea — who were excluded under the bill — pressed their claims. Mathilda Burling, now firmly considered the leading Gold Star mother, spoke up for mothers of those missing in action or lost at sea. "May we not include the mothers of the unknown dead on this trip?" she asked.

> These are so few. The Government [Graves Registration Service] has done such good work in identifying the bodies. I believe there are only about 300 left. What a comfort it would be to let these mothers kneel at one of the graves marked with

a marble cross with the words "Here lies an honored American soldier known but to God," and be comforted, thinking it might be her boy![37]

A New York Gold Star mother spoke for those lost at sea. Mrs. Charles Haas, New York state president of the War Mothers Association, urged Congress not to forget the mothers whose boys lie buried in the ocean. It is a terrible thing for a mother to see her son go to war," she testified, "thinking he may not come back, or come back seriously wounded, and those that do not know where they lie buried should at least have the satisfaction of seeing the spot and be allowed to throw a flower on the waves."[38]

Mrs. Thomas Spence from Milwaukee told Congress about her first-hand experiences. "My son was killed on the boat carrying troops from England and France, and the boat was torpedoed and his body lies in the English Channel," she told the legislators, "and we feel that we have just as much right to go over there and visit the spot and be privileged to sail over the spot where our sons lie as those who are buried there."[39] Mrs. Spence was disappointed the bill excluded mothers like her. "The son of one of our national officers was on the *Tampa* and the boat was torpedoed in the English Channel. Every year, if she can not go to France and friends are going over, she has them scatter flowers as they cross from England to France," she recalled.[40]

Another separate issue of eligibility concerned Americans who died in the war effort but were not in the U.S. armed forces at the time. Two groups were involved. One was Americans who eagerly joined the war, fighting for our allies before the United States entered the war. The second group consisted largely of the American Red Cross nurses who died in action. The nurses cared for AEF soldiers, but they were employed by the Red Cross, not by the army. Because the nurses were not in the armed forces, their mothers were ineligible for a pilgrimage.

Red Cross official Ernest P. Bicknell wrote to Congress to alert them to this situation.

> Nurses to the number of 101 lost their lives in France during the war while in military service, and certain nurses have inquired of us whether the provisions of this proposed law includes the mothers of nurses who died in the service in Europe will be eligible to the benefits which the law will give.[41]

The answer to Bicknell's inquiry was "no." Unless one died in the American uniformed armed forces, the mother or widow was ineligible for a pilgrimage.

The other aspect of this debate concerned American men who were eager for combat in the war. Hundreds of men joined the armed services of America's future allies to fight against the Germans. Men entered the military services of Canada, France, or Great Britain before the United States officially joined the war in 1917. The proposed law, Butler's bill, was clear: If these men died fighting under a foreign flag, their mothers and widows were ineligible for a pilgrimage.

Probably the best-known example was the flyers of the Lafayette Escadrille. The Lafayette Escadrille was an aviation unit composed of Americans who volunteered to fight for France. After the United States joined the war, the surviving members of the unit became part of the American military. While Congress heard that many mothers of Escadrille pilots were "pretty well off," many were too poor to attend the unveiling of the monument in the unit's honor in 1928.

Congress received a number of letters in support of these mothers. An attorney from Asheville, North Carolina, wrote one such letter on behalf of a Mrs. Loula Rockwell. "Mrs. Rockwell desires to make this pilgrimage, and it seems to me that this bill ought to be amended in such a way to include the mothers and widows of those boys who volunteered and went into the French service prior to our entry in the war," the letter stated. "The mothers and widows of these boys are as entitled to consideration in this regard, as the ones who actually fought in the American Army."[42] Mrs. Rockwell's plea failed; mothers of those who fought under foreign flags would never qualify.

Other objections to the pilgrimages emerged once the eligibility issue had been decided. Connecticut Senator Hiram Bingham questioned the constitutionality of the pilgrimages. He wondered whether the federal government should even be involved in such an activity. He stated "There has been quite a little discussion as to the constitutionality of this measure." Bingham challenged Senator Robert Wagner of New York to tell him what part of the Constitution covered pilgrimages.

"I had not thought very much about that question, because I had not heard it raised before," Wagner replied. "I do not see why this would not be regarded as a national project."

Bingham persisted. "Under what clause of the Constitution would you bring it?" he asked.

Wagner was clearly caught off-guard. He had not expected such a frank and extemporaneous exchange at a hearing. "You come at me rather suddenly. I will look into that question. I have not any doubt of the authority of the Government to expend money," Wagner replied.

"Several very distinguished constitutional lawyers have been consulted by the committee who believe it is not constitutional," Bingham assured the audience.

Wagner regained his composure. "I had not given that any thought, because I did not think that was a question which would be raised in a manner as sacred and humanitarian as this," he replied.[43] Bingham must have been satisfied just to raise the issue, because it never appeared as a serious hurdle to the pilgrimages.

Paying the Bill

Financial issues concerned Congress in 1928, just as they had back in 1924. The voucher-style provision of Dickstein's bill was gone. Congress also realized the pilgrimages were more than simply an issue of economics. "This is not the kind of bill or resolution that the Congress of the United States or the people of the United States should figure as to whether it is going to cost one million or two million or three million or five or ten million dollars," New York representative Sol Bloom told his colleagues in Congress.

> It can not be weighed on the scale of money or things of that kind, and I just want to say this, that ... to go over there and kneel down beside the grave of that boy and think that might be the grave of their boy, and that is one of the most beautiful thoughts I have ever listened to in my life and I am for it 100 per cent."[44]

Had Congress known the Great Depression was coming, the outcome may have been different. But no one could predict the future, so most shared Bloom's idea.

Supporters once again reminded their fellow legislators how the families had saved the government a lot of money by leaving their boys' bodies overseas after the war. Mothers and legislators made their point enough that it seemed beyond question. Yet Hamilton Fish made the point again. He failed to recall the exact amount leaving the bodies overseas had saved the government per person. He argued:

> I did not know it cost $500. I thought it was between three and four hundred dollars. I do not know what this bill calls for as regards appropriations for the widows and mothers. I do not think it is as high as $500 for the round trip. It is less than bringing back the body of the boy.[45]

Money, however, was far from the chief issue for Representative Fish. He felt the government owed a debt to the families, especially to the mothers, who decided to leave their loved ones overseas. "Now here is the point," Fish stated. "At that time there was a great deal written in the papers urging the Gold Star mothers to keep their boys' bodies in France, and those who left them there complied with the request of Congress and of the people who represented them in Congress."[46] Fish had always considered himself an ardent supporter of pilgrimage legislation. He argued, "This bill or some bill like it ought to be passed unanimously by this Congress."[47]

The final pilgrimage bill did pass, as Fish had hoped. President Coolidge signed the bill into law shortly before leaving office on March 2, 1929. The 10-year struggle was a series of false starts and passionate arguments, of wrong solutions to the right problem, and of legislative battles lacking any strong, visible opponent.

Perhaps no other explanation was needed except for the fact the pilgrimages were then (and remain today) a unique legislative event. The law had to be custom-made to fit a host of legislative, constitutional, and financial issues. "Anybody who knows anything about what goes on in Congress would not be surprised" by the 10-year process, William S. Prince observed.[48]

Congress also acknowledged the unique and difficult nature of the pilgrimage legislation. Representative John McSwain from South Carolina, a pilgrimage ally, stated on the floor of the House in 1930, "this is the most unusual piece of legislation. The sending of these Gold-Star mothers and widows to the graves in Europe, that could be contemplated, and I doubt there is another legislative body in the world that would have as much heart as this House."[49] Heart may have been an issue, but no other legislative body had the resources at its disposal to contemplate such a series of trips.

Perhaps a 10-year wait was just as well. The American cemeteries were just nearing completion in the late 1920s. Engraved tablets with the names of missing soldiers had just been installed at each cemetery in 1928. Ethel Nock felt the time was now right for a pilgrimage, especially for the mothers of the missing. "Then the mothers of the unknown will have a monument with their boys' names to which they can go," she testified.[50]

Some parents who had gone on their own felt the temporary wooden crosses were the only weak link in their experience overseas. Hamilton Fish argued the delay had probably been for the best. "They are just putting in the crosses and perhaps it is just as well that we have not passed this bill before," he stated.[51]

At the end of the 1920s, Representative La Guardia acknowledged his 1919 bill was premature. "It did not take hold," he said of his original bill. Everything was concentrated on getting those bodies back," he told his fellow legislators in 1928.[52] Yet La Guardia was not quite ready to let go of the past and move on.

"I was criticized very severely at the time, and abused, but of course, some of us get used to that. It is a source of a great deal of gratification to see that nine years later the bill is receiving serious consideration," La Guardia observed.[53] When asked who abused him, La Guardia declined to say. However, he did believe the abusive campaign was an organized one. La Guardia believed a targeted, organized letter-writing campaign had been in place to defeat his pilgrimage bill and to derail any subsequent efforts at passage. Was it the undertakers' lobby? He refused to speculate. He told his fellow legislators how he had received letters from across the country on the issue. "I received the same letter, rather abusive, from Oregon, one from one of the Southern States, and one from the Middle States, which indicated that these form letters were being sent out at that time," he stated.[54] He did feel, however, that the mothers who wanted their sons returned to the United States were part of this effort.

Despite the delays and debate, the efforts of Nock, McSwain, and La Guardia paid off. The bill Coolidge signed was a victory for these and thousands of other pilgrimage supporters. (Thomas Butler, who died shortly after his bill was introduced in 1928, was chief among them.) Signed into law as Public Law 70-952, the act was less than two pages long. It reflected the best efforts of Congress to resolve the decade-long debate. Its language had very special and significant implications for all subsequent pilgrimage activities. Section One read, in part,

> The Secretary of War is hereby authorized to arrange for pilgrimages to cemeteries in Europe by mothers and widows of members of the military or naval forces who died in the military or naval service at any time between April 5, 1917, and July 1, 1921, and whose remains are now interred in such cemeteries.[55]

Congress declared only mothers and widows of those who died in uniform were eligible. Their intent was clear: Fathers, mothers of Red Cross nurses and Lafayette Escadrille flyers, and remarried widows were all excluded.

Section Two contained eight crucial subpoints. This section provided for invitations to be extended to all eligible women for pilgrimages to be taken between May 1, 1930, and October 31, 1933. Special passport provisions were made, and the trips would take place along the most practicable route on U.S.-flag, cabin-class steamers.

The section also stated that "no mother or widow who has previous to the pilgrimage visited cemeteries described in section I shall be entitled to make any such pilgrimages, and no mother or widow shall be entitled to make more than one such pilgrimage."[56] The section also directed the War Department to issue regulations for the pilgrimages.

Congress was content to delegate most of the details to the Secretary of War.

Section Three authorized the appropriation of "such sums as may be necessary to carry into effect the provisions of this Act."[57] It also directed the War Department to determine the amount of such sums and report back to Congress with its findings not later than December 15, 1929. This provision, in other words, dispelled the fears the military had of being given a job to do but no money with which to do it.

Section Four, the final section, defined the words *mother* and *widow* as they related to the pilgrimages. A widow was the wife of a deceased member of the armed forces who had not since remarried after the war. A mother was a natural mother, stepmother, mother through adoption, or any woman who had stood *in loco parentis* to the deceased member of the armed forces for the year prior to the commencement of such service. Both the widow and mother of the same soldier were entitled to a pilgrimage, if they each desired to go.

Back to the Drawing Board

Yet the legislative debates were far from over. In fact, the carefully worded language of the final pilgrimage act all but invited revision. Mothers who were ineligible for pilgrimages and the military officers charged with carrying out the trips both returned to Congress several times to present their cases. Congress, for its part, was very willing to listen. Congress clearly wanted these trips to go forward successfully, and the members listened to the comments, made recommendations, and passed three bills to streamline the process and pay for the trips.

The first order of business was to pay for the pilgrimages. Congress appropriated $5,386,367 to pay for all four years of the trips. This appropriation, on February 7, 1930, followed the thorough examination of pilgrimage finances, as directed in Section Three of the original act. Army Col. William R. Gibson, a West Point graduate from Ohio, presented the War Department's analysis and proposed appropriation to the House Committee on Appropriations on January 21, 1930. Col. Gibson was well prepared and made a convincing case. He had his calculations down to the penny to cover all conceivable expenses of the trips. The budget he delivered to the House, along with his testimony, offered both an informative and thorough view of the military's planning of the trips.

The Quartermaster Corps did not simply plan for trips; it created a small, dedicated unit within its ranks to carry out their plans. In Col. Gibson's proposal, salaries for clerical and administrative staff were listed at

Col. Richard Ellis and Capt. Blanche Rulon decorate the grave of Percy Stevens, in the Brookwood American Cemetery, near London. Stevens was lost when his troopship was torpedoed by a German U-boat in 1918. The War Department planned and conducted the pilgrimages, and army officers served as tour guides, baggage handlers, and nurses. Col. Ellis headed the pilgrimage office in France, and Capt. Rulon oversaw pilgrims' nursing care. (National Archives photograph RG 92.)

$134,000. This total covered the hiring of additional staff in New York, Washington, DC, and France. An additional $782,315 was allocated for subsistence for staff and pilgrims, both while staying in New York and in traveling to Europe. This figure even allowed for tips in the United States and Europe. "Is that not a little high?" one of the legislators asked Gibson in regard to the tip portion of the allocation. Gibson acknowledged it was, but the amount was clearly necessary to cover any contingency.[58] Overhead expenses, such as rent, office supplies, and printing costs, were budgeted at just under $60,000. Another $20,000 was allotted for the construction of temporary buildings at the four largest cemeteries in France. These "hostess houses" had restrooms and seating areas for larger parties of pilgrims and were not part of the original cemetery layouts.

A miscellaneous category in Gibson's budget underscored the Quartermaster Corps' worst fears in its pilgrimage duty. Travelers' health was a prominent concern, and the army wanted to be prepared for any eventuality. Burial expenses were budgeted at $225 apiece for an estimated 21 bodies, representing the government's best guess on the number of women who would die during the pilgrimages. An additional $375 for transportation of these remains back to the United States was also included. The army estimated sick travelers would consume 17,600 days in the hospital, at a total cost over $350,000.

The largest category in Gibson's budget was $3,462,187 for travel, lodging, meals, and incidentals. Water transportation to and from Europe was by far the largest single component of this request, at more than $2.1 million. The original bills as introduced in 1928 called for transport on government-owned ships, most likely naval vessels. This provision proved impractical, and Congress knew it may have to pay a private steamer line to transport the pilgrims. The pilgrimage act acknowledged as much. It read, in part, "Vessels owned and operated by the United States Government or any agency thereof shall be used for transportation at sea wherever practicable."[59]

It proved not practicable at all, so the army recommended using the ships of the United States Line. Rail transportation to and from New York City was budgeted at $634,644. Tickets for the escort officers and nurses were included in this total. The original bill also foresaw free rail travel. It included a provision directing the Interstate Commerce Commission to require the railroads under its jurisdiction to provide free or reduced rate travel to each pilgrim. This provision was deleted from the final bill. The government had to pay for train travel, just as it did for steamer service. However, the railroad industry proved to be an especially cooperative partner.

Col. Gibson offered additional information in his testimony. He reported a total number of 11,630 eligible women. The Quartermaster Corps had contacted each one to inform them of the pilgrimage act's provisions. He said 5,649 stated a desire to go on a pilgrimage, and 5,026 lacked the desire or ability to go. Another 955 were undecided. Of the 5,649 who wanted to go, 4,135 wanted to go in the first year, 1930. A total of 1,348 did not state a year, whereas a few of the women chose 1931, 1932, or 1933.[60]

Congress seemed satisfied with Col. Gibson's report and his testimony. It expected the army to engage in "a little dickering" to save money but appropriated the full sum requested nevertheless. Congress wanted the pilgrimages to succeed, and it was not afraid to appropriate the full sum requested to see this vision become a reality. The stock market crash the previous year and the growing Depression did not dissuade them from their goals.

Appropriations were not the only subsequent pilgrimage issue before Congress. A second act, Public Law 71-155, became law on April 19, 1930. It obligated the government to pay for the medical care for women who remained in Europe after their pilgrimages due to illness. It also provided, in the direst circumstances, for funds for a casket and transportation of the body back home. The act also furnished the War Department full authority to contract for any pilgrimage services as it saw fit. Another provision recalled to active duty retired Maj. Gen. B. F. Cheatham, formerly the Quartermaster General, to supervise the pilgrimages. These technical issues, however, were minor compared to the issue of eligibility.

Rather than resolving the issue of who got to on a pilgrimage, the original act served only to increase confusion and controversy. Congress passed a bill, the third law, which made three important changes in eligibility. President Herbert Hoover signed the bill into law on May 15, 1930. The first change in this act, Public Law 71-227, was to strike out wording from the original act prohibiting women who had already gone on a pilgrimage at their own expense from taking part in an official government pilgrimage. This changed revealed a clean break from congressional intent as recently as 1924. During that earlier debate, law makers were opposed to government-sponsored pilgrimages for any but the poorest women, certainly not those who had already been to Europe.

Fairness, paperwork, and a bit of irony changed Congress's mind. First, the provision excluded some of the most beloved, if wealthiest, American women. Quentin Roosevelt's mother was prohibited, due to her 1919 pilgrimage to her son's grave, despite the strong but indirect role his death and burial had played in the pilgrimage movement. The Quartermaster Corps faced extensive paperwork because of this provision. If the army determined a woman had already been to Europe after the war, it made the assumption she had gone to visit her son's or husband's grave. Therefore, the burden was on these travelers to prove in some manner that although they had been to France, they had not indeed visited their loved ones' graves.

The Quartermaster Corps records in the National Archives are full of affidavits, sworn statements, and witness interviews stating how women had been to France during the 1920s but never quite made it to the cemeteries. Sudden illnesses seemed common, with women overcome by sickness just a few miles from their sons' graves.

Some in Congress said this restriction in the original act caught them by surprise. Representative A. Piatt Andrews told his fellow legislators this provision was one "of which I was unaware."[61] He told of two Gold Star mothers in his district who had already been to Europe to visit their sons' graves. Both encountered hardships just to make their private pilgrimage, and one of the women had less than an hour at her son's grave before she was compelled to leave with the rest of her tour group. Another woman in his district had traveled with the American Legion's second AEF visit to France in 1927, but she, too, was now ineligible.

Representative Andrews was eager to address this situation, as were many other legislators. He argued, "Such exclusion involves no economy to the Government that is worth considering, but it proposes a discrimination which seems harsh and unreasonable" in its application.[62]

The second change the May 15 bill made was to include the mothers and widows of men whose bodies were missing, buried at sea, or buried in isolated or remote graves separate from one of the eight permanent cemeteries. The original bill invited only those whose son or husband was buried in one of the official cemeteries or whose body was never found but whose name was nevertheless engraved on the Tablet of the Missing at one of the cemeteries.

Congress acted wisely here, too. Mrs. Roosevelt was ineligible under this provision of the original act as well — Quentin was buried in a remote grave "where the tree fell."

During the debate on this issue, opponents attacked this original provision. Representative Florence Kahn from California, always a zealous pilgrimage advocate, defended the change. "These boys certainly died in Europe," she said, referring to the missing.

> According to the War Department they [the pilgrims] will be taken to that particular sector, the neighborhood in which the boys died, and shown about where they were killed. It seems to me that is the least we can do for these mothers who gave their boys to their country. Certainly to visit once in a lifetime the grave of the boys who were lost abroad, or to be able to see once in a lifetime the place where their boys died, is mighty little comfort to give mothers.[63]

The third and final provision of the bill was a change in the definition of *in loco parentis*, the notion of occupying the place of a parent. Under the new act, pilgrimages were now available to any woman "who stood in *loco parentis* to the deceased ... for a period of not less than five years at any time to the soldier, sailor, or marine becoming eighteen years of age."[64]

This issue presented Congress and the War Department with both confusion and anguish. The Quartermaster General of the Army testified before Congress on December 17, 1929 and said this part of the original act "has given us more trouble than almost any phase of the bill in that our sympathies are involved."[65] Congress delegated sending the actual invitations and deciding on eligibility to the War Department. The Quartermaster Corps did the job but found it difficult to say "no" as often as it did. The Quartermaster General told Congress the War Department had rejected all but 35 of the 409 claims made under this provision of the act.

The somewhat narrow, legalistic language of the original bill was to blame. Most aunts, sisters, and stepmothers were ineligible because most men were 19 or older when they joined the service. The new act changed the wording, so most of those women who applied could now go.

Although Congress clearly was in the mood to expand the pilgrimages, it stopped short of allowing everyone to participate. This stance still held true for fathers and for those who fought and died in the military service of another nation. The issue of pilgrimages for fathers was raised again, as it had been in La Guardia's 1919 bill. The 1929 act, of course, excluded fathers and all other family members, friends, and companions.

Senator Henry Allen from Kansas introduced a bill on February 13, 1930, to allow Gold Star fathers to go on pilgrimages. His bill proposed a $3.5 million appropriation to pay for the trips. "I think that the fathers are as much entitled to see the graves of their sons as are the mothers," he said.[66] The fathers had no organized support and seemed intent on focusing their efforts on the soldiers' mothers. There is no record of a Gold Star fathers organization lobbying Congress for pilgrimages.

A number of men did eventually accompany their wives on pilgrimages, traveling at their own expense. In an era when few people traveled, and married women almost always traveled with their husbands, solo travel seemed a valid and familiar argument in favor of including the husbands.

One such husband was Canio Cerreta of Bridgeport, Connecticut, who wrote to Congress in 1928 with just this type of advice. He wrote,

> I would like respectfully to submit to your kind consideration the fact that very few mothers will benefit from such a bill unless their husbands have enough means in order to accompany them, as a great majority of them are not used to travel alone, without their husbands, even from one city to another. My wife, for instance, would not dare to go even to New York alone.[67]

Mr. Cerreta's comments would have made sense to the legislators.

Elmore, Ohio's William Oestreich accompanied Party B, 1930. Fathers were always permitted, of course, to travel at their own expense. Mr. Oestreich's party was preparing to travel, in fact, while this subsequent debate over eligibility continued. In a newspaper interview, he expressed reluctance at public grief that most men of his day shared. "Most of us men who lost our sons do not want to come over to visit their graves. We prefer to stay at home, let our losses remain memories, and our grief under cover of our daily lives," Mr. Oestreich said.[68]

In the end, however, Senator Allen's bill failed. Fathers and other companions were excluded, once and for all. This debate put the end to the pilgrimage movement in Congress.

Only one other bill was introduced, and that one not until 1935. Representative John Dingell from Michigan introduced a bill two years after the last pilgrim had returned. His bill attempted to resurrect the voucher-style payment to women who were entitled to go on a pilgrimage but were either unwilling or unable to go. His bill never passed.

The World War I pilgrimages were the only ones in which Congress seriously addressed sending Gold Star mothers (or any other relatives) overseas. There appears to have been no organized government support for such trips following the Civil War, World War II, the Korean War, or the Vietnam War.

Pause for Reflection

Many in Congress felt the pilgrimages offered a chance to show America at its best on the world stage. Legislators expressed this sentiment during the original debate on the bill and after the May 15 passage of the final piece of legislation. In a sense, Congress must have felt the quaint notion of "making the world safe for democracy" was not dead at all. The pilgrimages have always been an ideal canvas on which the audience, not the participants, fills in the background to create some sort of big picture meaning. Those who helped pass the bills were no different. Many in Congress and a number of the mothers themselves had almost sacred aspirations for the pilgrimages. Representative David O'Connell from New York felt the pilgrimages would become "a real peace mission to France, sending those women there as a moral lesson of the gratitude of a great country."[69]

Fiorello La Guardia agreed. The 10-year legislative fight had given the journeys a more solemn meaning.

> I think that it will be the greatest mission of peace that one country ever sent to another country. I think that this great mission of peace of these mothers who know what war means, who gave their sons for the cause of war, who gave their sons that we may put an end to war, meeting the mothers of the French boys and the English boys and the Belgian boys who died and getting together will be the greatest mission of peace, will be the greatest crusade of peace that the world has ever seen.[70]

Representative Loring Black from New York hoped the pilgrimages had a positive impact on how the rest of the world saw America. "It will do far more to bring about a better understanding, showing that we have a spiritual side to us, than anything that has been done heretofore by our diplomats and other representatives," he argued.[71]

Legislators assumed that pilgrimage efforts would put a stop to any future wars. Senator Robert Wagner from New York wrote that "such a holy pilgrimage to the American shrines in Europe would be a great living and moving monument to peace. The ranks of mothers and sweethearts would constitute a new expeditionary force and a first line of defense for peace."[72]

The Depths of the Great Depression

It is remarkable that the pilgrimage debate took place during the 1920s but was actually paid for and carried out during the Great Depression of the 1930s. The world had changed from the passage of the first bill to the subsequent act in 1930. The stock market had crashed, and many Americans were out of work. Perhaps the Depression and the desperate times it brought meant criticism of the pilgrimages was inevitable. Another force was at work, too. No one could find the slightest fault with Gold Star mothers traveling at their own expense to visit their sons' graves abroad. When public funds were involved, the movement found itself opened to criticism and ill will. Furthermore, most members of the public did not follow the bills through Congress during the 1920s. Yet when the laws were passed, and the pilgrims began to set sail, some members of the public did not like what they saw.

People wrote letters to the editor of major newspapers and to President Hoover, who had taken office right after the original act was signed. The first batch of letters was written in 1930, but letters were appearing in print as late as 1933. These letters had no effect; the pilgrimages went forward as planned and as funded. However, they revealed some of the prevailing public sentiment.

> Many of us are actually hungry and insufficiently clothed; yet, through taxes, we are compelled to pay for these expensive trips to European countries. It does not seem human, or even possible, that these "War Mothers" would expect or could enjoy this visit to the graves of their loved ones which would add to the burden of suffering in the country for which their boys gave all,

wrote John Sunnit in a January 17, 1933, letter to the *New York Times*.[73] The *Times* published another letter similar to Sunnit's. Eveline Alice Cohn suggested the Gold Star mothers should refuse the free trips, knowing how so many of their fellow citizens were suffering.[74]

The contentious issue of disabled soldiers made its way into the letters as well. Elsie L. Lewis's letter to the *Times* was published on February

8, 1930, and argued the $5 million voted for the pilgrimages would be much better spent on those who survived the war. "The interest on the sum Congress so blithely appropriated for travel would provide for hundreds of these disabled men," she wrote.[75]

Yet some letter writers defended the pilgrimages, often based on their own firsthand knowledge. Lottie Haas supported the pilgrimages in her own *Times* letter published April 18, 1932. In it, she elevated the debate over the pilgrimages from purely a monetary one. For this pilgrim, "the money expended can in no way compare to the comfort derived when these Gold Star Mothers place wreaths on the graves of their sons and look, perhaps for the last and only time, at the inscriptions on the white crosses, placed row upon row," she concluded. She declared the pilgrimages a "splendid gesture."[76]

President Hoover heard much the same from across the country. Many letters to the president faulted not the pilgrimages themselves but the timing of the trips. One New York City Gold Star mother, Clara Du Bois, wrote to the president on March 17, 1930. She told the president her son Norman was killed in action July 15, 1918, and is buried overseas. "He lies at Cuperly [France] at my wish, grave kept by me. I released the Government of his care. I have strong feelings about not moving him, as President Roosevelt felt about his son," her letter read in part. "I am opposed to this way for the Government to spend money for excursions for relatives to go the graves when our reconstruction work goes so slowly with our shattered men who suffer so desperately still."

Furthermore, Mrs. Du Bois was not entirely sure a journey would be beneficial for the pilgrims themselves. She preferred the money be kept at home "instead of sending mothers and wives abroad to see the graves and be harrowed by that unhealthy new touch with the Past."[77]

In the end, letter writers had very little impact on Congress and the president. Congress, for its part, was devoted to the pilgrimages. It took 10 years to pass legislation, but Congress got it right in the end. It listened to all participants, took feedback, and crafted law after law to meet as many objections as possible.

Some may have wondered, along with Mrs. Du Bois in fact, what impact the pilgrimages would actually have on the pilgrims themselves. Would they be beneficial? Or would they simply create an "unhealthy new touch with the Past?" If Congress wanted to answer these questions, they could have spoken to the hundreds of American woman who had already been overseas on their own, privately funded pilgrimages.

4

Do-It-Yourself Pilgrimages

Americans of the World War I generation did not wait for government assistance. They took matters into their own hands if at all possible. Gold Star mothers nationwide, rich and poor, journeyed to Europe to visit their sons' graves. Some went as soon as possible; Quentin Roosevelt's mother was in France just three months after the armistice. Others saved their money and waited 10 years or longer for the opportunity to go. For those who did go on their own, resources and assistance were available. Private tour operators helped with arrangements, and the American Legion took dozens of mothers along on its "Second AEF" visit to France in 1927. The Graves Registration Service's offices in Paris were ready to help. In fact, the service estimated over 1,000 Gold Star mothers had made private pilgrimages by 1924.[1]

Two prominent names deserve a closer look: Joyce Kilmer and Quentin Roosevelt. In a broader context, these individual journeys were part of a larger, worldwide trend in war grave and battlefield pilgrimages, which started almost as soon as the war ended. The private pilgrimages also serve to remind us that any mother who lost a son in the war may be properly called a Gold Star mother, not just those women who took part in an official government pilgrimage.

Ready to Assist

Long before Congress approved pilgrimages, many agencies and parties were ready to help individual families in France. The Graves Registration Service (GRS) joined with the Red Cross and other agencies to establish an Information Bureau in Paris to assist relatives coming to France to see the battlefields and soldiers' graves. The bureau was operational by 1920 and was located next door to GRS headquarters. Relatives were advised to make the bureau their first stop in Paris. Here, one could obtain the cemetery name and grave location of a loved one. These joint efforts overlooked no detail to assist with any arrangements a family member may request. "The Information Bureau is equipped with a Red Cross worker and a YWCA secretary, who furnish full information in regard to train schedules, hotel accommodations in towns near the cemeteries, and as to transportation from trains to cemeteries," one contemporary guidebook noted.[2]

Once families reached the cemeteries, they could count on additional assistance. This was especially true at the larger cemeteries. Near the Romagne cemetery, known today as the Meuse-Argonne, the army donated a barracks for relatives who wished to spend a night or two nearby. When refurbished, the barracks could sleep 20 people and hold even more at mealtime. Tea was served every afternoon, and a contemporary guidebook described the quarters as "cheery and homelike with bright furnishings and creton hangings."[3] The Red Cross provided transportation to and from the train station. At most cemeteries with hotels nearby, such as Belleau Wood, overnight accommodations on the grounds were unnecessary. Small cottages or service buildings with restrooms and seating areas were available in all but the smallest cemeteries.

At the Thiacourt Cemetery, even these small services were unnecessary. An interested French woman, a Madame Delcro, arranged for comfortable accommodations for American visitors all through the 1920s. The same guidebook assured all Americans that the French people and American volunteers in Europe stood ready to assist the pilgrimage abroad.

> They are all united in their desire to give aid and assistance to sorrowing relatives in locating graves, taking photographs of individual plots to be sent home to family and friends and procuring and arranging flowers which have been carried to the spot or sent from Paris."[4]

Many women used these resources to travel overseas. When they did, they often carried the hopes and dreams of others with them. When a Gold Star mother learned another woman was going to France to decorate her son's grave, she often asked for any information on the condition of her son's own cross. One such woman was Ethel Nock. Mrs. Nock was an outspoken pilgrimage advocate and testified before Congress in support of the trips. She made her own private pilgrimage to France in 1927. At Suresnes cemetery outside Paris, Mrs. Nock decorated the grave of Lt. William Rock. Lt. Rock was the son of Mr. and Mrs. William D. Rock of Pennsylvania. Both women were officers in the American War Mothers

4. Do-It-Yourself Pilgrimages 77

organization. This association included a broader membership than Gold Star mothers but welcomed any Gold Star mother in its ranks. Mrs. Rock, in fact, served as the Gold Star chairperson for the American War Mothers, and she argued "the idea for the pilgrimages had its inception in the American War Mothers."[5] No one group deserves sole credit for the pilgrimages; it was a broadly based effort that many patriotic and veterans groups supported, the American War Mothers among them.

Mrs. Nock wanted to decorate Lt. Rock's grave, not only as a tribute to a fallen soldier — Lt. Rock was awarded the Distinguished Service Cross — but also to his mother and her friend. She recalled how she "felt impelled to again pay tribute to this hero son of a woman who had given me such comfort in my own great sorrow."[6]

She compared the beautiful Suresnes to America's own Arlington National Cemetery. On the visit, Mrs. Nock had nothing but praise for the government and the men who tended the cemeteries in France. After meeting James Duncan, superintendent at Suresnes, Mrs. Nock asserted, "Our Government has placed remarkable men in charge of these cemeteries. They are men who guard the crosses as if they marked the places of their own sons."[7]

Mrs. Nock was an ardent supporter of pilgrimages because she knew firsthand how comforting and healing they were to the women who took them. It made no difference if the trip were a solo visit or an organized tour. Mrs. Nock realized for all Gold Star mothers, pilgrims or not, were joined together in ways only they could share. "All Pilgrims know the unbreakable bond that exists among those who have traveled together to the crosses overseas."[8]

Many women did wish to travel overseas, and they preferred to travel in groups. Two separate, private groups took place during the 1920s, while Congress continued to debate the subject. The first was a privately organized trip in 1925, sponsored by United States Lines steamer company. Press reports indicated the trip was offered in response to overwhelming public demand and interest.

Sailing aboard the *S.S. George Washington*, the party left New York on May 16, 1925, and landed at Cherbourg on May 22. American ambassador to France Myron Herrick and French President Doumerge received the mothers in an official ceremony in Paris the next day. Battling rain and cold weather, the women decorated France's Tomb of the Unknown soldier on May 27. The party visited cemeteries and other World War I sites around France over the next few days. Reports indicated as many as 15 women took the trip, although up to 8 were ill at any one time. The party returned to the United States aboard the *S.S. Leviathan*. The all-inclusive trip sold for $225, and this price included steamship travel plus hotels and meals in France.⁹

The second and far larger group was the American Legion's Second AEF in September 1927. The Second AEF was composed primarily of former doughboys. (In fact, the Legion held several postwar trips to France. It offered an official tour in 1921, and several hundred legionnaires took a battlefield pilgrimage in 1937.) Their objective was the Legion's 10th annual convention, held in Paris September 19–23, 1927. The Second AEF was designed strictly for legionnaires and their families; however, passage was opened up to others, including Gold Star mothers. Almost 16,000 people sailed with the group in what was surely one of the most complex, costly, and well-organized private trips ever conducted up to that time.

Legion planners overlooked no detail to make it easy for members to travel overseas. The Legion secured special, discounted round-trip train tickets to and from New York City for its members. They received so many inquiries about the proper type of suitcase for foreign travel that it designed its own model and contracted with two luggage manufacturers to make the bags and sell them to legionnaires at a group rate.¹⁰ Getting time off to take a European trip was a challenge. Many workers did not have vacation time available for such trips. The Legion made its best efforts to assist its members.

> A campaign was carried on through magazines of the country and through appeals to large associations requesting the cooperation of employers of ex-service men to grant increased vacations in order to make it possible for legionnaires to attend the Paris convention,

the Legion's official report on the Second AEF observed.¹¹

Five separate steamer lines were necessary to transport the attendees, and virtually every available hotel room in Paris was booked for members of the Second AEF months in advance. The Legion promoted these liners as luxury ships, nothing like the troopships most doughboys used to and from France. "Each one is a floating palace! No bunks, mess lines or restrictions. Instead—spacious staterooms, beautiful dining salons and full freedom of the ship. There will be no class restrictions on the transports of the 2nd AEF," one of the Legion's ads stated.¹²

Other organizations were glad to assist the Legion. The American Red Cross established aid stations as well as a 24-bed hospital in Paris to care for sick legionnaires. The Salvation Army brought 27 staff from the United States to equip a lunchroom for legionnaires in convention headquarters. The menu included tea, donuts, ham sandwiches, and familiar American-style coffee. The Knights of Columbus brought 31 secretaries from the

United States to help legionnaires with their correspondence and even passed out 327,000 bars of soap, an amenity the Americans learned French hotels never provided for their guests.[13]

The highlight of the Second AEF was a grand parade of the legionnaires in Paris. Hundreds of thousands of cheering Parisians joined thousands of French soldiers to watch the legionnaires march the five-mile parade route. The Legion was delighted with the response it received. "The parade was moving amidst a welcome so whole-heartedly sincere that cheers, applause, and tears throughout the entire length and breadth of the march became a gigantic demonstration of mixed emotions without single untoward incident," the Legion's report on the convention noted with obvious pride.[14]

The convention was more than just parades and parties. (Parties, no doubt, were part of the Second AEF, as many of the former doughboys failed to observe Prohibition while on their European convention.) Battlefield visits and cemetery tours were part of the program. A photograph in *American Legion Monthly* showed five legionnaires kneeling at the grave of a fallen comrade in an unidentified cemetery.[15] In addition, some 243 Legion officials took a postconvention tour throughout Europe. The party found a very warm reception in several European capitals. England's King George pronounced the party a "fine looking lot," and the pope received the group at a special ceremony in Rome. They were disappointed, however, to learn Italian Premier Mussolini would be unable to meet with them, due to the recent birth of a son.[16]

Gold Star mothers were welcomed on the Second AEF and encouraged to attend. Several dozen Gold Star mothers accompanied the Legion on its trip. Some traveled solo, whereas others accompanied their husbands or other family members. The Legion embarked on a fundraising and public relations campaign during the summer of 1927 to enable Gold Star mothers to make the trip. "Do you know of some mother whose boy fell in France?" a Legion-sponsored story asked in a major city newspaper. "Whose son is sleeping today for all time in one of the American cemeteries in France? Would it not be a wonderful thing for you women [readers] to send such a mother to France?"[17]

The newspaper urged its readers to get together and form Gold Star Mothers to France clubs and raise funds to send the women overseas. (The Legion urged its own members to establish savings accounts, not unlike today's Christmas club accounts, to help save money for the Second AEF.) It also published newspaper subscription renewal forms where readers could, if they desired, send in extra money earmarked for the Gold Star trips.

Fundraising appeals were patriotic, sentimental, and effective. The appeal pleaded,

> Consider the psychology of mothers. How faithful, how eternally devoted they are in their love! Is there anything to match it? Poets have sung and with truth the changelessness of a mother's love. It is she who faithfully and in all seasons goes to graveyards when all the remainder of the family has forgotten or become calloused in their grief, over the passing of loved ones.[18]

"Remember that the mother of any soldier, any lad who gave his life for this, our country, is the worthiest of all," the appeal continued.

> With gratitude she would cross the broad Atlantic ocean simply for the privilege of kneeling at the grave of a gallant son whose memory never has been diminished in her heart. With something of pride she would witness the honors that will be paid to his memory by his comrades. He will not be forgotten by the great legion which will cross the sea next September. Nor should the mother who gave him his life and who suffered worse than death when that life was taken away be forgotten now.[19]

A number of Gold Star mothers went with the Second AEF. The women found peace and solace on the trips, as they would in the Gold Star pilgrimages a few years later. Most of the women traveled with a husband or Legion companion. One such couple who made the pilgrimage to France was Mr. and Mrs. M. F. Boechat of Buffalo, New York. The Boechats went to decorate the grave of their only son, Sgt. John A. Boechat. He served with the 27th Division and is buried in the Somme Cemetery.[20] The women had a day, at most, at the cemeteries as the Legion party ventured out into the French countryside. At least one of these women presented a heartbreaking sight at one of the cemeteries. Her son was Private Joseph Murphy. He was killed in action, but his body was never found. A reporter noticed that the "woman in black moved along the eastern slope of Belleau Hill, kneeling first beside one white stone and then another. Each cross at which she paused to pray bore the inscription, 'Here Rests in Eternal Glory an American Soldier Known But to God.'"[21]

Her experience is that of a mother of a missing soldier. The pilgrimage would have brought some comfort, seeing the cemeteries, but there must have remained some doubt. Which grave was her son? Perhaps he is still missing or captured? The pilgrimage experience would have been different, certainly less of a closure than for women who had a specific grave to decorate.

Private Murphy's mother explained her journey. "His comrades say he is here among the unknown," she stated. "I brought with me a little bag of Pennsylvania earth from the yard of our home where Joe used to play. I sprinkled some of it on each of the unknown graves so that Joe would get his share."[22] To the Murphy and Boechat families, the Second AEF would have been an invaluable healing experience.

To America's former allies, however, the Second AEF had quite a different impact. This impact is certainly not what the Legion itself would have wanted. British observers objected to the large American contingent and its assertion that America won the war single-handedly.

> The American Legion tour was an unprecedented event, which was reported in newspapers throughout the world. In many countries journalists instigated a growing demand for ex-servicemen to travel to the battlefields, if only to show that the Americans were not the only ones who had won the war!

argues David Lloyd in his book *Battlefield Tourism: Pilgrimage and the Commemoration of the Great War in Britain, Australia and Canada, 1919–1939*.[23]

The Second AEF spurred a pilgrimage by the British Legion the following year, a trip attended by over 10,000 British veterans and their families. In planning for their pilgrimage, the British wanted to avoid the reprehensible behavior of the Americans on the Second AEF. Reports indicated some Americans treated Paris as both a bar and a brothel. The British Legion noted this behavior and worked to insure there would be no "repetition of the preposterous opera-bouffe scenes which attended the visit to Paris of the American Legion."[24] One group of legionnaires shouldered their way into King Albert's palace in Belgium, looking for the Belgian war hero.[25] Whether the legionnaires were all that bad, or whether the British were peeved the Americans beat them to the punch, remains a mystery. In either case, the Second AEF deserves credit for being both the largest American Great War pilgrimage and for shaping the pilgrimages efforts of our allies in the years which followed.

Joyce and Quentin

Two of America's most well-known families figured prominently in the do-it-yourself pilgrimage story: the Kilmers and the Roosevelts. Both families lost sons in the war, and members of both families made their own private pilgrimages to France as soon as possible. Quentin Roosevelt was shot down over France, and Joyce Kilmer was killed by machine gun fire while lying in an exposed position next to his commanding officer. In an era of nearly universal participation in the war effort, Joyce and Quentin stood apart. Either one could have easily avoided combat, but both sought it out, eager to do his duty to his country and his family.

Alfred Joyce Kilmer was born in New Brunswick, New Jersey, in 1886. He is best remembered for his 1913 poem "Trees." ("I think that I shall never see / A poem lovely as a tree.") He received is bachelor's degree from Columbia University in 1908. He was married shortly after graduation. His wife, Aline, was also an accomplished poet and writer.

When war was declared, Kilmer was eager to join. Although he was over 30 and had wife and children, he wanted to do his part. He was no mere dilettante; he wanted to be a real soldier.

One man who saw him as a soldier, not a poet, was his priest, Father Francis Duffy. Father Duffy was the chaplain of Kilmer's unit, the 27th Division. It's hard not to like Kilmer as we meet him through Father Duffy's eyes. "Nothing of the long-haired variety about him — a sturdy fellow, manly, humorous, interesting," Duffy observed in his book, *Father Duffy's Story*.[26]

Duffy speculated that many men in Kilmer's position would have been content to stay at home. Not so with Kilmer. "But he is bound to do his share and do it at once," the priest wrote, "so there is no use taking the fine edge off his enthusiasm. He sees what he considers a plain duty, and he is going ahead to perform it, calm and clear eyed and without the slightest regard to what the consequences may be."[27]

Kilmer's 27th Division was an Irish American outfit composed of New York men. Its officers had names such as O'Ryan, Donovan, and Hurley. The men were proud to be both Irish and American. Kilmer told his comrades "cold steel propelled by Irishmen was said to be what the Germans chiefly feared."[28] He felt the energy and enthusiasm of his fellow soldiers, a feeling he believed was uniquely Irish. "The feeling of the officers and men was one of stern delight, of that strange religious exhilaration with which men of the Celtic race and faith go into battle, whether the arena be Vinegar Hill, Fontenoy, or Rouge Bouquet," Kilmer observed.[29]

Kilmer's poem "Rouge Bouquet" is especially moving. During a mass on St. Patrick's Day 1918, Father Duffy read the poem to the assembled troops in France. "The last lines of each verse are written to respond to the notes of 'Taps', the bugle call for the end of the day which is also blown ere the last sods are dropped on the graves of the dead."

Duffy wrote of the ceremony, "Sergeant Patrick Stokes stood near me with his horn and blew the tender plaintive notes before I read the words; and then from the deep woods where [bugler] Egan was stationed came a repetition of the notes like horns from elfland faintly blowing." Duffy instructed the musicians to break the somber mood with some "rollicking Irish airs." "We can pay tribute to our dead but we must not lament them overmuch," Duffy concluded his account.[30]

Joyce Kilmer and Father Duffy, poet and priest, became close friends. What little free time they could find they spent in each other's company. "My chiefest joy in life is to have Joyce Kilmer around," Duffy wrote. "In the army it matters little whether a man was a poet or a grave digger—he is going to be judged by what he is as a soldier. And Joyce is rated highly from everybody from the K.P. [kitchen police] to the Colonel because he is a genuine fellow."[31]

For Kilmer's part, wartime camaraderie suited him just fine. He always had time to visit with Father Duffy and other soldiers. "Whenever he gets a day off he is in to see me and we break all the rules by chatting till midnight and beyond," Duffy recalled of Kilmer's late night visits.

> Books and fighting and anecdotes and good fellows and things to eat and religion; all the good old human interests are common to us, with a flavor of literature, of what human-minded people have said in the past give them breadth and bottom.[32]

Kilmer and Duffy lived soldiers' lives in France. As much as they enjoyed each other's company, they knew death was all around them. Even Duffy knew the risks. "Kilmer or I, one of us, may see an end to life in this war, but neither of us will be able to say that life has not been good to us," he wrote.[33]

Unfortunately, the priest was right; one of them didn't make it through the war. Sgt. Joyce Kilmer was killed in action on July 30, 1918, in heavy fighting near the Ourcq River. His commanding officer, Lt. Col. William J. Donovan, described the poet's last mission.

> Sgt. Kilmer, at his own insistence, went with me. We were lying together along the Bois Coles [Colas]. Machine gun fire was coming down the draw from the village of Seringes [-et-Nesles]. A bullet hit him full in the head, killing him instantly. Not only did Sergeant Kilmer find a soldierly joy in the conflict and actually seek danger, but he was a cool headed soldier. On the day of his death and on the day preceding, he performed the very trying duties of adjutant and was full of eagerness at all times to give his full measure of service.[34]

Donovan's remarks are preserved in an affidavit he wrote, kept in the burial file on Joyce Kilmer at the National Archives in College Park, Maryland. (Donovan gained fame as "Wild Bill" Donovan in World War II, the man who founded the OSS, considered the forerunner of the CIA.)

The decision to return Kilmer's body fell to his widow, Aline. Their son Kenton recalled how he and his mother talked over this difficult issue. The decision reminded them of a stanza from Joyce's war poem, "Rouge Bouquet." "There is on earth no worthier grave / To hold the bodies of the brave / Than this place of pain and pride / Where they nobly fought and nobly died."

"We both agreed that we should respect the sentiments Dad expressed in his lines," his son wrote. Joyce Kilmer's body remained in France, where he had certainly nobly fought and nobly died.[35]

Kilmer's parents were prominent people. They had the means and interest to visit his grave in France, and they made a private pilgrimage in September 1920. (His sons Kenton and Christopher and his daughter also visited his grave several times in later years.) His mother, Annie Kilburn Kilmer, was something of an amateur playwright and poet. Mrs. Kilmer dedicated several of these poems to her fallen son. She wrote these poems, she said, not so much to demonstrate her ability as a poet but "rather to show the throbbing of a mother's heart."[36] Joyce's father was a chemist and an early officer in the company Johnson & Johnson.

The circumstances surrounding this personal pilgrimage are somewhat confusing. Mrs. Kilmer felt as if she had been refused permission to go visit her son's grave soon after the war. It is unclear, even today, why permission was needed to visit France. If indeed permission was needed, and it was refused, why was she allowed to go in 1920?

As we've seen, the GRS worked with other interested parties to facilitate cemetery and battlefield visits. Mrs. Kilmer was offered a chance to participate in one of the organized pilgrimages, but she refused. Mrs. Kilmer returned her letter of invitation from the War Department with this handwritten note: "Was refused permission by your Dept. in 1919 — so I went without it in 1920 and again this summer."[37]

In any event, Joyce's parents were pleased with their pilgrimage to his grave in the Oise-Aisne Cemetery. His mother described her visit in her 1925 book, *Leaves from My Life*. "How can I describe the sad journey to his grave?" she wrote. "I can see it as I write. The grave was covered with flowers, but I took those at the head, and placed them further down, and put my flowers in their place," she recalled.[38]

Mrs. Kilmer learned from the cemetery attendant that her son's grave is never without flowers. Many visitors bring their own to decorate his grave. Her account is also a unique one. It is the only book-length, published account written by a Gold Star mother after the war that described in any detail what the pilgrimage experience — solo or organized — was like.

Kilmer's parents were pleased with their trip. Today, their son still rests in the Oise-Aisne Cemetery, just a few hundred yards from where he was killed. During their 1920 visit, his body was not yet buried in a permanent cemetery. His grave would have lacked a final marble cross. Nevertheless, the Kilmers both found the situation a soothing one and very much to their satisfaction.

Joyce Kilmer's father, F. B. Kilmer, wrote a letter to the War Department to express the satisfaction he and his wife both felt after their pilgrimage.

> In our journey to the cemetery, and upon our arrival at the cemetery, the sadness was greatly softened when we witnessed the condition of the American cemeteries; all seemed in perfect order, kept with the most scrupulous care, and in charge persons who were in love, and in sympathy, with the work. We could utter words of praise for each and every individual with whom we came in contact, and we feel, as one deeply interested and perhaps from the nature of the case, quite able to judge the efficiency of the entire work, including the courtesy which we received from your office in Washington.³⁹

The condition of the graves and cemeteries always concerned the relatives. Perhaps they expected unmarked graves and unkempt cemeteries. Even the temporary cemeteries of the early 1920s dispelled their fears, and the permanent ones were then and remain today immaculate and beautiful.

Mrs. Kilmer felt the intense pain of her son's loss. Given her son's fame, she was especially proud of his wartime accomplishments. She took the opportunity in her published accounts to share the loss and pride she felt. She was delighted the French government presented her with a miniature Croix de Guerre. "I am most proud to wear my French flag and my service pin, whose blue star miraculously turned to gold days after I received news of my son's glorious death," she wrote in *Memories of My Son Sergeant Joyce Kilmer*.⁴⁰

"I do not claim to be like the Spartan mother who told her sons when going to battle to return bearing their shields or upon them, but I *do* claim to be the very proudest mother in all the world because Sergeant Joyce Kilmer was and *is* my son," she continued.⁴¹

Mrs. Kilmer wrote several poems about her son. The most moving was "To My Boy Who Lies in France," published in her 1920 book, *Memories*.

To My Boy Who Lies in France

Are you lonely, Dear, beneath the shining Lilies?
Do you miss the tramp of marching feet all day?
When the 69th had left you for the Home-land,
With their bright young faces resolute and gay —

Did you think "My mother longing for my presence,
Cannot bear to see my Comrades marching by —

> Through the streets where she and I often lingered,
> In Manhattan, underneath its bright blue sky."
>
> "Ah! My mother's heart was always beating for me,
> And she never cared for aught when I was near —
> Now the stormy, stormy, stern Atlantic rolls between us —
> But her soul is in the Poppies over here."
>
> Oh! My darling, rest quiet 'neath the Lilies,
> God is good, and gives me courage for your sake!
> For the mother of a Hero should not falter,
> And the bitter cup He gives, I will take.[42]

On the organized pilgrimages almost a decade later, many of her fellow Gold Star mothers were indeed willing to take the bitter cup, be strong, and visit the graves of their own heroes. Although is it unknown how many of her fellow Gold Star mothers read Mrs. Kilmer's accounts, there is no doubt many of these mothers shared her feelings once they had crossed the stormy, stern Atlantic.

Poor Quinikins

The other name in the do-it-yourself pilgrimage movement was even more prominent than Kilmer — it was Roosevelt. The story of young Quentin Roosevelt, his death in battle, his parents' plea, and his mother's pilgrimage is a vital part of the Gold Star mothers' story. In a sense, Quentin's death may be viewed as the very beginning of the pilgrimage movement.

Quentin was born to Teddy and Edith Roosevelt on November 19, 1897, in Washington, DC. He attended school in the Washington area while his father served his two terms as president, from 1901 to 1909, of the energetic Roosevelt children, Quentin was the youngest and grew up in front of the American public while TR was in office. Called the "White House gang," the children were noted for their pranks, stunts, and general good-natured mischief. (Quentin was as well known to most Americans as were John and Caroline Kennedy some 60 years later.) Quentin was enrolled at Harvard when the United States entered the war.

Quentin's military career began earlier than that of most Americans. He attended the noted Plattsburgh cadet training camps during the summers of 1915 and 1916. The Plattsburgh academy offered patriotic men a chance to learn military drill and tactics prior to joining the service, and it provided a small measure of preparedness to an otherwise unprepared America as the war began. Given Teddy's Rough Rider image, it is no surprise that Quentin was eager to see action. He wanted to be a pilot and entered the Army's Air Service in 1917.

4. Do-It-Yourself Pilgrimages

Teddy and Quentin Roosevelt on Family Picnic. The Teddy Roosevelt family at rest on the family estate, Sagamore Hill, New York. Teddy Roosevelt is in the foreground, in a hat. Quentin Roosevelt is at his right, second from left. Teddy Roosevelt had six children. Alice was his first child, born to his first wife, who died shortly after childbirth. Teddy married Edith Kermit in 1904. They had five children together: Theodore Jr., Kermit, Ethel, Archibald, and the youngest Quentin. The undated photograph was probably taken 1916–17. (Sagamore Hill National Historic Site, National Park Service.)

Commissioned an officer, young Lt. Roosevelt arrived in Liverpool, England, on August 8, 1917, and was immediately assigned to the aviation operations at Issoudun, France. After completing training at various bases in France, Quentin served as an instructor pilot. He was eventually assigned to the 95th Aero Squadron at Toul, France, on June 24, 1918, his first combat position. Quentin was delighted to be in the thick of battle, but his aviation career had trouble getting off the ground. As the son of a former president, young Quentin found that his superiors were unwilling to assign him to combat duty. "Throughout his Air Service career he found that no officer wanted the responsibility of assigning him to hazardous duty. In fact, it had been a real struggle for him to escape a desk job to take flight training," one aviation historian observed.[43] Even so, Quentin was determined to get into battle, not to use his name and family position to avoid combat. Much like Joyce Kilmer, Quentin pulled every string he could, not to avoid danger but to put himself in the best position to help his country win the war.

He eventually did get into battle and served his country. He shot down his first enemy aircraft on July 10, 1918. He became separated from his squadron over Chateau-Thierry while on a mission. He finally spotted a large formation of friendly aircraft heading home and joined the group. Suddenly, Quentin realized he had joined a flight of German planes heading east over enemy lines. He reacted quickly, firing a short burst into the Fokker fighter in front of him and then dove sharply away from the enemy formation. Quentin was eager to confirm his kill. Before the Germans turned to follow him, he recalled,

> I could half watch him looking back, and he was still spinning when he hit the clouds three thousand meters below. Of course he may have just been scared, but I think he must have been hit, or he would have come out before he struck the clouds. Three thousand meters is an awfully long spin.[44]

A kill was a kill; now Quentin had to live long enough to get back home to tell the story.

Quentin's account of his escape is dramatic. In a letter home, he wrote, "I had a long chase of it for they followed me all the way back to our side of the lines, but our speed was about equal so I got away. The trouble is that it was about 20 kilometers inside their lines, and I am afraid, too far to get confirmation."[45] This letter, along with several others Quentin wrote in the service, is preserved in a remarkable book edited by his brother Kermit. *Quentin Roosevelt: A Sketch with Letters* was published in 1921. It collected not only Quentin's wartime letters home but also those of friends, military officials, and other well-wishers who were affected by Quentin's death. He emerges as a likable, open, genuine fellow, and one can't help feel he and Kilmer had much more in common than just prominent prewar notoriety.

With this one confirmed kill under his belt, Quentin was under no illusions about either his skill or life expectancy. His was a very dangerous business, and luck played a very big part in day-to-day survival. His letters revealed he was exceptionally accepting of these risks. Quentin showed this side in another letter home. In referring to a fellow flier who was shot down, Quentin believed,

> still, — there's no better way, — if one has got to die. It solves things so easily, for you've nothing to worry about it, and even people whom you leave have the great comfort of knowing how you died. It's very fine really, the way he went, fighting hopelessly against enormous odds, — and then thirty seconds of horror

and its all over,—for they say that on average its all over in that length of time, after a plane's been hit.⁴⁶

For Quentin himself, this letter, straight out of a Hemingway novel, could not have been more prophetic.

It was all over in a matter of minutes for Quentin Roosevelt on July 14, 1918, Bastille Day in France. Over the shifting lines of the western front, a force of approximately 12 American aircraft attacked a smaller formation of German planes. After what a German report described as a "long fight," Quentin was shot down with two bullets through his head.

Lt. Edward Buford Jr. witnessed the dog fight. In a letter to his own father dated September 5, 1918, Lt. Buford wrote about the battle.

> About half a mile away I saw one of our planes with three Boche [Germans] on him, and he seemed to be having a pretty hard time with them, so I shook the two I was maneuvering with and tried to get over to him, but before I could reach them, our machine turned over on its back and plunged down out of control.⁴⁷

Even with Lt. Buford's eyewitness account, American officials searched for any hard information on Quentin's disappearance. Hamilton Coolidge, one of Quentin's buddies from back in the States, also served with the 95th Aero Squadron. (Coolidge later lost his own life in the war.) He tried to piece whatever information together he could and conveyed these facts to Quentin's mother in a letter dated July 16. Coolidge learned witnesses had seen an American plane "piquing sharply, but not in flames and apparently under control" during the dogfight.⁴⁸ He concluded the aircraft was indeed Quentin's. His letter speculated as to the evasive actions Quentin had taken. Unfortunately, Coolidge's conclusions were wrong. Buford's eyewitness account of an American plane "out of control" matched the circumstances surrounding Quentin's death. Confirmation came from an unexpected source.

Two days after the battle, American radiomen intercepted the following German message:

> On July Fourteen seven of our chasing planes were attacked by a superior number of American planes north of Dormans. After a stubborn fight, one of the pilots—Lt. Roosevelt—who had shown conspicuous bravery during the fight by attacking again and again without regard to danger, was shot in the head by his more experienced opponent and fell at Chamery.⁴⁹

Something remarkable happened when Quentin died. In a war remembered for millions of forgotten dead, Quentin's enemies paid him the respect of holding a funeral in his honor. The Germans buried Quentin with full military honors on July 15.

American Capt. James Gee of the 110th Infantry was a German POW and witnessed the funeral. Captain Gee described the event in this manner:

> In a hollow square about the open grave were assembled approximately one thousand German soldiers, standing stiffly in regular lines. They were dressed in field gray uniforms, wore steel helmets, and carried rifles. Officers stood at attention before the ranks. Near the grave was the smashed plane, and beside it was a small group of officers, one of whom was speaking to the men.
>
> I did not pass close enough to hear what he was saying; we were prisoners and did not have the privilege of lingering, even for such an occasion as this. At this time I did not know who was being buried, but the guards informed me later. The funeral was elaborate. I was told afterward by the Germans they paid Lt. Roosevelt such an honor not only because he was a gallant aviator, who died fighting bravely against odds, but because he was the son of Colonel Roosevelt, whom they esteemed as one of the greatest Americans.[50]

How many other times during the carnage of the Great War did enemies stop fighting and bury a member of the opposing forces? Perhaps we'll never know, but the episode is both rare and remarkable, and we are fortunate Capt. Gee took the effort to record his experiences and share them with Quentin's family.

American infantry, on the move, captured the ground where Quentin was buried on July 18. Doughboys found a small grave with a wooden cross at its head, which read "Lieutenant Roosevelt Buried by the Germans." Alongside the German cross, Americans decorated his grave with his aircraft's damaged propeller and wheels. In addition, a regiment of engineers engraved the following inscription on a cross at the grave: "Here rests on the field of honor Quentin Roosevelt Air Service U.S.A. Killed in Action July, 1918."[51] (The Americans were unsure of the actual date of death.)

Meanwhile, news of missing soldiers traveled slowly, and even a former president and first lady could do little but wait for final word of a fallen son. Teddy Roosevelt's first clue something was wrong came on July 16, two days after Quentin was shot down. A reporter friend came into possession of a cable saying, "Watch Sagamore Hill," the Roosevelt family's Long Island compound. TR assumed something had happened either to Quentin or Theodore Jr., who also fought on the western front.

On the following morning, Associated Press reporter and Roosevelt confidant Phil Thompson delivered a cryptic, one-sentence cable. It stated that Quentin had been shot down, but his fate was unknown. Fearing the worst, his parents put up a brave front in public. They issued a joint state-

4. Do-It-Yourself Pilgrimages 91

Burial services for Lt. Roosevelt. 2nd Lt. William Preston places a cross on Lt. Quentin Roosevelt's grave. Quentin was shot down over France on July 14, 1918. According to his parent's wishes, his body remained in France. (National Archives, RG 111, Photo no. 18913.)

ment the same day, which read, "Quentin's mother and I are glad that he got to the front and had a chance to render some service to his country, and to show the stuff that was in him before his fate befell him."[52]

Losing a child is hard for any parent. Once Quentin's death was confirmed, the former president took the news especially hard. Some speculate the loss hastened TR's death, which took place about six month's after Quentin's. Shortly after confirmation of Quentin's death, a maid spotted Theodore Roosevelt in a rocking chair at Sagamore Hill muttering to himself, "Poor Quinikins, poor Quinikins."[53]

However, it was not until some four months after the young flier's death that the full significance of the loss began to emerge. In a letter to army Chief of Staff Peyton March, the Roosevelts pleaded to let their son's remains lie in France. The former president wrote, "Mrs. Roosevelt and I wish to enter a most respectful but most emphatic protest against the proposed course as far as our son Quentin is concerned. We have always believed that where the tree falls, there let it lay."[54] Roosevelt urged the government to let his son remain right where the Germans had buried him, and the letter even announced their intent to visit their son's grave in France. The "proposed course" to which the letter referred was the wartime plan to disinter all the remains in Europe and return them to the United States. If Teddy had had his way, all American bodies would have probably remained overseas. Nonetheless, he was probably satisfied with the policy letting the families make this difficult decision.

Although the Roosevelt's letter to Gen. March was dated October 25, it was not published until after the war ended. It ran in the *New York Times* on November 18, for example. It ran in many other newspapers across the country. TR's admonition, "where the tree falls, there let it lay," was tremendously evocative. Coupled with his enormous popularity, the letter was greatly responsible for the thousands of Americans who left their sons' and husbands' bodies in Europe after World War I. Although one may never know to what extent the Roosevelts' decision influenced other families, there is no question the former president played a part in this decision.

Quentin's body did indeed remain right where it fell in rural France. Quentin's isolated grave became a magnet for American pilgrims and visitors as soon as the war ended. Teddy Roosevelt died on January 6, 1919, so he was unable to complete his stated goal of a pilgrimage to his youngest son's grave. However, his wife and son Theodore Jr., who survived the war, visited Quentin's grave the following month. Mrs. Roosevelt, a Gold Star mother, carried an armload of flowers to decorate the grave. A family member who accompanied the pair "marveled at her tearless self-control as she knelt and recited the Lord's Prayer."[55]

Unlike Joyce Kilmer's mother, Mrs. Roosevelt never published an account of her graveside visit. She kept her feelings to herself or perhaps chose to share them with a few close family members and friends, as most of the other Gold Star mothers elected to do. Other prominent people immediately made Quentin's grave a stop on any battlefield tour. New York Senator Royal Copeland visited Quentin's grave after the war and brought back a flower from it for Mrs. Roosevelt.[56]

Others remained at home but found a way to pay tribute to the Roosevelt family. Minna Irving wrote a poem called "Star of Gold," and this poem was collected in Kermit Roosevelt's book for his brother. Irving's poem was written just after the war, and it demonstrated how fully Americans had adopted the gold star symbol.

The Star of Gold

A Viking of the air was he
Who sailed his fragile plane
Through vast uncharted spaces blue,
As Norsemen sailed the main.

> He met the foeman and he fought
> Unflinching in the sky,
> And died as his brave sire would wish
> A soldier-son to die.
>
> The Prussian airmen wrought his grave
> And laid him down to rest,
> His shroud the leather tunic wrapped
> About his gallant breast.
> The guns a thunderous requiem
> All day above him sound,
> America in spirit mourns
> Beside his lonely mound.
>
> When twilight over No Man's Land
> A veil of purple weaves,
> An escadrille of stars appears
> Above the hangar's eaves
> With one that speeds on wings of light
> In ether fast and far,
> The Allied aviators say
> "Tis Quentin Roosevelt's star."[57]

As the Gold Star mothers' pilgrimages moved toward reality and after the trips had begun, the images of Quentin Roosevelt's death and burial were still important symbols. In the 1928 House hearing on the pilgrimages, New York Congressman James M. Fitzpatrick shared his views on overseas burial of the dead.

> The way I feel on this matter that the body should remain in Europe to remain in the grave on the other side, that the tree should lie where it fell and they [the mothers] should be given at least the opportunity to go over there and see the graves of their sons."[58]

His audience needed no reminder as to the fallen tree metaphor; Teddy Roosevelt's remarks were so well known no attribution was necessary. Even though Congress knew Quentin's case, it did not prevent legislators from a major oversight in the first pilgrimage act. Mrs. Roosevelt, Quentin's mother, was ineligible to go on a pilgrimage on two counts: She had already been to France, and Quentin was buried in a remote grave, not in one of the official American cemeteries. Amended pilgrimage bills cleared the way for her to go, but she declined her invitation.

If Congress had forgotten, momentarily at least, about Mrs. Roosevelt, her fellow Gold Star mothers remembered her and her son on almost every pilgrimage party. At least one vocal Gold Star mother urged all pilgrims to visit the grave. Ethel Nock addressed Congress in 1929 with this message: "And I hope every mother who will be anywhere near Quentin's grave will be taken there." Mrs. Nock asserted the "inscription on his grave is the most comforting thing any woman can have said of her soldier son who has gone on. It is this: 'He has outsoared the shadow of the night.'"[59]

From the very first group of pilgrims, Party A in 1930, Quentin's grave became an impromptu stop for hundreds of women. On May 23, 1930, members of Party A passed nearby Quentin's isolated grave. The grave sat on a hillside and was surrounded by a white picket fence. It was plainly visible from the road. Most mothers were unable to make the muddy climb up the hill. "Many, however, would not be content until they had stood beside the tomb of the hero and bravely trudged through the mud," to see the grave, the *New York Times* reported.[60] Rain and mud seemed to be constant companions for the mothers, just as they had been during the war for their doughboy sons. Pilgrim parties continued to visit the grave, some as soon as the following month.

Ironically, Quentin's body was moved a few decades later. He now lies buried in Normandy Beach cemetery, next to his brother, Theodore Roosevelt Jr. Theodore Roosevelt was a Medal of Honor–winning general killed during the D-day invasion of Europe in World War II. After the war, Quentin's body was exhumed and buried next to his brother. The decision to let the brothers lie together was technically in violation of the plan to separate dead from each war. However, the presence of at least one Great War soldier in the heavily visited World War II cemetery is a grand gesture and very appropriate.

Conclusion

Private pilgrimages are an important part of the Gold Star mothers' story. They remind us one did not need to take part in an organized pilgrimage to be considered a Gold Star mother. Americans of means visited the graves of their sons as soon as practicable. Prominent families such as the Kilmers and the Roosevelts found both assistance and solace in their private pilgrimages. The Second AEF helped dozens of mothers who could not have afforded to go on their own.

In the broadest context, the private, do-it-yourself pilgrimage movement should remind Americans of the pilgrimage experience of mothers from other nations. Their war graves pilgrimages, though organized in some cases, were entirely left up to the individual families to pay for. Congress realized private pilgrimages took place and probably wished all families could afford to go.

5

The Quartermaster Corps in Peace and War

Congress delegated the planning and conducting of the Gold Star mother pilgrimages to the War Department. The War Department, in turn, chose the Army's Quartermaster Corps to carry out the trips. The Corps not only had experience with large-scale logistical operations but also operated the Graves Registration Service (GRS) for the military. The military may have been reluctant to act as tour guides during the 1920s, but the Quartermaster Corps was determined to carry out the pilgrimages as best it could. This it did in a very remarkable mission, taking several thousand aged civilians overseas in a very public military operation whose single goal was the alleviation of private, personal grief.

The pilgrimage experience greatly affected all the officers, overwhelmingly men, who participated in it. In fact, their observations, combined with the pilgrims' letters of thanks to the military, form perhaps the largest single body of firsthand accounts of the Gold Star mother pilgrimages.

The mission assigned to the Quartermaster Corps was both monumental and unprecedented. Given the barest of outline of the original pilgrimage act, which was less than two pages long, the Corps had many tasks ahead of it. It had to identify all potentially eligible women, contact them, and determine their eligibility under the statute. It had to extend invitations to the women and provide them with travel documents and detailed directions.

It next needed to make all domestic travel arrangements—getting the women to New York City and back home again. Lodging had to be secured in New York, as well as steamship travel abroad. The Corps negotiated favorable rates and schedules from United States Lines, the only company that qualified to carry pilgrims abroad. Passport arrangements had to be cleared with the State Department, as well as with the governments of Belgium, France, and England. The United States found its European allies very willing to assist. "The French government cooperated beautifully," Kurt Piehler observed.[1]

With the pilgrims' arrival in Europe, the Quartermaster Corps' biggest challenges began. Staff met the liners in Cherbourg Harbor, France, and escorted the women to special trains to Paris. The army secured the finest Paris hotels and arranged for official receptions along with sight-seeing and even a little shopping in the French capital. Local guides, drivers, and interpreters were hired.

The Corps divided women into smaller subgroups, based on which cemetery they were to visit, and then bused the parties to their cemetery for several days of private visits and reflections. Each woman was provided with a bouquet of flowers at the graveside, as well as a photograph

Busloads of Gold Star mothers arrive at the cemetery. The army hired comfortable buses to take the pilgrims from Paris into the countryside to visit the cemeteries. The army divided the full parties of mothers in Paris by cemetery. Buses transported the mothers to their cemetery, with plenty of time for visiting battlefields and other World War I sites of interest. (National Archives, RG 92.)

of herself at her son's or husband's grave. The visits took several days and were dignified, quiet, and reverent. The army even added "hostess houses" at some cemeteries, complete with kitchens and American-style bathrooms. Connie Potter from the National Archives believes that "although this is never stated specifically, they wanted to make sure that the bathroom facilities were what the women were used to, and they were not the kind frequently in hotels [or cemeteries] in France at the time."[2]

Pilgrims were returned to Paris, where they were reunited with their full parties. The train trip back to Cherbourg led to the voyage back to New York City. Women stayed in New York for an additional night or two before the final train trip back home. The full pilgrimage experience took approximately four weeks, and the Quartermaster Corps was responsible for every single minute of it.

The Corps Sets to Work

To take care of the pilgrimage duty, the Quartermaster Corps set out to custom-build a flexible, responsive organization staffed by some of the army's most capable young officers. The first order of business was creating a clerical and support staff in both the United States and France to coordinate the effort. The Pilgrimage Section of the Corps' Washington, DC, office served several functions. It coordinated all pilgrimage activities, including transportation and accommodations. It also created, maintained, and updated lists of eligible travelers. Staffing for this office was projected to cost at least $70,000 per year and required the hiring of 32 clerks, typists, stenographers, and other support personnel.[3] (These and other budget figures come from Col. William Gibson's testimony before Congress in 1930. Congress appropriated the full amount the army and Col. Gibson requested.) The Corps also established a Pilgrimage Port of Embarkation in New York City. Staff in this office met the incoming pilgrims at the train stations, escorted them to their hotels, arranged transport to the port, and helped them return to their homes safely.

Coordination with leading New York hotels and United States Lines were an important part of this office's job. Col. (later General) A. E. Williams supervised this office. The army projected a staff of 22 in this office, with an initial annual payroll exceeding $24,000. The total of 22 employees included, among other personnel, 8 nurses, 3 typists, and 1 baggage master.[4] (Many of these employees worked on a seasonal basis, only when the pilgrimages were in session.)

Col. Richard T. Ellis headed the Pilgrimage Headquarters in Paris. Col. Ellis was also the commander of the GRS European Division, so his office already had plenty of experience in helping American travelers visit the cemeteries. The Paris office was responsible for all pilgrimage activities from the time a woman landed in Europe until she returned to Cherbourg Harbor to depart for the United States. The Paris office's staff was projected to number almost 40 people, again mostly on a seasonal basis. Annual staffing costs were projected at approximately $40,000. The Army staff here included 2 finance clerks, 3 baggage clerks, 8 interpreters, 6 typists, and 10 nurses.[5]

Col. Ellis and the Paris office did a remarkably effective job for four years in a row. One officer observed,

> That no complications arose in carrying out his plans, which provided at times for as many as fifteen distinct groups [parties] to be in various parts of Europe at one time, speaks well for the thoroughness of the arrangements and the elasticity of his organization.[6]

The large staff in Europe and the United States was necessary to handle the mountainous paperwork the pilgrimages produced. Every step of the trips generated correspondence. The Washington, DC, pilgrimage alone sent out over 450,000 communications during its first year in operation.[7]

The correspondence survives intact to this day. Copies of army documents along with original cards, letters, and telegrams from the pilgrims themselves are in the National Archives facility in College Park, Maryland. Securely tucked into acid-free folders in archival boxes reside handwritten notes from the women that — even today — have the raw immediacy of an open wound or a broken heart.

To begin the pilgrimage process, the Quartermaster Corps' staff compiled a list of some 30,000 potentially pilgrimage-eligible women — the next-of-kin of the troops buried in European graves. Each woman then received a steady stream of mail from the pilgrimage office. The first such letter was generally a letter of introduction. It contained a one-paragraph summary of the pilgrimages and included a copy of the brief act itself. If the letter was addressed to a mother, not a widow, it inquired if the deceased soldier or sailor had a wife, and if so, asked for her name and current address. The purpose of this initial mailing was to learn the number of women who were interested in a trip. Each form letter included a box in which an army clerk could insert the name of the dead soldier.

The volume of letters must have been overwhelming, if the hurried nature of the typing was any indication. Mrs. Anna Norris of Cincinnati received her letter on June 29, 1929, with the name of her dead son, Alexander Norris, typed crookedly, barely fitting in the allotted space.[8] Mrs.

Norris was a typical Gold Star mother. She took her pilgrimage in 1930. The National Archives file on her son runs some 40 pages in length. For Mrs. Norris and others, more correspondence followed if she responded to the first query.

The next letter was a brief one, and it requested answers to three questions. Is the deceased survived by a widow? If so, what is her address? Will you make the pilgrimage to Europe? The Quartermaster Corps followed up with another letter if the answer to the third question was yes.

This next piece of mail was more detailed. Its purpose was to determine the number of women desiring a trip and in which year they wished to sail. Each letter contained five questions for the potential pilgrim to answer. First, the letter asked if the woman wished to make a pilgrimage. Second, it asked if she wanted to go in 1930, the first year for the trips, or in a later year. Next, the letter asked if she had made a prior trip to Europe to visit her son's grave. (Under the original pilgrimage act, such a visit would have made her ineligible for a trip. Revised pilgrimage legislation overturned this prohibition.) Fourth, the letter asked for her age and state of health; she had the choice of circling either "good" or "poor." Finally, the letter, which was written in English, asked if she spoke English or any other language.

Mrs. Norris received such a letter from the Quartermaster Corps dated October 7, 1929. Her letter read in part: "The records of this office show that you are the mother of the late Pvt. Alexander Norris, Co. H, 127th Infantry, whose remains are now interred in the Meuse-Argonne American Cemetery, Romagne-sous-Montfaucon, Meuse, France."

She responded that she did want to make the pilgrimage, and she wanted to travel in 1930. She had not been to Europe to visit her son's grave. She was 62 years old at the time and considered herself in "poor" health. She spoke English.[9]

After receipt of this letter, the army verified the information before extending the Gold Star mother her formal pilgrimage invitation. The invitation letter came with a small post card for her reply. The card read: "I _____ the invitation extended me to make a pilgrimage to Europe at the expense of the Government of the United States under the provisions of the Act of Congress approved March 2, 1929." The line left space for the woman to write in "accept" or "decline." Once the woman accepted the trip, she was considered invited to sail on a pilgrimage, and a formal invitation and even more correspondence was on the way.

Each pilgrim received in the mail prior to sailing her official Gold Star mothers pilgrimage badge. The badge was to be worn at all times on the trip to identify the woman as a pilgrim, as one who was to receive special treatment. The badge consisted of a gold medallion suspended from a red, white, and blue ribbon. The circular medallion contained a gold star inside a larger circle. The ribbon was attached to a small, horizontal metallic bar. The woman's name and home state were engraved on this strip of metal. The words "Pilgrimage of Mothers and Widows" were engraved on the medallion. Leaves of oak and laurel were underneath this inscription.[10]

The women also received a seven-page mailing, which contained the key points from the War Department's pilgrimage regulations. (The War Department issued a detailed set of pilgrimage regulations in 1930.) The mothers may have been quite surprised at how the government was mothering them. Every aspect of the trip was spelled out in complete detail. They were told they could bring only two pieces of luggage. The government instructed the mothers to bring two pairs of comfortable shoes, galoshes, an umbrella, full-length coat, sweater, and enough underwear, nightgowns, stockings, handkerchiefs, and other clothing to last about two weeks without laundering. Laundry facilities would be available only in New York City and Paris.

The mothers were assured, "the climate of Europe is much colder than that of the United States, [and] each woman should provide herself with sufficient warm clothing to stand the motor bus trip and the visit to the cemeteries."[11] The mothers were informed medical care provided by army doctors and nurses would be available all during the pilgrimages. Army officers would serve as escorts for the trips, and the Quartermaster Corps would add interpreters, drivers, and other guides as needed. Her newly received pilgrimage badge was to be worn at all times, from when the woman left her home until she returned safely from Europe.

> Special care and attention will be given the wearer of this badge by railroad, Pullman and hotel employees and the police of all the cities you may visit, and it should, therefore, be worn from the time you leave home until the time your return thereto,

the regulations advised each pilgrim.[12] Also, they could bring a friend, relative, or companion along. This travel would not be at government expense; however, the government would assist with arrangements.

The woman also received a check in the mail to cover incidental expenses and meals on the train trip to New York. The letter that accompanied the check read, in part, "under no circumstances must this check be cashed and used for any purpose other than that specified. If for any reason, you are not able to sail on the date mentioned in your invitation, the check must be returned to this office immediately."[13] Mrs. Norris received her check for $10 with a letter from the War Department dated April 21, 1930.

Pilgrims were entitled to a no-fee U.S. passport to make the trip. Prospective travelers received a detailed, two-page letter with passport instructions, covering everything from photographs to a list of places to apply. Many mothers and widows were U.S. residents, not citizens, and as such were ineligible for a U.S. passport. However, State Department officials issued special documents to allow these women to enter France.

Even today, widows, mothers, and other close relatives of deceased service members are eligible for a no-fee U.S. passport when traveling abroad to visit the graves of a loved one.[14] This no-fee passport courtesy is perhaps the last trace of the Gold Star mother pilgrimages and the courtesies extended them. With passport, train tickets, and per diem check in hand, most of the women were ready to travel.

One of the most intriguing documents issued the pilgrims was a one-page itinerary for their party. It is unclear if they received this prior to sailing or once they arrived in France. In either case, their pilgrimage itineraries "to and from the cemeteries and the daily itineraries while at the cemeteries have been varied so as to take in points of historical interest as well as some parts of the battlefields where American troops were engaged."[15] The itinerary listed daily stops and activities, from sight-seeing detours to cemetery visits.

World War I may be viewed as the beginning of the impersonal world of form letters and fill-in-the-blank correspondence. "As the first widely known example of dehumanized, automated communication, the post card popularized a mode of rhetoric indispensable to the conduct of later wars fought by great faceless conscripted armies," Paul Fussell observed in his landmark 1975 book, *The Great War and Modern Memory*.[16]

The Quartermaster Corps had little choice in the matter of its pilgrimage mail. With something like half a million pieces of correspondence, speed and volume were the keys, not personal formalities. Much of the correspondence was in response to letters from the Gold Star mothers themselves.

Eligibility Issues

The original pilgrimage act was very clear on who was eligible to go on a trip — and who was not. Congress sketched the big picture, and it was eventually left up to the Quartermaster Corps to fill in the details. In each case, the army had to determine if a soldier died, where he was buried, who his next-of-kin were, whether he was married, and whether the mother and widow were eligible for a pilgrimage.

The Corps did this job exceptionally well, following the letter of the law as best it could. The army also kept Congress informed of its experiences, and Congress revisited the original pilgrimage statute several times, as we've already seen.

If the pilgrimage law was unclear to some women, the Corps took time to explain it to them. Mrs. Henrietta Haug wrote the army on May 6, 1930, to inquire about a pilgrimage. "I wish very much to join the pilgrimages to France. I am 59 years old, in perfect health, and perfectly able to take care of myself," she wrote from her home in Arizona.[17] Mrs. Haug moved to Arizona after the war. The body of her son, Corp. Oscar Haug, was returned from France and buried in Calhoun County, Illinois, in 1921. Haug was killed in battle on November 11, 1918, the final day of the war.

Capt. A. D. Hughes of the Quartermaster Corps replied to Mrs. Haug in a letter dated May 13th. He wrote to inform her, "There is no provision of law which would enable you to make a pilgrimage to the grave of your son in America, at the expense of the government." Hughes further informed her the law provided only for trips to European cemeteries, not to burial sites in the United States. His reply did offer that she could sail to France with the pilgrimage party but at her own expense.[18]

The loss of her son haunted and pained Henrietta Haug for decades. On the brink of World War II, she decided to collect experiences of other Gold Star mothers and share them with the world. She compiled the recollections of World War I Gold Star mothers into her book, *Gold Star Mothers of Illinois*. Illinois mothers were encouraged to share their memories of loss in what was hoped to be an important plea for peace. Many of the mothers had not been on the pilgrimages, such as Mrs. Haug herself, but many of them had. The book was dedicated to the memory of her son, and it collected memories of pilgrims we shall meet throughout this book.

If the Quartermaster Corps found some cases, such as Mrs. Haug's, easy to dismiss, others were much more difficult. Nothing caused more anguish than the twin topics of *in loco parentis* and a previous visit to the dead son's grave. The Quartermaster Corps' decisions in these cases were always fair, that is to say, by the book. Yet the army acknowledged the decision to say "no" to a pilgrimage request was always painful.

The issue of a previous cemetery visit, as spelled out in the original pilgrimage law, created substantial headaches and paperwork for the army. When the Quartermaster Corps determined a woman had her passport stamped for any European travel after the war, it made the assumption she had been overseas to visit her son's grave. This assumption was true more often than not, but it was an assumption nevertheless. Therefore, any

European travel was suspect enough to yank a woman's pilgrimage invitation.

Sometimes, even the mere issuance of a U.S. passport was enough to derail a pilgrimage effort. One such case was that of Elizabeth Penry of Ohio. Mrs. Penry had planned to accompany three Canadian friends to France in the summer of 1926. Mrs. Penry canceled her trip at the last minute, when her brother died unexpectedly. The Quartermaster Corps records indicated the issuance of a passport for European travel. Therefore, Mrs. Penry's pilgrimage invitation was revoked. She requested assistance from her friends. Two of her Canadian companions signed an affidavit stating that Mrs. Penry had never sailed for Europe in 1926. The affidavit read in part, "that the aforementioned Mrs. Thomas Penry has not left the United States at any time for the purpose of visiting France and the battlefields, where her son, a private in the American Expeditionary Force, is buried."[19]

This was sufficient evidence for the army, and Mrs. Penry was permitted to sail after all with her pilgrimage party to visit her son's grave.

Even more remarkable was the case of a Baltimore Gold Star mother named Nina Reid. Mrs. Reid had received her check to cover expenses, along with her invitation to sail on a pilgrimage in May 1930. However, the Quartermaster Corps wrote her a letter dated May 2, 1930, revoking her invitation. The letter read in part, "It is requested that you return the identification emblem bearing your name and that of your state, together with the check sent you to cover your subsistence on the trip to New York preparatory to sailing on S.S. *Harding* May 14th."[20] The

Gold Star mother Nina Reid from Baltimore. Nina Reid was a prominent Baltimore woman. Her son, Lt. Howell Reid, was killed in the war. She raised funds for the war effort and was related to French commander Marshal Joffre. (National Archives, Howell L. Reid Burial File, RG 92.)

reason for this change of heart? Mrs. Reid was told she had evidently "made a previous visit to France in the vicinity of the cemetery in which is located the grave of your son, the late Howell Lewis Reid, and are, therefore, ineligible under the provisions of the above Act to make this pilgrimage at the expense of the Government."[21]

Mrs. Reid relied on the same solution Elizabeth Penry had the month before: a sworn affidavit. In her notarized reply, she stated: "I, Mrs. Andrew Melville Reid, of 1210 North Calvert Street, Baltimore, Maryland, mother of Lieutenant Howell Lewis Reid do hereby make oath that I did not visit my son's grave when in Paris in 1927, owing to the fact of my being ill whilst there."[22] Her plea worked, just as it did for Mrs. Penry. Mrs. Reid was told she could go on the pilgrimage with the rest of her party, and the army instructed her to keep her badge and check. She was back on schedule for her pilgrimage.

Mrs. Reid's case revealed, if anything, the evenhanded treatment the Quartermaster Corps gave pilgrims and even prospective pilgrims. Mrs. Reid objected to the revocation of her invitation, but she would not have been able to say it was unfair.

Women from all walks of life received the same sad message in the mail from the army. A number of women, Mrs. Reid included, had powerful friends who lobbied the army for special treatment. There's no evidence the women sought this treatment for themselves, but there is plenty of evidence to suggest the Quartermaster Corps declined the advice.

During early planning for the pilgrimages, the army learned "Mrs. Reid is an unusual woman and I think it is only fair the officer referred to should know who she is and know of her attainments. She doubtless can be of considerable assistance to those in charge," Maj. Gen. Fred Sladen wrote to his army comrades on May 7, 1930. Sladen continued: "Any special attention that can be shown her in stateroom accommodations and otherwise will be greatly appreciated by me and a host of her prominent friends here in Baltimore."[23]

Mrs. Reid did indeed possess unusual abilities that probably did come in handy to the pilgrimage officials. She was born in France and was related to Field Marshal Joseph Joffre, the French commander-in-chief during the war. She was considered a well-known and successful wartime fundraiser in Maryland, and she had volunteered her efforts during the war in France, Russia, and Belgium.

Her son was an officer, Lt. Howell Reid. During this era in the military, many officers came from more prominent, noteworthy families. (Lt. Howell L. Reid was a member of the Army Air Service and died on October 20, 1918.)

Mrs. Reid received special treatment on her pilgrimage trip. That is to say, she received the same treatment all the other pilgrims received. The army made no special allowances or arrangements for prominent or VIP pilgrims. It didn't need to: The "routine" pilgrimage experience was so carefully planned that it would easily satisfy the most privileged of passengers. Mrs. Reid sailed with Party C in late May and early June 1930. She arrived in Paris with her party on May 23, after her transatlantic voyage aboard the *S. S. Republic*. Mrs. Reid's portion of Party C remained in and around Paris during her pilgrimage; her son was buried in Suresnes Cemetery. She was scheduled to visit his grave over five separate days. She also had some time to see the sights of Paris, and she visited Napoleon's tomb, Versailles, and the Louvre, among other places. The rest of her party rejoined the Suresnes pilgrims in Paris prior to sailing back to the America on board the S. S. *George Washington* on June 5th.

"I feel I must send a few words of thanks to the War Department and thank them for the marvelous trip you gave to the War Mothers," Mrs. Reid wrote to Maj. Gen. DeWitt upon her return from Europe.

> Words fail to express to you how grateful I am for having given me the privilege and comfort to visit my son's grave. The whole trip was wonderful. We were surrounded by every comfort, besides having the privilege of seeing so many wonderful sights.[24]

Her brief note was typical of all those the army received from the Gold Star mothers: grateful, appreciative, and to a degree, at peace. Nina Reid died in Baltimore in 1937 at the age of 81.

The case of a Congressional Medal of Honor winner's grave posed an even stickier problem for the Quartermaster Corps. Lt. Erwin Bleckley was awarded the Congressional Medal of Honor for his exploits in finding and rescuing the Lost Battalion. Lt. Bleckley's mother never denied making her own private pilgrimage; she visited her son's grave in the newly built Meuse-Argonne Cemetery in 1920. Rules were rules, and the army declined to offer a pilgrimage invitation to Margaret Alice Bleckley.

Bleckley's father thought this was unfair, so he wrote the army to protest. "As no doubt you are aware that our son was awarded the D.S.C. [Distinguished Service Cross] and the Congressional Medal of Honor and it would seem to me as though his mother should be permitted to make this trip if she desired to," Mr. Bleckley wrote to Maj. John Harris on July 8, 1929.[25] Mr. Bleckley did not advocate for his own pilgrimage; he was content to leave the focus on Lt. Bleckley's mother.

The Bleckleys enlisted help in their fight. Representative W. A. Ayres from Kansas wrote a letter to Maj. Harris on their behalf. He acknowledged the pilgrimage law gave the army little latitude in this matter, which was an understatement, but he still wanted to plead his case. Ayres made a good point; Mrs. Bleckley's 1920 visit took her to a temporary cemetery with wooden markers. Indeed, the permanent cemeteries with their lush landscaping and marble crosses did bear little resemblance to the makeshift cemetery Mrs. Bleckley would have seen.

In addition, Ayres assured the army,

> I happen to know Mr. and Mrs. Bleckley personally and wish to state that Lt. Bleckley who was killed in France was an only child. His parents have never recovered from the shock of his death. Shortly after the close of the War, at a considerable financial sacrifice, Mrs. Bleckley made a trip to France to visit the grave of her son. At that time, however, he was buried in a little, out of the way cemetery, and not where the grave is now located.[26]

Ayres made a very strong case, but the army admitted it had no choice but to decline Mrs. Bleckley's invitation.

Maj. Gen. B. F. Cheatham sent a personal reply to Congressman Ayres. "I appreciate Mr. and Mrs. Bleckley's position and am sure that you can realize that I am helpless to make any other decision in this case."[27] Mrs. Bleckley's invitation was declined. Officers such as Cheatham and Harris and Representatives such as Ayres realized the unfair nature of the original law, and one of the amendments to the pilgrimage act removed the barrier to women who had already made their own private trips. This cleared the way for Mrs. Bleckley to make her pilgrimage, and her case demonstrated remarkable flexibility on the part of both Congress and the army.

Mrs. Bleckley sailed to Europe with other Gold Star mothers for a late summer pilgrimage in 1931. She sailed with Party O, leaving New York aboard the *S. S. President Harding* on August 6, and arriving at Cherbourg on August 13. The party visited the Arc de Triomphe the next day for the traditional pilgrims' wreath-laying. Mrs. Bleckley and her party spent two more days sight-seeing and getting accustomed to Paris before departing for the cemeteries on August 17.

Mrs. Bleckley was part of the Meuse-Argonne group, which visited the cemetery on three consecutive days, August 18, 19, and 20. The Meuse-Argonne mothers departed Verdun the next day, joined the rest of the pilgrims from their party, and arrived in Paris on the evening of August 21. Mrs. Bleckley and her party spent the next five days in and around Paris, shopping and visiting attractions such as the palace at Versailles, the French Colonial Exposition, and the Louvre. The Party left France on August 27 and arrived safely back in New York on September 4.[28]

If the Quartermaster Corps found the issue of previous pilgrimages difficult to resolve, as indeed the cases of Mrs. Penry, Reid, and Bleckley were, the issue was mild in comparison to that of *in loco parentis*.

This issue got at the heart of what Congress had wrestled with for over a decade: who, precisely, is a mother? If this issue caused the Quartermaster Corps plenty of grief, the case of an Ohio woman showed why. Grace Moran's case also demonstrated the enormous amounts of paperwork and correspondence that accompanied each and every pilgrim's voyage.

Grace Moran was the stepmother of army private Ray Moran. Private Moran, 166th Infantry, 42nd Division, was killed by artillery fire on November 1, 1918, during a heavy bombardment in the Meuse-Argonne offensive. "Moran had always shown great courage," his commander wrote, "and had at different times gone through heavy fire, he being one of the platoon liaison runners."[29]

News of war casualties, burials, and other information surrounding soldiers' remains traveled very slowly back to the United States. Sometimes, in fact, families had to press for details on their own behalf. The Morans learned of their son's death shortly after the war ended. A year later, however, the family had received very little additional information. They had never received his personal effects or any back pay he may have been owed.

Mr. Moran wrote the local American Red Cross chapter for assistance. "Sgt. Darle McGough of West Mansfield, Ohio, reported in a letter to the Red Cross that they were being relieved that morning and that the Company did not bury Roy," Mr. Moran wrote. "One member of his Company told me that he waited to call the Red Cross and then had to hurry on, leaving Roy on his hands and knees. One year has now passed and I feel like again asking for information," Mr. Moran wrote.[30]

Knowing his son was left alone, dead or dying, in a foreign land was bad enough for Mr. Moran, but having no other information on his son made the situation even worse. The Moran family would have eventually learned Roy Moran was disinterred on September 21, 1921, for permanent burial in the Meuse-Argonne American Cemetery. At the time of his reburial, Moran's body was "badly decomposed, features unrecognizable." He was buried in his uniform raincoat, burlap, and a wooden box, according to the army's records.[31]

Grace Moran married Charles W. Moran, on October 14, 1916. When the Quartermaster Corps realized Grace Moran was Private Moran's stepmother, not his natural mother, it wrote her a letter dated October 25, 1929. In the letter, she was asked the date of her marriage to Mr. Moran. The letter also inquired if she were married to Private Moran's father when he entered the service and if she were still married to Mr. Moran when Private Moran was killed in battle.

She provided her wedding date and answered "yes" to both questions. The army was satisfied with her answers and extended her a pilgrimage invitation. She met the revised criteria for serving *in loco parentis*: She had served in the role of mother for at least one year prior to his death in the service. (Note, Grace Moran was ineligible for a pilgrimage under the original law, which required a five-year period. Only due to the army's feedback did Congress revise the act. This revised statute was the one which let Mrs. Moran and hundreds like her make pilgrimages.)

Mrs. Moran sailed with Party A in 1931. Her stepson was buried in the Meuse-Argonne Cemetery, and her group of pilgrims was able to visit the graves of their loved ones on three successive days, May 19–21, 1931.

The Moran family case is significant for one other reason. Grace Moran brought her eight-year-old daughter, Lula, with her on her trip. Pilgrimage regulations, of course, forbade free trips for family members. However, many pilgrims brought with them, at their own expense, husbands, sons, daughters, grandchildren, friends, and even private-duty nurses.

I estimate approximately 500 women brought such companions with them. Most were adults in their own right, but a number were children. The army made an attempt to book these companions in the same hotels, on the same ships, and in the same buses as the pilgrims themselves. The army realized these companions would be of comfort to the pilgrims, so it ensured that "every effort was made to assist these accompanying relatives and friends in making their arrangements."[32] Such arrangements even included medical care. Young Lula became ill in Paris with a fever, and army doctors treated her twice at her hotel.

In short, the Quartermaster Corps was responsible for handling thousands of pieces of correspondence and keeping records for the pilgrimages. The broad outline of the original act gave it substantial power to extend or decline invitations for pilgrims. The army did this duty in a humane, dedicated, and very professional manner. In keeping Congress informed, it ensured the true spirit of the pilgrimage act, rather than the letter of the law. The cases of Nina Reid, Grace Moran, and Mrs. Bleckley revealed how the army got it right in the end.

Health Care Concerns

The army handled the paperwork admirably, but the health of the pilgrims concerned it most. The Quartermaster Corps frankly expected the pilgrims to die in unprecedented numbers once they reached Europe. The mothers' average age would be approximately 65 years. Moreover, stress and strain were expected to take a heavy toll. "You must consider the temper of the women and take that into consideration with the object of the pilgrimage, which does not tend to a calm mental condition," the escort officers were warned.[33]

Army estimates showed 10–12 women could be expected to die in a year had they remained at home. Therefore, the army prepared for an equal or even greater number to fall ill and die while on an arduous, emotional pilgrimage. In fact, one figure estimated as many as 65 pilgrimage deaths. These estimates were more than 90 percent off—only four women died during the trips. This excellent performance was due in equal parts to superb medical treatment and to the unexpected nature of the pilgrimage experience itself.

Press accounts reported that only four women died on the pilgrimages, all during 1930. One of the deaths was on board a train to New York City to begin the pilgrimage. Mrs. A. O. Jacobson of South Fergus Falls, Minnesota, was found dead in her Pullman sleeping railroad car in Pennsylvania on the morning of June 23, 1930. Maj. A. M. Halpine was dispatched from New York City to accompany Mrs. Jacobson's body back to Minnesota.

Mrs. Rose Fox of Annville, Pennsylvania, died aboard the *S.S. President Roosevelt* on her way back from her pilgrimage in August 1930. Mrs. Fox had completed her trip to the grave of her son, Private Joseph T. Conner, who was buried in the Meuse-Argonne Cemetery. An officer was assigned to escort her body home once her liner docked in New York.

Just two women died in France, both in Verdun hotels on separate trips in 1930. Mrs. Harriet Bates was the first. She died on August 14, 1930, at Verdun's Nouvel Hotel. The Pennsylvania woman, traveling as part of Party O, was stricken with apoplexy at her son's grave. She died a few days later. The army medical staff feared this scenario the most—grief-stricken pilgrims collapsing during the cemetery visits. This happened in just a few instances, and only Mrs. Bates died during such an episode.

Mrs. Elizabeth Kingsbury of Smith Centre, Kansas, died at the Verdun Hotel the following month. An army doctor and two nurses were with her at the time of death. She traveled with Party S, the next-to-last group of 1930. She became very ill shortly before leaving Paris with the rest of her party, and press reports said she was "cheated by death" from visiting her son's grave before she died.

Nevertheless, only four deaths were considered a remarkable showing by the mothers. At least some of the credit went to the women themselves. One of the many army nurses who traveled with the mothers glimpsed a partial explanation for the low number of fatalities. She felt the pilgrims possessed an unusual supply of strength, fortitude, and vitality. "They must be the fit that have survived. Had they been weak, they never would have reached their present age," she observed.[34]

Medical care for the pilgrims was excellent. Army doctors and nurses were always ready to lend a hand. Nevertheless, some pilgrims probably needed more personal attention and treatment than each nurse could provide.

Col. Richard Ellis received a very colorful letter from a Mrs. E. H. I. Robinson after her pilgrimage in 1931. Mrs. Robinson, an outspoken woman of some means, brought her own private-duty nurse on the trip with her. Mrs. Robinson had some very definite ideas about medical care and treatment. "Confidentially I think your nursing service is the weak spot," she told Ellis.

> Not in severe or "bed" cases of which I know nothing of but in being on their jobs during sight-seeing. In Notre Dame, one tottering wreck nearly fainted three times on my Miss Holmes, the official nurses being too occupied ... to notice. Finally a Doctor (out of uniform) helped us out. I believe the truth is *each* totterer should have a keeper or a "special"!!! Like me. *I* did the Louvre and Versailles with the Mob and then went to the [1931 Paris] Exposition."[35]

In any case, medical care was more than adequate, and the pilgrims' showing was exemplary. Before the first year of the pilgrimages, the army estimated sick travelers would consume 8,000 hospital bed days in Europe. By the end of the 1930 season, however, only 17 women were sick enough to require advanced medical care. They used only 500 hospital bed days. Far fewer women died on the trips than had they just remained at home, according to insurance industry estimates. Largely because of the pilgrims' sturdy showing, the army found the trips much cheaper than anticipated.

The War Department had asked Congress for and received approximately $840 per woman. After the first year of the trips, however, figures showed the total was closer to $700 each, a substantial savings.[36] In fact, the entire four years' worth of pilgrimages cost less than anticipated, and the women's surprisingly good health, coupled with very efficient management by the Quartermaster Corps, were the two main factors.

Officers and Gentlemen

It is one of the great ironies of the pilgrimage movement that this mission of peace was carried out as a military operation. Dozens of men and women from all parts of the army, not just the Quartermaster Corps, carried out the pilgrimages in a remarkably efficient, humane, and caring manner. Furthermore, the army did this duty against a backdrop of low pay and benefits and very little chance for advancement in the peacetime military.

Although the army emerged to win World War II, it faced serious challenges after World War I. If the men complained of expensive overseas duty and separation from families, they did so in private, not wanting to detract from the pilgrimages' success.

The Quartermaster Corps attached great importance to the pilgrimages, and all participants from the top down made sure this was a consistent message. When the first group of officers prepared to sail for France in spring 1930, the Quartermaster General himself was present.

Maj. Gen. J. L. DeWitt traveled to New York City to address this initial group of hand-picked officers in a speech at the Pennsylvania Hotel on the evening of April 15, 1930. DeWitt fully realized the importance of the pilgrimages, and he wanted to set the tone for the trips right from the start. "I want you to perform your duties in the spirit in which that law was conceived," he told the officers. "Bear in mind, I am emphasizing it because I want no doubt in your minds as to what Congress intended and as to what the Secretary of War expects."[37]

DeWitt's speech demonstrated that the army's concern for the Gold Star mothers was genuine. It was not artificial. He told the officers the duty would be unique and difficult. Nevertheless, the pilgrims' comfort and convenience were paramount.

"Let me enjoin upon you now that you must exercise patience, forbearance, good judgment, tact, and have a sense of humor, and at no time fail to appreciate the unusual conditions under which you are serving," he told the officers. "I want to be perfectly frank with you. A great deal is expected of you."

"If you are not diplomats now, you will probably be diplomats by the time you get back," DeWitt added.[38]

Moreover, DeWitt had some idea of what the escort officers would face. He knew the pilgrimages brought together women from all walks of life, from all across the country. In some ways, diversity and unity were highlights. However, DeWitt knew this diversity would challenge the officers.

"You must remember that these women will be from all classes of society and will be just as true a cross section of the country as was the draft during the War," he reminded the officers.

> Some of them will be highly refined women. Some of them will be illiterate. Some of them will not be able to speak English. Some of them will be absolutely

poverty stricken and will be dependent upon you and the Government and the organization to pay all their expenses.... The majority of them will be in an environment in which they are utterly unfamiliar. Many of them are from small towns and farms. They will depend absolutely on you.[39]

In addition, until the very end of the pilgrimages, America was a dry country. (Prohibition ended in late 1933.) The Quartermaster General made it clear his officers would observe Prohibition, even while stationed in Europe for pilgrimage duty. No champagne toasts for these sober officers. "No officer must indulge even slightly in intoxicants ... you must be up to the mark at all times," DeWitt warned the men.[40]

Pilgrimage duty for most of the men, however, was not really considered a luxury duty or even a plum assignment. Although the glamour of foreign travel certainly expanded many horizons, the duty was probably seen as useful but tangential to military service.

Leading World War I historian Edward Coffman agrees. "I don't think regular army officers consider this a particularly good assignment. It was not career-enhancing, I'll put it that way," Coffman observed.[41]

Furthermore, the cost of overseas duty posed a real burden to the officers, especially those who chose to bring their families along. Dissent and controversy were certainly rare in the military, but a few officers griped privately. A *New York Daily News* article, relying on unnamed sources, reported "most of the captains and majors selected for the assignment are anything but joyful over the assignment...."[42] The reason was primarily financial.

The officers were provided a basic daily subsistence rate, which Congress refused to change to expensive European conditions. An unidentified married officer with a large family calculated his "summer vacation" in Europe with the pilgrimages would cost him over $2,000 out of his own pocket, a small fortune during the Depression.

The same article cited Paris hotel rates of up to $5 a day, while the average officer received only $36.40 per month for living expenses. "The honor has been generally accepted without protest ... because rejection would be equivalent to insubordination," the article stated.[43]

"If you think that's a junket, you can have the job any day you want it," the officer stated.[44]

Moreover, the so-called glamour of on overseas assignment in reality meant long weeks away from one's family. The men had to focus on the pilgrims completely and attend to their needs. DeWitt foresaw this situation and brought it to the attention of the initial group of escort officers.

> You must understand that you are on a permanent change of station status. In the performance of your duties you will unquestionably be separated for many days from your families. So, after you arrive in France and have located yourselves and your families your wives must understand that.⁴⁵

But DeWitt need not have worried. The officers selected for pilgrimage duty performed remarkably well. The quality of the officers was superb. Several officers served in both World Wars. John W. O'Daniel was decorated in both, earning the Distinguished Service Cross and the Purple Heart in World War I and the Silver Star in World War II.

Col. Benjamin O. Davis was the highest ranking black officer in the army during the pilgrimages, and he volunteered for escort duty in Europe. Many officers were West Point graduates, such as Francis Pope and Leo Paquet. Paquet's story is especially noteworthy. He was born in New York in 1897 and graduated from West Point in 1919. He had been trained for tank duty by the time he served as a pilgrimage escort officer. He stayed in the army and served in World War II. He was the Executive Officer of the 31st Infantry Battalion in the Philippines. Paquet's unit was among those that surrendered to the Japanese. He survived the brutally infamous Bataan Death March, only to die as a POW in 1945 at the age of 48.

Another equally intriguing escort officer was Robert Ginsburgh. Ginsburgh was born in Russia in 1895, came to the United States as a child, and graduated from Harvard Law School. (Many officers such as Ginsburgh used the interwar years to earn advanced degrees because promotions were rare; Ginsburgh served as a captain for 17 years.) Ginsburgh was a field artillery officer who served as one of the escorts in the last year of the pilgrimages, 1933. After the pilgrimages were finished, Ginsburgh shared his recollections of the trips in an article for *American Legion* magazine titled "This Too Is America." Ginsburgh was in the perfect position to observe the pilgrimages effects, not only on the pilgrims themselves but also on their officer escorts. Far from anticipated scenes of hysteria, Ginsburgh and his fellow officers witnessed numerous acts of kindness, bravery, and forthright beauty on the part of the mothers.

> Of course there were tears. However, signs of hysteria seldom manifested themselves. Those who seemed to bear up best usually were walking around to cheer up others less capable of handling strain. Often it was the officer and not the Pilgrim who had to turn his back on the scene to hide the sight of his own tears.⁴⁶

Ginsburgh was equally affected by sentimental cemetery visits. His daughter remembered how her father told her about one pilgrim who barely spoke English. She was overcome with grief during her graveside

Sarah Dyson and fellow Gold Star mothers sail for Europe accompanied by an army officer. Army officers accompanied the pilgrims every step of the way. The officers won widespread praise for their efficient and courteous service. (Courtesy Janet Payne, whose grandmother Sarah Dyson is second from left.)

visit. However, she wanted to remain strong, for herself and for the other pilgrims. In broken English, she repeated, "Julie, she no cry. Julie, she no cry." "It affected father greatly," his daughter recalled.[47]

In fact, Ginsburgh and his fellow officers were well positioned to observe such scenes. Ginsburgh and several other men wrote articles about the trips, and their notes and letters are housed with the pilgrimage files in the National Archives. These records and recollections are especially important, because the women themselves left almost no published accounts of their trips.

"The comments that do survive are basically from the officers who conducted them in New York, or on the ships, or in France, and most of the officers commented that the women really enjoyed what they were doing," Marvin Fletcher noted in his documentary interview.[48]

There can be no doubt the pilgrims did indeed enjoy what they were doing. The army's planning deserved a great deal of the credit, too. The National Archives records of the pilgrimages are full of brief notes and longer letters from pilgrims, expressing their sincere appreciation for their experience. Mrs. Dellah Mae Miller of Lodi, California, for instance, took a few moments to write a short note to the Quartermaster General after her 1932 pilgrimage. She felt she lacked "words to tell how much I appreciated the trip, and the staff who took care of us were marvelous beyond expectations. They did all in their power to make us happy. No favoritism shown or neglect either."[49]

In short, the Quartermaster Corps did a commendable job in organizing and conducting the trips. It is a testament to the military's flexibility (not rigidity) that it could accomplish such a high-profile, unique task in a time of tight budgets and manpower shortages.

The army responded by building a custom made operation to handle pilgrimage workload. Leadership and support from the highest levels ensured the troops knew the letter as well as the spirit of their mission. Furthermore, the army succeeded by keeping Congress informed of the difficulties it faced, and they were fortunate that Congress listened and passed amended pilgrimage bills in response to this information.

These changes made eligibility issues that affected Grace Moran, Nina Reid, and Mrs. Bleckley, among others, much easier to manage. Medical care was a major challenge, but not as great as first feared. This was in large part due to the unique and quite unexpected nature of the pilgrimage experience. However, for all the War Department's success and attention to details large and small, one of its decisions threatened to swamp the pilgrimages in controversy: segregation.

6

Black Stars and Gold

"Invitations to mothers and widows of the Negro race shall be extended for such time as will permit the organization of separate groups of such mothers and widows," the War Department decided at the outset of the pilgrimages.[1] With this one-sentence declaration, the War Department announced a policy that opened the most controversial element of the entire Gold Star mother pilgrimages.

Despite protest and controversy, the War Department stuck to its decision. It segregated black mothers and widows from their white counterparts for the duration of the pilgrimages. In one sense, this order should not have come as a complete surprise. America in the early 1930s was a segregated society: separate but equal in theory, but more separate and unequal in practice. Blacks and whites did not eat together, learn together, or play together. And they most certainly did not travel together. Even the armed forces were segregated until after World War II.

This systematic segregation was called Jim Crow, after the stereotypical black cartoon character of the 19th century. It should have surprised no one, in fact, that the pilgrimages were segregated. It also should have surprised no one that the black pilgrims laughed and cried, mourned and behaved just like the white pilgrims did. Perhaps the biggest surprise of all was the chance to learn just how free from racism French society actually was for the dozens of black women who went overseas on their pilgrimage.

Black Soldiers Go Over There

Black soldiers made important contributions to the AEF, despite the fact they were segregated and used primarily as laborers. "If you want to say what is the typical black soldier in World War I, he would not be carrying a rifle, he would probably be carrying a shovel," Marvin Fletcher noted in *Gold Star Mothers: Pilgrimage of Remembrance.*²

Unfortunately, U.S. military officials wanted our allies to offer this same type of segregated treatment found in the United States. AEF leaders informed the French they were not to treat black troops as equals of whites. According to Professor Edward Coffman's summary of World War I racial attitudes, "You have to understand we're a segregated society, and we don't want you treating these people [black soldiers] as equals."³

Many African Americans paid the ultimate sacrifice for war experience. Despite segregation, many black troops did participate in combat. They did so as segregated units, commanded by white officers, in the AEF. Black troops also served in a more integrated and successful capacity with the French. For these young troops, the chance to be treated as equals was a unique experience. Hundreds of black troops were killed or wounded in the war, both in integrated and segregated units. A total of 1,268 black troops are buried in America's World War I cemeteries.

As the pilgrimages began, the Quartermaster Corps estimated that 600 mothers and widows of these men were eligible for a pilgrimage. Once these women had been contacted, the NAACP reported that 219 black mothers and widows had accepted invitations by May, 1930; 151 of them expressed an interest to sail in 1930, the rest in 1931 or a later year.⁴

Decision and Response

The War Department's decision to segregate the pilgrimages prompted black protests. The NAACP and its leaders led the way. It compiled a petition signed by some 55 eligible black women who planned not to go on their European pilgrimage. The petition was sent to President Hoover in May 1930, shortly after Party A had departed for Europe. It was signed by 55 women from 21 different states. "As a Gold Star Mother who happens to be colored," the petition read in part,

> I wish to protest against the gratuitous insult in attitude of the War Department and the United States in segregating colored Gold Star Mothers who are entitled to go to France to visit the graves where our loved ones are buried.
> When the call to arms came from our government in 1917, mothers, sisters, and wives, regardless of race, color, or creed, were asked to give their loved ones to the end that the world might be saved for democracy. This call we answered freely and willingly. In the years which have passed since death took our loved ones, our anguish and sorrow have been assuaged by the realization that our loved ones who rest in the soil of France gave their lives to the end the

world might be a better place in which to live for all men, of all races and all colors.

Twelve years after the Armistice, the high principles of 1918 seem to have been forgotten. We who gave and who are colored are insulted by the implication that we are not fit persons to travel with other bereaved ones. Instead of making up parties of Gold Star Mothers on the basis of geographical location, we are set aside in a separate group, Jim Crowed, separated and insulted.

We appeal to you as Chief Executive of our nation and as Commander-in-Chief of the army and navy, to issue an order abolishing this unjust ruling. If you as President of the United States refuse to abolish this ruling we respectfully decline to make the trip to France, preferring instead to remain at home and retain our honor and self-respect.[5]

The protests against segregation only increased once the details of the segregated pilgrimages emerged. In two important aspects, they indeed were separate but not equal. First, black travelers who gathered in New York City for a day or two of rest before departure for Europe were lodged not in first-class Manhattan hotels but in the Harlem YWCA. The second, and far more contentious issue, was the ocean liners chosen to transport the black pilgrims. Black mothers and widows were not to be transported aboard United States Lines top-drawer ships. Rather, they crossed the ocean on second-tier ships, from the *S.S. American Merchant* class of liners.

These were not cattle boats as some asserted; they were legitimate passenger ships. However, they were not as luxurious as the liners on which the white pilgrims traveled. The *S.S. American Merchant* class ships had started their service as freighters, especially during World War I, but they were fully refitted as comfortable (if not opulent), passenger ships. They were also smaller than their luxury counterparts. (The War Department argued the difference was due to the smaller size of the black parties. The average party of white pilgrims in 1930 approached 200, whereas the average of the two black parties was fewer than 50. In fact, at least one party of white women did travel on the smaller class of ship during the pilgrimages.) Nevertheless, the image of cattle boats stuck, and this type of treatment especially infuriated the black women and their supporters.

With segregation on land and on sea the order of the day, a number of white journalists and observers joined the protest. These writers balked at the inherent injustice of the situation, but they also saw the political reality behind the decision.

A magazine called *The World Tomorrow* ran an editorial against segregation titled "Government Goes Jim Crow." The piece concluded:

> The Government of the United States should be too big to stoop to such a thing as running Jim Crow [ocean] liners. It will be interesting to see whether

President Hoover's reputed lack of race prejudice is genuine and sincere or whether the bugaboo of lost Southern votes will lead him to evade the issue by the familiar political device of lying low and saying nothing.⁶

"There is no record, so far as we know, that any officer of the late war refused a Negro soldier the inestimable privilege of dying for his country because of his color," *The Nation* stated in its own article on segregated pilgrimages.⁷ The magazine criticized the War Department's decision, which it considered a disgrace not just to black pilgrims but indeed to all Americans. Segregating the black pilgrims served only to highlight what the magazine's editors believed the racist and undemocratic nature of American society.

The editors argued it was reprehensible for America to

> make the incredibly stupid and ungracious gesture of drawing attention to the Negro women, putting them in a group by themselves, providing for them a different sort of accommodation in hotels and on shipboard. Their sons died as white men died. The mothers are not to visit the graves as do white mothers. The article also put the Hoover administration on notice of the political price it would pay. "They are American citizens with a vote," the article reminded the War Department on behalf of the black pilgrims and their supporters.⁸

The article continued:

> If there were a few white women from any section of the country so delicately constituted that they could not endure to travel on the same ship with a black woman whose son or husband was killed in France, the War Department might with good grace have received cancellation of their passages. But we believe that such cancellations would have been few and far between. We believe that American white women are less prejudiced than the War Department itself. We believe the Negro women in a group would have been as welcome as Italian women or Jewish women or Polish women, for whom it was not thought necessary to provide separate accommodations. The government must learn that the Negroes are no longer property to be shunted around back alleys or smuggled in at side doors."⁹

It should be noted that white America should not be viewed as one solid mass of equal citizens. In the early part of the century, native-born whites looked down on newly arrived immigrants from Europe. This point of view was true, even though all groups, both native and immigrant, were "white." As *The Nation* viewed it, some would have seen almost as much reason to segregate Italians, Jews, or Poles as it would have blacks.

The political angle was worth considering. Up through the Hoover administration, blacks generally voted Republican, the party of Abraham

Lincoln, when they were permitted to vote at all. The pilgrimage decision, coupled with other perceived civil rights blunders during the Hoover administration, threatened to drive blacks into the arms of the Democrats.

Hoover heard as much from Tom Canty, one of his supporters from Chicago. Canty was acquainted with officials in the Hoover White House, including Hoover's personal secretary, George Akerson. Canty sent Akerson a telegram on May 30, 1930 to register his displeasure. Canty felt

> the person who discriminated against the colored gold star mothers pulled the worst boner contributing to the ever increasing unpopularity of your administration.... You may rest assured, George, that it will take some hokus pokus raised to the nth power to repopularize Mr. Hoover with our people in the Middle West.[10]

Another civil rights leader, Maurice W. Spencer of the National Equal Rights League, wrote a letter to Hoover with much the same theme. He was especially bitter because he believed the desire for segregation stemmed from the desire to cater to the prejudices of white Southerners. He argued the move was unconstitutional, bacause blacks were taxpayers as well as whites. "The colored mothers and widows are to be segregated by the federal government itself," Spencer wrote. "There is neither liberty nor equality in segregation. It is applied legitimately and usually only for the protection of the community against criminals, diseased, insane. To this category, it inferentially reduces Americans of color."[11]

It should be noted the segregation policy was directed solely against African Americans. At least one Native American was deemed worthy enough to travel with the white pilgrims in her party.

Even the host nation, France, joined the criticism of the segregation decision. A French newspaper noted shortly after the pilgrimages began that the black women "are carefully segregated from the others. Alas! The antipathy of the races still hold, even in the similitude of war."

Although French society was far ahead of the United States in eradicating racism, in 1930 it was far from colorblind. The same article referred to the African American pilgrims as "black mammies."[12]

Despite all the protest and controversy, President Hoover's mind was likely made up. The War Department policy remained unchanged, and the pilgrimages were segregated. One can assume that most whites would have agreed with Hoover's decision at the time, given the fact America was then a segregated society. There is very little recorded sentiment in favor of segregation; there is just one telegram in support of it in the files of the Herbert Hoover Presidential Library in Iowa. It came to the White House in May 1930, from the Chatham Unit, American Legion Auxiliary in Savannah, Georgia. The telegram "wishes to thank the President for his action in upholding the War Department in its arrangements for the voyages of the several groups of Gold Star Mothers to France in spite of the attitude taken by the negro Gold Star Mothers in this matter."[13] The unit's president and secretary signed the telegram.

Although it was just one telegram, it very likely represented the feelings of President Hoover, Secretary of War Hurley, and the majority of Hoover's Cabinet and advisors. This was especially true of Hurley, who was considered to be an "avowed segregationist."[14]

The Georgia women got their way. Hoover and Hurley failed to intervene. In fact, it is likely both of them approved of the segregation and probably supported it in the first place. The administration launched several defenses of its policy, saying it had made a thorough study of the issue. The War Department stated it had no objections if white and black pilgrims wished to travel together, provided all members of each group agreed. This scenario, of course, is impossible to imagine in 1930, since the War Department could not picture groups of white women lobbying to travel overseas with black pilgrims.

Barbara Ransby, from the University of Illinois at Chicago, concludes, "the Government was really symbolizing in some of the most painful ways the devaluation of black life."[15]

The Pilgrimages Begin

When the decision on segregation stood, the planning for separate black pilgrimage parties began. Invitations were extended, parties were formed, and reservations were made. The planning took on a new dimension when a new army escort officer was added, Col. Benjamin O. Davis. Davis was America's highest-ranking black military officer. He achieved this rank in a segregated army, which numbered no more than 3–4,000 black soldiers in the 1930s. Because he was black, he was not allowed to command whites, and he was denied admission to the army's advanced training and leadership schools. Despite segregation, Davis was an enthusiastic and professional soldier. He wanted nothing other than a long and successful army career. Edward "Mac" Coffman recalled his impression Davis gave of army life. "You could tell that he loved it," Coffman remembered. "I would talk to him about being a cavalry commander on the frontier. They'd go out and hunt elk. They wouldn't shoot deer. They were too little. That's the thing. He loved the horses, he loved hunting. He loved the Army."[16] Dissatisfied with a series of dead end assignments by 1930, Davis actively sought duty as a pilgrimage escort officer with the black pilgrims. His request for transfer was granted.

Davis took his wife, mother, and son with him to Europe (at his own expense) for the pilgrimages in 1930. Then in 1931, his teenage daughter, Elnora, accompanied the rest of the family. Elnora recalled how she got seasick on the trip over. "After crossing the English Channel without getting seasick, I resolved not to get seasick on the way home. Thus I enjoyed the trip."[17] None of the family spoke French, so Col. Davis hired a tutor, who gave Elnora daily French lessons and took her to points of interest around Paris.

Davis's European duty was no vacation for him; his full-time pilgrimage duties occupied him. His family was free, however, to spend time learning about France and visiting countries such as England, Belgium, and Holland. As a full colonel, or "bird" colonel, Davis had more means than junior escort officers to pay for extras such as tutors on the trips. Most escort officers were lieutenants or captains, who often had difficulty making ends meet in Paris.

Benjamin O. Davis, pilgrim escort officer. This photograph of Benjamin O. Davis was taken in 1918. By 1930, Davis was the highest-ranking black officer in the U.S. Army. Davis volunteered for escort officer duty and conducted trips for the segregated African American mothers. He later become America's first black general during World War II. (Benjamin O. Davis Sr. Collection, RG590S-BOD.43. U.S. Army Military History Institute.)

Davis's salary at the time was close to $10,000 per year, putting him in the top 1 percent of all wage earners in the United States.[18] However, his escort duties kept him busy, and he generally traveled with the pilgrim parties on their transatlantic voyages. Davis did indeed serve as a Steamship Liaison officer, as this duty was called, with the very first party of black pilgrims in 1930.

Party L began to assemble in New York City after July 4, 1930. As they prepared to sail, Secretary of War Hurley waged a public relations campaign to ease the controversy over the segregated pilgrimages. He continued to argue the pilgrimages, though admittedly segregated, were indeed equal. He also stated the army's desire to reduce stress on the pilgrims as much as possible, and this ideal extended into whites and blacks traveling separately.

> After a thorough study the conclusion was reached that the formation of white and colored groups of mothers and widows would best assure the contentment and comfort of the pilgrims themselves. No discrimination between the various groups is contemplated. All groups will receive like accommodations, and the representatives of the War Department will at all times be as solicitous of the welfare of the colored mothers and widows as they will be for the welfare of those of the white race.[19]

Comfort and convenience of the pilgrims were considered paramount. However, Hurley injected a racial spin into this area. Any unusual strain would tend to upset the pilgrims, who would already be in a fragile emotional state. Hurley believed,

> the journey will be a severe tax on those making it, and it will take them into strange surroundings and away from families and friends for a period of about six weeks. The War Department has been motivated by the desire to relieve this strain in so far as possible by not disturbing the normal contacts of the individual pilgrims. It would seem natural to assume these mothers and widows would prefer to seek solace in their own grief from companions of their own race.[20]

In short, Hurley and Hoover saw little need to change the "natural" order of things, and the pilgrimages remained segregated. Hurley's words did little to change the mind of the NAACP and other critics of segregation. In fact, the War Department continued to receive black pilgrims' cancellations up until Party L sailed.

Despite segregated lodgings, army and government officials organized a full-scale sendoff for the party on the afternoon of July 11 at City Hall in New York. Acting New York City Mayor Joseph McKee presided over the ceremonies, which included guests from each branch of the military. McKee was conciliatory in his remarks.

"We feel that you come to us consecrated with the blood of your young sons," he said to the assembled party of mothers and widows.

> You are going on a journey — perhaps a sad one. America's great contribution to the World War was a united people, and you can find consolation in the

thought that your boys died in an effort to uphold that dignity.... I am sorry that a different note [of dissent] had to be struck here, but in this city there runs a great, deep vein of gratitude. We go with you with thanks in our heart."[21]

Several pilgrimage supporters were on hand, including Representatives David O'Connell, John Boylan, and Samuel Dickstein. Each had been vocal congressional supporters of the pilgrimages during the 1920s.

Leading black Alderman Fred Moore struck a defiant tone in his speech at the ceremony. His audience, black and white alike, knew his belief that segregated pilgrimages insulted the black pilgrims. "When our boys went to France they felt they were fighting for democracy," he said.

> But that democracy lasted only a few days after the reception to the heroic members of the [all-black] Fifteenth Infantry. Then we were criticized, degraded, and humiliated, but we have borne that with Christian fortitude. We don't want to be regarded as things any longer; we want to be regarded as humans. We are proud to be Negroes."[22]

After the speeches, bands from the New York City Sanitation Department and the 369th Infantry sent the pilgrims on their way. Once the pilgrims reached their ship in Hoboken Harbor, the *S.S. American Merchant*, another small ceremony took place. Speakers included Paul W. Chapman, president of United States Lines and an ardent pilgrimage supporter, retired Quartermaster Gen. of the Army Maj. Gen. Frank Cheatham, and Col. Davis. "After an appropriate ceremony, the presentation of medals to the pilgrims, the ship got under way at noon," July 12, Colonel Davis wrote in his official Liaison Officer's report.[23] The report is preserved today in the U.S. Army War College's Library in Carlisle Barracks, Pennsylvania.

Davis's notes from this and later segregated pilgrimages offer an unprecedented, detailed, and sometimes unvarnished view of pilgrimage duty. Davis emerges as a professional, competent, and observant officer in his reports. He had nothing but praise for the ship and her crew on this and all subsequent voyages. Other parts of the military were equally cooperative.

> Too much cannot be said of the value of the services rendered by ... Port Quartermaster Agent. He spares no pains, not only in the rendering of services but seemed to delight in rendering some courtesy or kindness to members of the Party and the Liaison Officer.[24]

Party L's voyage was a smooth one. Davis noted that no unusually heavy seas or bad weather were encountered. The only glitch in the voyage was a medical one. The army feared distraught women causing harm to themselves or others in the unfamiliar surroundings of a pilgrimage. This is exactly what Davis witnessed on his first stint as Liaison Officer.

The pilgrim "suffered from hallucinations. She declared that she was in direct communication with the Devil who was trying to influence her to jump overboard. The case was very trying, but was well-handled" by the ship's medical staff.[25] Col. Davis was no doubt relieved when Party L reached Cherbourg Harbor on the morning of July 21, and he was able to turn the party over to Col. Richard T. Ellis.

Davis pronounced the party in good health and joined the pilgrims, Ellis, and Maj. Gen. Cheatham on the train to Paris. An enthusiastic and unusually large crowd, including both French citizens and the "American Negro Colony," welcomed the pilgrims. Peyton's jazz orchestra played the French and American national anthems along with popular tunes. Young black women from a Paris cabaret raised money for flowers for the pilgrims, and each mother and widow received a purple aster as she entered the train station.

The French press gave an intriguing account of the women's arrival. "Stirring and strange was the arrival yesterday of the 55 colored Mothers debarking at 2:05 P.M. at the Gare des Invalides," the story in *Le Matin* began.

> 55 women were there on the platform, with childish and tired faces, hesitating on that platform where everything seemed so strange to them. One by one, dressed in black or bright colors, they walked up the steep stair which leads to the esplanade. Some colored people handed them flowers, and all of a sudden a jazz band of colored musicians started to play the first notes of a moaning song. Then we saw the strange band, led by an enthusiastic man, started to play the National Anthem and the Marseillaise. Stirred, and amused at the same time, the mothers who came on that sad pilgrimage agitated their small flags. Awaiting buses took the party on a brief Paris sight-seeing tour, including the Place de la Concorde and the Tuileries Gardens before dropping the party off at its hotel.[26]

Party L received its official welcome the next day, July 22. The military governor of Paris, Gen. Henry Gourard, welcomed the party on behalf of the French government in an afternoon ceremony at the Arc de Triomphe. A large and enthusiastic crowd again greeted the pilgrims. U.S. ambassador to France Walter Edge, along with Cheatham, Ellis, Davis, and Lt. Col. George G. Bartlett escorted the party to the now customary wreath-laying at the French Tomb of the Unknown soldier.

Party L's honor pilgrim, Laura Newton of Bennettsville, South Carolina, placed a wreath at the tomb. Newton's son Isaac died while serving with the 370th Infantry and was buried in the Meuse-Argonne Cemetery.

After the ceremony, the party attended a reception in the Louis Quinze Salon of the Laurent Restaurant. While eating a light meal, Gen. Pershing and Ambassador Edge welcomed the party to France on behalf of the U.S. government. The women were scheduled to visit the Louvre and take a boat ride on the Seine the next day, Wednesday, July 23. The full party was scheduled to leave Paris and visit the cemeteries beginning on Thursday, July 24.

Press coverage did not follow the black pilgrims to the cemeteries. Neither the *New York Times* nor the *Paris Edition* reported on the pilgrims' visits to their loved ones' graves. One may speculate this was because the white press did not want to witness blacks mourning their dead in a very touching and altogether human way. However, one cannot be too sure of this point.

After Party A's visit earlier in 1930, the press seldom traveled to the cemeteries with parties, white or black. When parties were covered, correspondents usually reported only on the women's movements in and around Paris. For example, the same *New York Times* story that reported on Gen. Gouraud's reception for Party L devoted just one paragraph to the activities of white Parties J and K in their cemetery visits in the French countryside.

In fact, one gathers that the press and even the War Department were somewhat uncomfortable with the black pilgrims, especially in 1930. Neither group knew how to treat them. That the black pilgrims received equal treatment, in Europe at least, is beyond question.

Yet what today would be considered pure racism was the order of the day for the white press in the early 1930s. For example, before Party L left Paris to visit the cemeteries, the *Paris Edition* reported the mothers would be treated to a traditional Southern fried chicken dinner when they returned to the French capital. American chef Willis Morgan, who ran the famous Chicago Inn in Paris, planned a menu that included Maryland fried chicken, corn on the cob, sweet potatoes, ham, and cornbread. He even planned to import an entire railcar of watermelons from Algeria. The *Paris Edition* reported this story without the slightest hint of irony.[27] In fact, considering black and white disliked French food, the army likely thought a down-home menu was a grand gesture. In any case, the press gave more space to the black pilgrims' diet than to their cemetery visits. This enhanced coverage of food and parties held true for the black parties throughout the pilgrimages.

However, this type of coverage may have been just as well. Plenty happened in Paris for the black pilgrims. The sizable African community in Paris embraced its black pilgrims. The most visible proof was the talent show that bandleader Noble Sissle hosted for the pilgrims in Paris after Party L returned from their cemetery visits. Sissle and his orchestra joined noted acts such as the Two Black Dots, Norman Thomas, and club owner Brick Top at the Hotel Imperator. Other acts were household names then but largely lost to history now: Snow Fisher, Herbert Parker, Vance Lowrey, and jazz pianist Sam Wooding. Sissle envisioned the show as a way to cheer up the mothers and take their minds off the sad sights they would have seen at the cemeteries. The press noted that one could not find such a collection of black talent even in Harlem. Ambassador and Mrs. Edge, Gen. Pershing, General Gouraud, Gen. Cheatham, Col. and Mrs. Ellis, and Col. Davis and his wife attended the festivities. Brick Top thanked the pilgrims for attending. She broke down on stage during her brief speech, but the *Paris Edition* quoted what she managed to say. "No matter how much pleasure you may have received this afternoon, dear mothers, it cannot half equal the joy with which we have given it to you."[28]

Despite the reporting, racism and prejudice made their way into this unsigned news account. "The rhythm and music inherent in the Negro race manifested itself triumphantly yesterday," at the charity concert.[29]

If black pilgrims faced segregation in the United States, an ironic thing happened once they reached Europe. In one notable area, black pilgrim parties fared much better than white. The world of white expatriate Paris, those American artists and bohemians who had left the United States, by and large ignored the pilgrims completely. Perhaps the pilgrims reminded the assorted poets, writers, and artists too much of their own mothers back home. The black community of Paris, by contrast, welcomed the black travelers with open arms. Entertainers, athletes, churchmen, and other dignitaries greeted, entertained, and feted the black mothers during their trips, as Noble Sissle had done for Party L. Several hundred blacks living in Paris turned out to welcome the pilgrims, not just in 1930 but in later years as well. While America continued to practice segregation and intolerance in 1930, the black pilgrims found themselves moving in what was the most accepting, tolerant, and free society they had ever known.

Wherever the pilgrims went, prominent black people were there to welcome them. Names ranged from boxing champion "Panama" Al Brown to classically trained composer Clarence C. White. Other entertainers included dancer Thaddeus "Teddy" Drayton, Norman Thomas, Fanny Cotton, Herbert Parker, and journalist J. A. Rogers. Ada "Brick Top" Smith was omnipresent. Her nightclub was the toast of Paris and the setting for at least one party for the pilgrims. (Her nickname came from her reddish hair, inherited from her Irish and African-American mother.) (Brick Top died in 1984 after decades as a successful nightclub owner in both the

United States and Europe.) Eddie South was another noteworthy name. South was born in Missouri in 1904 and studied classical music in Chicago in the 1920s. Finding the world of classical music closed to him, South studied and performed in Europe from 1928 to 1931. He recorded with such names as Stephane Grappelli and Django Reinhardt and released records on popular labels such as Mercury and Chess. He died in 1962 and is still considered one of the finest classically trained jazz violinists.

The most prominent name of all was that of Noble Sissle. His name and music weave in and out of the black pilgrimages like notes from a familiar melody. Sissle was born in 1889 in Indianapolis. He was a drum major during World War I in the noted all-black 369th Infantry Band. Sissle gradually earned fame as a bandleader and arranger. He cowrote and coproduced with longtime partner and pianist Eubie Blake a pair of landmark musicals, *Shuffle Along* and *Chocolate Dandies. Shuffle Along* was the first Broadway musical featuring an all-black cast. The musical was a huge hit, especially with white audiences. It toured nationally and played in white theatres. *Shuffle Along* also gave the first big break to a 16-year-old dancing prodigy, Josephine Baker. Blake and Sissle's follow up, *Chocolate Dandies*, was successful if not equally popular. Sissle and his band were international sensations and toured Europe throughout the 1920s and early 1930s.

Celebrities such as Cole Porter, Tallulah Bankhead, and Jascha Heifitz enjoyed the music. In 1930, Sissle played for the British royal family in London, and the duke of Windsor even sat in as the band's drummer. Musicians including singer Lena Horne and clarinet genius Sidney Bechet at times performed with Sissle and his band. During the 1950s, Sissle served as Harlem's honorary mayor. He had by this time gained respect from white audiences. His band broke the color barrier at the Park Central Hotel in New York City and toured with USO shows. The 1948 Truman presidential campaign revived one of *Shuffle Along*'s numbers, "I'm Just Wild about Harry," as a theme song. In 1953, Sissle and his band later played President Eisenhower's inauguration.

In later life, Sissle was a club owner, disk jockey, and music publisher. He died in Tampa in 1975. Although virtually unknown outside of jazz circles today, Sissle was a superstar in the 1930s. Black pilgrims would have recognized his name and have enjoyed the presence of such a big star.

Once the merrymaking, parties, and cemetery visits were finished, Party L prepared to conclude its six-week pilgrimage. The party embarked on the *S.S. American Merchant* on August 3. Col. Davis took charge of the party on their voyage back to America, and he reported how the ship's crew "lined up on the deck and gave the Party a cordial welcome."[30] The voyage home was a rough one, not smooth like the trip to Europe. "Quite heavy seas were encountered and the weather did not permit the Pilgrims to spend much time out on decks," Davis noted in his report. "However, other than sea sickness there were only a few cases of tonsillitis, which were successfully treated by the Surgeon Dr. Densleo."[31]

Davis's report praised the ship's crew for their excellent work in conducting the pilgrimages. "The *American Merchant* was well suited for this mission," he wrote.

> The cabins were large and comfortable. Due to the small size of the Party all older Pilgrims were assigned rooms with private baths and toilets.... The entire ship was placed at the disposal of the Pilgrims, and the entire crew left nothing undone or failed in any way whatsoever to make the voyage a pleasant one.[32]

As a good officer, Davis took time to review the performance of the individuals assigned along with him to pilgrimage duty. He singled out the ship's purser, surgeon, stewardess, and nurse for special praise. The nurse received the most attention. "It is hoped that the services of Miss [Henrietta] Forrest can be secured for the next trip. She was always present for duty," Davis wrote.[33]

However, he reserved a few choice words for the trip's hostess.

> I regret to report that the Hostess ... was of practically no help during the voyage to and from Europe. Shortly after the ship got under way going and returning, she retired to her cabin and was reported seasick. A hostess who cannot render assistance afloat is not any help to the Pilgrimage, and it is hoped that in the future an effort will be made to insure the employment of a hostess who will not be incapacitated most of the time while afloat. In this case, [the hostess] was just one more sick person to be waited upon and rendered practically no service at all afloat.[34]

A substandard hostess aside, the black pilgrims from Party L had nothing but praise for their trip. Several of the women prepared a statement after landing in New York. It read, in part,

> the exquisite cleanliness of the boat and tidiness of the staterooms gave evidence at once of the thoughtfulness of the management. The beautiful and tastefully decorated dining room and delicious food served by spotless and courteous attendants gave proof that somebody meant us to be happy.[35]

Davis observed much the same gratitude. He reported the pilgrims were uniformly delighted with their trip. "The Pilgrims have been very profuse in their expressions of satisfaction, happiness, and appreciation on the way they have been handled on this trip," he wrote. "They are returning to their homes with a feeling of gratefulness to the Government and with renewed faith in the principles upon which our Government is founded; and the feeling that their sons and husbands have not died in vain."[36]

Davis should well have counted himself among the reasons for the trip's success. His efficient service and caring demeanor surely improved the pilgrimage experience for the 54 women who sailed with him on Party L, 1930.

The second and final African American group of 1930 was Party Q, which included 43 mothers and widows. Party Q experienced less controversy but also less press coverage than Party L did earlier in the season. The party reached France aboard the *S.S. American Merchant* on August 25. Davis again accompanied the party overseas, and Noble Sissle and his orchestra once again welcomed the pilgrims to Paris. Honor pilgrim Louise Kimbro placed the traditional wreath at the French Tomb of the Unknown soldier.

The party divided up for visits to the individual cemeteries. Thirty-six women went to the Oise-Aisne Cemetery, while seven members left the group for the voyage across the English Channel to Brookwood Cemetery outside London.

One of the Oise-Aisne pilgrims was West Virginia widow Katherine Bell Holley. Her husband died from illness on October 4, 1918. (African American parties usually had a larger percentage of widows than did the white parties.) Holley and her fellow Oise-Aisne pilgrims experienced much the same type of trip that white pilgrims did. The group left Paris on August 29 and paid its first visit to the cemetery on August 31. They returned to the cemetery the next day, September 1. On the way to the cemetery, the group stopped at now-familiar locations, such as Quentin Roosevelt's grave, Belleau Wood, and the small village of Reims. The full party reformed in Paris on September 2 and then departed for the United States on September 7, once again aboard the *S.S. American Merchant*. The party arrived back in the United States after its pilgrimage on September 16.

Party Q enjoyed itself as much as did Party L. Honor Pilgrim Louise Kimbro wrote a sincere thank-you letter to the War Department. She singled out two army officers, both white, for their kind treatment. Her letter read in part,

> I never will get through talking about the grand time we had. Everyone was happy over the way Col. [Capt.] Maroney and his wife treated us so nice. Also Mr. [Col. Richard] Ellis and his wife.... How can anyone forget such a trip ... we

never can.... I want to thank the whole War Department and everyone concerned with the courtesy and kindness shown to the Gold Star Mothers and Widows.[37]

Another Party Q pilgrim shared the same view. Her letter went beyond mere praise for the army; it addressed the soothing and healing nature of the pilgrimage experience itself. Mrs. G. A. Buckley from Michigan wrote to Col. Williams to express her appreciation.

> I am going to write our United States Senator of how the Gold Star Mothers appreciate this great thing the Government is doing for them. I feel that a gap has been filled, and that now I have seen my dear son's resting place, and know that it will be forever kept beautiful, I am more contented.[38]

Pilgrims black and white universally shared this same view. The trips did fill a gap, and women did return more contented than when they left.

The first black party of 1931 was Party E, which assembled in New York City in late May. United States Lines organized the customary farewell party on May 29, just as the pilgrims boarded the *S.S. American Farmer*.

Paul W. Chapman, president of United States Lines, welcomed the party.

> And while *we* must remain at home, nevertheless, our thoughts go with you together with our gratitude for the sacrifices you and yours have made in the name of the United States of America and of the World. There is nothing we can add to or detract from the glory that is yours alone—God bless you all and make *us* worthy of the deeds of your loved and lost.[39]

Col. Davis also addressed the pilgrims, and his remarks revealed how privileged he felt to be serving as a pilgrimage officer. "Who could be more interested in the success of this mission than those of us who trained, marched, and fought beside your sons and husbands?" Davis asked the pilgrims.

> The United States has placed this ship at your command enroute to France. I have been selected to accompany you as the representative of the United States. I feel deeply this great honor conferred upon me. As far as human intelligence can foresee everything has been done that will make for your safety and comfort. The crew, the War Department personnel, and all connected with this Pilgrimage are consecrated to the mission of making this a safe, comfortable, and pleasant voyage for you — our Gold Star Mothers.[40]

The party landed in France on the evening of June 7. The members of the party arrived at the Gare des Invalides at exactly 9:53 P.M. Noble Sissle, his band, and several hundred well-wishers met the party. Sissle's band welcomed the pilgrims with what was reported as a "lusty" version of "Onward Christian Soldiers." The women also heard a sizzling hot jazz tune, "Happy Days," which kept their toes tapping. Sissle played other songs, ranging from "Mammy" to the French anthem "Le Marsellaise." Waiting buses took the tired pilgrims to the Hotel Splendide.[41]

The party of 28 (accounts varied) pilgrims assembled for a wreath laying ceremony. Amanda Mitchell, the Honor Pilgrim from Washington, DC, laid the wreath. The ceremony was especially moving for one pilgrim. "One old gray-haired mother who asked the translation of the inscription on the slab [on the Tomb of the Unknown] wept silently on hearing the answer. Her son has an unknown grave, somewhere in the Atlantic."[42] After the ceremony, the pilgrims traveled to the Restaurant Laurent for a welcoming tea. A who's who of American society in Paris, both black and white, were present. Dignitaries included U.S. ambassador to France Walter Edge, Gen. Pershing, Ellis and Davis, French representative Capt. Delafonde, along with Sissle and musician Cameron White.

Edge told the pilgrims he was glad they were in France. He expressed concern how the public in both France and the United States had lost interest in the war and had forgotten the soldiers and sacrifices they made. He was glad to report to the pilgrims that many French people, along with the French government, were glad for their presence.

Pershing also assured the pilgrims he was glad they came. He admitted sad times were ahead at the cemeteries, but he knew from personal observations that visiting the graves would help ease the pain of their losses. Pershing expressed his view that black troops were the equal of whites when they received similar training and leadership. He told the party "mothers would realize ... when they looked out over the white crosses of the cemeteries where their sons and husbands lie, that the sacrifice was not in vain, and that their memories would be tenderly cherished down through the years."[43]

Press coverage expanded for the black parties in 1931. Perhaps white newspapermen felt more comfortable with the black pilgrims after the two successful trips in 1930. The *Chicago Tribune*'s *Paris Edition* followed the party extensively in Paris. The paper noted how the pilgrims adjusted quickly to Parisian life. The women praised their escort officers, two white men from Georgia, and were delighted at how kind the French were to them. One mother was quoted as saying the French "are plumb fine the way they are so nice to us and all."[44] Mothers visited Napoleon's Tomb and remarked to each other how he was the French equivalent of a Lincoln or Washington. The freedom to drink alcohol, while Prohibition was still underway back home, struck the pilgrims as unique. Marion Sealey, a Long Island pilgrim, proclaimed she liked wine and beer and that Prohibition "is stupid and it makes only a lot of drinkers."⁴⁵ Family back home urged Sally Ann Anderson to taste Cognac, but she hadn't the nerve to order any. French-style food always posed a problem for the American pilgrims. The black pilgrims missed American-style white bread. They were served American-style coffee at the hotel, which proved ideal for dunking the hard French bread. Mrs. Anderson liked the bread and butter dunked in coffee so much she was too full for dinner one evening.⁴⁶

The American press covering the black pilgrims reported most of their words in stereotypical black dialect. This was especially true in the *Paris Edition*. In the only story on the black pilgrims to carry a byline, the *Paris Edition* ran a piece by Will Barber on the black pilgrims in its June 30, 1931, edition.

Barber's article was replete with "yessir" and "ummmm." One black pilgrim was quoted as saying "Lawdy, jes' think of that" when she saw Napoleon's Tomb. Another pilgrim was identified only as "Po'k Chops" Griffin; her real name was never used. When the reporter asked her about this nickname, here's how her answer was given: "Dey calls me Po'k chops, chile, because I likes my meat. I spends a dollar every Satiday for my po'k chops, 'cause I'se got to have 'em. Dey tols me I can't eat meat, but I does. Sure, I got it on the boat."⁴⁷ Other pilgrims were called names such as Aunt Sarah and Grandma Sally Ann. (Aunt Sarah was Sarah Downes from Baltimore.) The liveliest member of Party E, Sally Ann Anderson, was a 44-year-old grandmother from Asheville, North Carolina. (It is not clear from the press coverage how Mrs. Anderson qualified for a pilgrimage. At that age, she was probably a soldier's widow.)

Nevertheless, Barber also saw the women as individuals. He remarked on how much they enjoyed the experience of just sitting in the hotel lobby watching the American Davis Cup tennis team walk by. He reported the women liked the freedom they found in Paris, and many simply wanted to remain in France.

Barber was a young man in his early 20s when he wrote this story. He became a veteran correspondent, reporting from all over Europe for the *Tribune*. He met his death on the eve of World War II in Africa. Barber was working in London when Italy prepared to invade Ethiopia. He wanted to get vaccinated before traveling to Africa. He asked permission from the *Tribune*'s imperious owner, Col. McCormick, if he could postpone his departure until he had had his shots.

As *Paris Edition* veteran Waverley Root told it,

> the colonel fired back one of his lapidary cables on which he prided himself: Are you a Historian or a Newspaperman?

"Barber left London the next day, and for six months sat idly in Addis Ababa waiting for something to happen. On the day the Italians invaded, he died of blackwater fever."[48]

The mothers left crusty bread and the Davis Cup team behind them. It was time to embark on the purpose of the pilgrimages. The party split up to visit the cemeteries. Some went to Brookwood in England, but the majority boarded busses for the larger American cemeteries in France. The press did not follow the women to the cemeteries, so we know nothing of what took place there, but it was waiting for them when they returned to Paris.

Sissle once again organized an all-star concert at the Hotel Splendide on Friday, June 19. Sissle and his band led the festivities. "Every time Noble stepped out on the floor and rolled his eyebrows, that band of his just played for all it was worth," the press reported.[49] Brick Top sang and danced and served as master of ceremonies. Snow Fisher and Fanny Cotton also performed. Jimmy Ferguson and Theodore Drayton each danced for the pilgrims, and the team of Marino and Norris entertained with dance numbers as well.

In the midst of the entertainment, Robert Ephraim, a University of Chicago student, delivered a stirring address to the mothers and widows. The women, for their part, loved the show. Their remarks, as usual, were reported in dialect. One woman said, "Lawdy, listen to this heah jazz, sistah."[50] Pilgrim Hattie Campbell's remarks were reported as "It's gran'. Fact is, it's better than that."[51]

By way of contrast, this is a good spot to examine the most noted instance of a white expatriate in France interacting with the Gold Star mothers. Merrymaking and celebration are replaced by a rejection of the world the pilgrims represent. F. Scott Fitzgerald used an encounter with a party of Gold Star mothers in the 1933 novel *Tender Is the Night* to contrast the middle America of the new world with the Lost Generation in the old. Fitzgerald's character Dick Diver is having lunch with his wife and another woman. "There was a party at the next table that they could not account for. It consisted of an expansive, somewhat secretarial, would-you-mind-repeating young man, and a score of women," Fitzgerald's account began.

> The women were neither young nor old nor of any particular social class; yet the party gave an impression of a unit, held more closely together than a group of wives stalling through a professional congress of their husbands. Certainly it was more of a unit than any conceivable tourist party.
>
> An instinct made Dick suck back the grave derision that formed on his tongue; he asked the waiter to find out who they were.
>
> "Those are the gold-star muzzers," explained the waiter [in broken English.]

Aloud and in low voices they exclaimed. Rosemary's eyes filled with tears.
"Probably the young ones are the wives," said Nicole.
Over his wine Dick looked at them again; in their happy faces, the dignity that surrounded and pervaded the party, he perceived all the maturity of an older America. For a while the sobered women who had come to mourn their dead, for something they could not repair, made the room beautiful. Momentarily, he sat again on his father's knee, riding with Moseby while the old loyalties and devotions fought on around him. Almost with an effort he turned back to the two women at the table and faced the whole new world in which he believed.
Dick asked: "Do you mind if I pull down the curtain?"⁵²

To Fitzgerald's credit, he observed the natural cohesiveness of the Gold Star mothers party, a trait that characterized them as pilgrims, certainly not just "any conceivable tourist party." He is quick to acknowledge the women's dignity. Symbolically, however, millions of Americans turned their backs and closed the curtains on what the pilgrims represented. The African American parties, by contrast, did not experience the closed curtains or turned backs presented by the white members of the Lost Generation in Paris. Stars such as Noble Sissle and Brick Top ensured they received the warm welcome they deserved.

Meanwhile, Party E, 1931, left Paris the next day, June 20. The press did not chronicle its ocean voyage or return home. Party E received more press coverage than any other black party, however. Just as with white parties, the coverage focused on parties, receptions, and other ceremonies. The press, for its part, was probably growing more comfortable with the black pilgrims. Although the press often quoted their conversations in stereotypical dialect, it was also able to observe how much freedom the women enjoyed in France. What the black pilgrims thought and felt at the graveside died with them.

"The Gold Star mothers really saw a contrast when they traveled to Europe," Professor Barbara Ransby from the University of Illinois at Chicago observed.

> They could eat in restaurants and didn't have to take their meals out and eat them in the car, or eat them in back, as would be a commonplace practice in the south in the United States. They didn't have to look for white signs or colored signs in order to navigate public space. And so there was a sense of seeing new possibilities and also seeing the anger that existed in the restraints and constraints that existed in this country.⁵³

Party K was the second and final black group to travel in 1931. The group, 34 strong, sailed aboard the *S.S. American Merchant*. Davis again served as liaison officer with the group. His report was especially detailed and offered a glimpse into the world of the escort officers. His description

Party K, 1931, on its pilgrimage. African American pilgrims were segregated from white women during the trips. They sailed on less luxurious liners than white pilgrims. On European soil, however, they stayed in the same hotels and ate at the same restaurants as the white Gold Star mothers. The War Department's decision to segregate the trips was controversial, and many black mothers decided not to travel under separate conditions. Col. Benjamin O. Davis is in the back, escorting the group. (National Archives, RG 92.)

of greeting the pilgrims sounded more like an amphibious assault than a welcome for bereaved women.

> On the afternoon of July 10th, I took station on the deck near the gangway, greeting all the pilgrims as they came aboard, and arranged with the Chief Steward to have all the baggage immediately placed in the pilgrims' cabins under the supervision of the Port Quartermaster Agent just as soon as it was placed aboard ship. Baggage was actually checked in each pilgrim's cabin and found to be correct.[54]

The ship sailed promptly at 4 that afternoon. The voyage overseas was not especially eventful. Seasickness affected several pilgrims, but most recovered quickly. A memorial ceremony was held on July 15. The weather was nice, and all pilgrims felt well enough to be on deck together for the first time since departure, Davis reported.

The only item of note in his report was the injured knee of Mrs. Zelina Carrington. She injured her knee getting out of her berth in the stateroom on July 18. Davis looked into the matter with true military precision.

> Investigation disclosed that Mrs. Carrington had used the upper berth in her Cabin. She had been advised by the Bed Room Steward and the two nurses that she had been assigned a lower berth and should occupy it. I questioned Mrs. Carrington and she admitted that she had been told to use the lower berth, but that since nobody was using the upper berth and she preferred it, she used it.[55]

Mrs. Carrington recovered and joined the rest of her party when it docked in France on July 19 Davis again praised the ship's crew for their uniformly professional and courteous service to all pilgrims.

The 34 pilgrims, including honor pilgrim Eva Bush from Columbus, Ohio, laid the ceremonial wreath at the Tomb of the Unknown. Two of the party visited Brookwood Cemetery while the remaining 32 women visited cemeteries in France.[56] The party returned home safely to New York City in early August.

By 1932, the press and the public back home had begun to lose interest in the pilgrims, black or white. Whereas the coverage of Party A in 1930 was front-page news, pilgrimages by 1932 and 1933 received no more than a column inch or two of newspaper coverage, if that much. Moreover, reports were now relegated to the style or women's pages of the newspaper, far removed from the front pages.

Press coverage for the black parties followed the same pattern; the first black party of 1932 received a grand total of one column inch in the *New York Times*, a simple announcement the party had arrived in France.[57] Therefore, what we can learn of the black pilgrims comes largely from their experiences in 1930 and 1931.

For all the controversy of the segregated pilgrimages, they achieved their goal. They help relieve the suffering and ease the grief of a deserving group of war widows and mothers. Their sincere notes and letters of gratitude showed that the mission was accomplished. Something else was accomplished, too.

For anyone who cared to look, this mixing of the races in international travel worked just fine. White officers from the South escorted the women professionally and without incident. The shipping line transported them with courtesy and harmony back and forth to Europe. The white population, through the white newspapers such as the *Paris Edition* did learn the black and white pilgrims had much more in common than was expected. Will Barber, noticed as much. Despite referring to the mothers' speech in dialect, Barber was won over by the women's mixture of grace and good humor. "They were all very happy, and they were all very charming, regular folks," he wrote. "Each had given a son or husband or brother in the War with quiet patriotism, without fanfare."[58] No one should have expected anything more or anything less.

Racism Takes a Holiday

The pilgrims along with Col. Davis and his family noticed the freer, less racist conditions in Europe. Many of the women wanted to remain in France once they arrived. "Some of them are so pleased they want to stay," Barber wrote. "The freedom, the courtesy, the charm of Paris urge them to obey the words of Mrs. Emma J. Parker of Virginia.... 'I've made my will. I'se fixed my things. Jes' let me stay. I don't want to go back home. Why? I likes it over here, that's all."[59] Knowing her remarks would have been reported in dialect would probably have sealed Mrs. Parker's decision.

The pilgrimages highlighted how much African Americans had to fight simply to participate in the military. Davis fought for promotions and choice assignments during his entire career. He became America's first black general during World War II; President Truman officially desegregated the army in 1948.

However, Davis was a loyal soldier who was proud to serve his country. Davis's son, Benjamin O. Davis Jr., loved the military life as well. He enrolled as the only black cadet at West Point in 1932. Outside of official conversations, none of the white cadets spoke with the younger Davis during his four years at West Point. He graduated in the top 10 percent of his class in 1936 and served with the famed Tuskegee Airmen during World War II. Davis followed his father's trailblazing footsteps; he became the air force's first black general. He retired in 1970 with the rank of lieutenant general. He died in 2002 at the age of 89.

Davis Sr. shared the frustration of being a black officer with his son. The freedom of France made this frustration all the more difficult. Davis wrote his son a letter from France during the pilgrimages that read in part,

> I am enjoying freedom and find it hard to think that I have to return to the place [the United States] where before I try to enter [any white establishment], I've got to be sure I'll be accepted, even though I have the price.... After the freedom I've enjoyed here American restrictions will be hard for a time.[60]

The tragic irony of the black pilgrimages remains that blacks had to leave the United States to experience the freedom and equality that America at the time barely promised and scarcely delivered to its citizens of color.

7

Pilgrim Profile: Louise and Grace Ziegler

On Thursday, July 28, 1932, Louise Ziegler and her daughter Grace were on the next to last day of their pilgrimage. They had already visited the grave of Private Fred Ziegler in the Meuse-Argonne Cemetery. The Zieglers were enjoying a few days of sight-seeing as their party made its way back to Paris for departure. Thursday was a busy day for the women, with a morning trip to view the medieval artifacts at the Cluny Museum and then an afternoon boat ride on the Seine through Paris.

Grace kept a detailed daily diary of her trip, and it was published in her hometown newspaper, the *Rockford Morning Star*, on her return. It remains one of the longest, most observant first-person accounts any pilgrim ever produced. Of her experiences on July 28, Grace wrote in her diary:

> Thursday, we visited the Cluny Museum where most of the exhibits were medieval and were three or four hundred years old. We speculated on how those knights ever blew their noses when they had a cold. The guide told me to pick out the jewelry I wanted, but it took me too long to decide so I had to come away without it. In the afternoon, we went to Suresnes and took a boat ride down the Seine River. We saw an old woman washing her clothes along the bank and went by the bridge where there is a replica of the Statute of Liberty.[1]

"I'll wager her knees got sore. The water was dirty!" Grace added in a caption to the photo album she also kept from the trip.[2]

Meanwhile, half a world away in Washington, DC, July 28 took on a very different meaning for another segment of the World War I generation. Maj. Gen. Douglas MacArthur led armed infantry and cavalry troops against the so-called Bonus Army. MacArthur and his men used tear gas, fixed bayonets, and even tanks to drive thousands of unemployed Great War veterans from the nation's capital.

His forces, which included Maj. Dwight Eisenhower and George Patton, scattered the protesters and chased them across the Anacostia River to their shanty encampment. MacArthur's troops set fire to the Bonus Army's camp, thereby ending the group's Depression-era plea for government funds.

The Bonus Army was the culmination of a veteran's movement that began during the 1920s. By 1924, Congress passed (over President Coolidge's veto) a plan to pay World War I veterans up to several hundred dollars each for their wartime service. The payment of this bonus, as it came to be known, was to be deferred until 1945. By 1932, however, the Great Depression was at its worst. Former soldiers wanted their money immediately; they did not want to wait 13 more years for payment. Approximately 20,000 veterans and their families made their way to Washington, to lobby Congress for their bonus during the summer of 1932.

Although some in Congress were sympathetic to their plight, President Hoover and other leaders felt the country could not afford to give relief to any one group of citizens at the expense of others. That decision applied even to a deserving group, such as the Bonus Army veterans. In addition, many in Washington were afraid of such a large mass of unemployed, disgruntled citizens. Therefore, the president and Secretary of War Patrick Hurley ordered MacArthur to clear the marchers from the nation's capital. By pursuing the men across the Anacostia River. MacArthur exceeded his orders. Nevertheless, his efforts put an end to the Bonus Army and their claims.

The Bonus Army and its men put the military in a very awkward position. The army's official history acknowledged this challenge.

> The troops cleaned up the situation near the Capitol without firing a shot, and then proceeded with equal efficiency to clear out all marchers from the District of Columbia. From a military point of view the Army had performed an unpleasant task in exemplary fashion, with only a few minor injuries to participants; but the use of military force against civilians, most of them veterans, tarnished the Army's public image and helped defeat the [Hoover] administration in the forthcoming election."[3]

The juxtaposition of the Zieglers' river cruise against the treatment of the Bonus Army is yet another reason the Gold Star mother pilgrimages are so fascinating. While the Zieglers enjoyed their cruise and museum visit at government expense, armed troops forced thousands of veterans out of Washington. More specifically, one part of the army treated the mothers to a remarkable pilgrimage experience, while another part of the same military establishment gave veterans the bum's rush. The Gold Star pilgrims had succeeded in their decade-long struggle to secure government funding for themselves.

At the same time, the veteran Bonus Army left Washington with no financial rewards to show for their years' worth of effort. The same government that treated a segment of World War I soldiers to violent ejection from the capital then lavished the mothers of their dead comrades with European pilgrimages.

Rebecca Jo Plant called the Bonus Army episode "one of the great ironies" of the pilgrimage story. She commented on this irony during her interview.

> So there you have the very men who had fought alongside the sons of these women, and their demands for compensation from the state are being ignored entirely, and are being forcibly denied, whereas the women overseas are still being pampered and treated to this kind of luxury tour, even at the height of the Depression. And that had to cause some reflection, at the heart of the American people, because the disparity would've seemed too great between how these two different groups were treated.[4]

None of these issues or ironies concerned Grace Ziegler and her mother during their pleasant day in Paris on July 28. Nor should they have. The Bonus Army, for its part, would probably not have begrudged the mothers their pilgrimages, nor would the mothers have wanted their sons' fellow comrades in the Bonus Army to suffer. Louise Ziegler had earned her pilgrimage, and she and Grace had every reason to enjoy it.

A Soldier's Death

The Zieglers traveled to France to visit the grave of Private Fred M. Ziegler. Ziegler served in Company D, 132nd Infantry regiment. His outfit was part of the 33rd or "Prairie" Division, composed largely of Illinois men. The division was formed in August 1917 at Camp Logan, Texas, from units of the Illinois National Guard. Elements of the 86th and 88th Divisions added to its numbers prior to sailing for Europe. Ziegler accompanied his division on a long trip to Camp Logan in April 1918. Starting with this first post, Ziegler kept the folks back home well aware of what he was doing in the army. He mailed at least 16 letters and 4 postcards to his sister Tressa back in Durand.

The young man who wrote those letters is hard not to like. He comes

Fred Ziegler. Private Fred M. Ziegler, 33rd Division, was killed during the Meuse-Argonne offensive on October 11, 1918. He is buried in the Meuse-Argonne Cemetery. His mother, Louise, and his sister Grace visited his grave during their pilgrimage in 1932. (Courtesy Ed Bliss.)

across as cheerful, easygoing, and ready to do his duty. He wasn't a complainer, but the long train trip to Texas, with a 4:30 A.M. arrival was a little too much to take for the young recruit. He and his buddies were sleeping eight to a tent at Camp Logan. "It is hot as hell here and dusty so you can't see across the street," he wrote Tressa.[5] Ziegler stayed with his unit for about a month's worth of training in Camp Logan. The duty was hot and tiring, and the men were always on the move. Later in April, Fred recalled how "we came back from the rifle range Friday morning and have been busy as the dickens washing dirty clothing and everything."[6]

The 33rd then traveled across country by train to prepare for their overseas voyage to Europe. The men stayed in Camp Upton, New York, for several days prior to their short trip to the Hoboken docks. Fred found the trip across the Atlantic a grand adventure. "We are on a German ship which the Kaiser was on when war was declared," he wrote to Tressa, in reference to one of several German ships the Allies seized for their own wartime use.[7]

Once overseas, the division served honorably in the war, fighting in some of the AEF's largest battles, including the St. Mihiel and Meuse-Argonne offensives. The division spent 38 of its 100 days on the front lines in combat. Ziegler's division captured 4,000 prisoners and advanced 22 miles into enemy territory during its time at the front.

This success came at a high price. The division suffered 6,800 casualties, including some 993 who were either killed in action or died of wounds received in combat.[8] It also had the dubious honor of being the most gassed division in the AEF.[9]

Fred's letters gave a textbook history of a soldier's training regimen. The men got acclimated to France and began to serve short stints in trenches away from the action. "We are going to the trenches again tomorrow," Fred wrote on June 28, "I guess for 48 hours. The Kaiser said he was going to be in Paris today, but he is just as close as he will ever get I think."[10] The men gradually received more training and more equipment in preparation for putting them in the front lines. This process took approximately two months. Although the French would have preferred to see Americans fight as soon as they arrived in Europe, most of these troops were untrained and unready.

By the end of July, Fred felt he was ready. "They issued me a .45 automatic and a trench knife, and if they would issue me a couple more arms I think I could go clear through to Berlin myself."[11] Nevertheless, Fred and his unit still had time for some reflection in mid–September. He wrote a letter to Tressa on September 12, which happened to be his 22nd birthday. "I wonder where the devil I will be next year at this time," he mused.[12]

Private Ziegler and his unit were by now in the midst of the Meuse-Argonne offensive in October 1918. Their job was to dislodge the Germans from their heavily defended positions along the Meuse River. October 10 and 11 were days of bold advance for the 33rd Division. Ziegler and his fellow members of the 132nd Infantry, approximately 2,200 strong, dug in to hold its previous gains, and the remainder of the division moved through Ziegler's unit to advance along a broad front on the west bank of the river. The 33rd Division formed part of the III Corps, along with the 4th and 80th Divisions. The 33rd Division was involved in a truly multi national war effort. It served shoulder to shoulder with British and Australian troops; French colonial troops from Africa fought nearby.

The combat experience gave Ziegler and his Prairie Division comrades all they could handle and more. "By mid–October," Edward "Mac" Coffman wrote in his history *The War to End All Wars*,

> the men in this division were exhausted; many of them had worn their clothes to shreds; the skin on some men's feet peeled off with their filthy socks. They had been in the Meuse-Argonne front for over a month, and, since September 26, they had been under constant gas and high-explosive harassing fire. During most of this period they were unable to change clothes or to get water with which to wash.[13]

Ziegler's own letters confirmed this assessment. His last letter, dated October 3, was his longest — nine pages. He was in the thick of the fight. He had to read Tressa's last letter in a trench by the light of a cigarette. "I have been in the [front] lines 24 days today and no relief in sight," he wrote. "I have just shaved today for the first time in three weeks, and believe me I was a pretty good looking kid."[14] The 33rd was making good progress for all the troops' exertions. Ziegler told Tressa he and his buddies were now occupying trenches held by the Germans since 1915. Even so, Ziegler had no way of knowing the war had less than one month to run. "I don't know but I think it will be over by next July if not before."[15] Yet Ziegler, one can sense, knew the danger he faced. He did not want to alarm his sister, but it is easy to tell he knew the end could come for him at any time. He closed his last letter on an upbeat and solemn note. "I am fine and dandy and hope you are all well. Lots of love to all. As ever your brother," he closed.

Then he did something rather unusual. He signed his full name. All his other letters were signed with only his first name, "Fred."[16] Perhaps he wanted to make this letter, which he knew could be his last, somehow more official and final. No one can know with any certainty, but the "Fred M. Ziegler" at the end of this final message is a haunting close to his correspondence.

Unfortunately, the end was close at hand. Ziegler was killed in action between Sivry-sur-Meuse and Consenvoye on the east bank of the Meuse River. "I saw Pvt. Ziegler killed by shrapnel on the morning of Oct. 11, 1918. Death was instantaneous," wrote Private John Hanses, one of Ziegler's comrades from the 33rd.[17]

Ziegler's body was buried in a temporary American graveyard near Sivry, approximately 20 miles northwest of Verdun. The cemetery contained bodies from Ziegler's unit, along with men from the 30th and 357th regiments. Unlike many of his comrades, Ziegler's body was readily identified and buried in a properly marked grave. Army identification of his remains was "conclusive." Identification tags on the body had name and serial number. In addition, army records noted "a Knights of Pythias medal found on the body. Shows: Ziegler, Fred, member of lodge #726, Illinois."[18] Dental records showed two gold crowns, two silver filings, and one cavity. "This lad being but 22 years of age evidently had not cut his wisdom teeth," a doctor noted on the burial records. Ziegler stood 5'9" and weighed 155 pounds. He had brown hair.[19]

As with most families who waited at home for news during the war, the Zieglers did not learn of Fred's death for several weeks. Mrs. Ziegler learned of her son's death in a hastily written telegram dated November 7, 1918. It was written in pencil, and its informal, hurried nature would surely have shocked many families. It read: "Deeply regret to inform you that Private Fred M. Ziegler, infantry, is officially reported as killed in action on October 11th." The signature on this scrap of paper is illegible.[20]

The Ziegler family wanted Fred's remains to rest in France. He was disinterred for permanent reburial on August 17, 1921. The Knights of Pythias medal and his identification were still with the body. His body had decomposed, because most hasty wartime burials were not embalmed. His remains were "partially disarticulated, features not recognizable," according to the GRS report on his final burial. He was buried in a permanent grave in the new Meuse-Argonne American Cemetery, in "pine box and burlap."[21]

The Ziegler family had lost their son, and his remains were buried in a foreign land. They could take solace, if it was solace at all, in the kind words of Illinois Governor Frank Lowden, who wrote a letter to Mrs. Ziegler dated November 29, 1918. It read:

> I have learned with deep regret that Private Fred M. Ziegler was recently killed in action, and I want to extend to you and to the other members of his family my heartfelt sympathy in the loss you have sustained. It must be some consolation to you, however, to know that he died as a brave soldier should die, and that he gave his life in as sacred a cause as the world has ever known. Illinois feels a great pride in the supreme sacrifice he made for humanity."[22]

Given the spirit of those times, Governor Lowden wrote not simply what he thought the Ziegler family wanted to read. He wrote what all of America knew to be true.

Pilgrimage

Louise Ziegler accepted the Army's invitation to sail to Europe on a pilgrimage in 1932. In addition to the regular pilgrimage, Mrs. Ziegler expressed interest in a side trip to Germany. Army correspondence assured Mrs. Ziegler she could make the trip and then return to the United States with her party at government expense. Although such side trips were beyond the scope of the pilgrimage regulations, the army stood ready to assist travelers in planning their excursions. "If you are willing to forego some of the sight-seeing trips that have been arranged for your party in and around Paris," the army wrote to Mrs. Ziegler, "it will be possible for you to pay a short visit to Germany."[23]

Pilgrims such as Mrs. Ziegler who were interested in side trips often relied on the American Express Travel Department and United States Lines for the assistance the army was unable to provide. American Express, for instance, prepared a six-page travel brochure for the mothers, outlining its available services. The brochure, issued in 1931 and titled "A Message to Friends and Relatives of Gold Star Mothers," gave details on the official pilgrimages plus other services available for extra cost. Seven optional tours were highlighted, ranging from 7 to 11 days in length. These were strictly tourist excursions, with no stops planned in cemeteries or battlefields. Five of the tours included stops in Germany, and it is likely Mrs. Ziegler or Grace had this information in hand when planning their excursion.

Prices for a relative or friend to accompany a pilgrim ranged from $142 to $205, depending on which cemetery was visited.[24] Despite these helpful options, the Zieglers decided to save the money and skip the side trip to Germany.

A side trip to Germany was perfectly understandable. Louise Muller was born in Germany on January 27, 1872. She came to the United States when she was eight years old. She married Martin Ziegler, a German-born man, in 1893. Martin Ziegler died in 1913. The couple had four children: three daughters, twins Grace and Gladys, Tressa, and one son, Fred. Hundreds of other Gold Star mothers were born in Europe, with dozens of them born in Germany. Many pilgrims also had children still living in Germany, even a number who had fought for the Kaiser against America. By the time of the pilgrimages, overt anti–German sentiment had all but faded. In fact, there is no evidence, either in Grace's diary or in any other source, that pilgrims of German ancestry faced any discrimination on their trips at all.

If Mrs. Ziegler passed on her German trip, she did take advantage of the army's assistance in another matter: she brought Grace with her. The army informed her the pilgrimage regulations did not provide for free trips for relatives or other companions. However the army assisted travelers in bringing family along if they chose to do so. On her official pilgrimage information card, for instance, the army noted, "Miss G. Ziegler is authorized to accompany her mother on all bus trips."[25] The Ziegler party, Party E, contained at least two other mother-daughter combinations: pilgrim Sophia Sehrt and her daughter Della from Wisconsin and Mrs. A. F. Mosely and her daughter Lily.

Grace was born in Durand, Illinois, in 1906. She and her twin, Gladys, graduated from the University of Illinois with degrees in home economics in 1931. Grace married Edward Thoren, another man of German ancestry, in Rockford, Illinois, in 1935, after having taught school for a couple of years. She was a Rockford homemaker for 38 years and moved the few miles back to Durand after her husband's death. The couple did not have any children. She worked in the family grocery store, where her nephews Fred and Ed knew her. When her nephews sat down to be interviewed in Fred's house in Durand on a rainy day in March 2002, they recalled Grace as a determined and generous woman, with a stubborn streak.[26] They both admired her ability to save the hundreds of dollars from her teaching job during the start of the Depression to pay her own way to France to escort her mother.

Both believed Louise would probably not have gone if Grace had not gone with her. Louise Ziegler was lucky her daughter went with her, and anyone who wishes to understand the pilgrimage experience in detail is lucky, too. Grace's diary, scrapbook, photo album, and family recollections form the most complete, well-rounded accounts of the pilgrimages to survive. Her diary reveals her to be a likable, friendly, thoroughly Midwestern woman. She wrote well and was a good observer of all around her.

The pilgrimage began for the Zieglers as it did for almost all others: with a train trip to New York City. The Zieglers left Durand on July 4, 1932, at 1:35 in the afternoon. They changed trains in Chicago and took the Pennsylvania Railroad to New York City's Penn Station, and they arrived at P.M. the next day. Grace Ziegler's diary of her pilgrimage started with this train trip from Durand.

"I think I will plunge in at the beginning," she wrote.

> Here Mamma got her first taste of real service. The porter hung her coat on a hanger and put a cushion under her feet. We grinned at each other after he left. I told her she would have to get used to service, but I didn't realize how much truth I spoke.

The train trip also included their first stay in a Pullman sleeper car berth. The experience was fine, aside "from sticking our feet in each other's eyes" all night long.[27]

The women reached New York City on the evening of July 5, and escort officers met them and took them to the Commodore Hotel. The officers took their passports and return tickets and held them for safekeeping. The ladies ate a light dinner and checked into a spacious room with twin beds and a private bath. Grace's mother and some of her fellow pilgrims "dared me to take them to a show" on Broadway. Grace cleared the outing with an escort officer, who told them to "stay out of jail." The party went to see the play *Grand Hotel* at Broadway's Astor Theatre. The cast was remarkable and included Greta Garbo, Joan Crawford, Wallace Beery, and both John and Lionel Barrymore. The Illinois women were somewhat unimpressed with their evening, however. Grace wrote, "It cost so much I'd rather have had the sleep."[28]

The party was to sail the next day. After an early breakfast, they traveled on four buses to the pier in Hoboken. The U.S. Marine Band welcomed the mothers. Many waved small American flags, a gift from New York City mayor Jimmy Walker. Grace recalled how

> the boat left the pier so easily I never knew we were moving until people's faces got further away. The band played the "Navy Song" and everybody was laugh-

ing, waving, crying and shouting all at once. We must have made a pretty picture as we left because all the mothers were waving their flags.[29]

Party E sailed aboard the *S.S. President Harding*, with Commander A. M. Moore in charge. They were part of 255 cabin-class passengers, most of whom were neither Gold Star mothers themselves nor connected with the pilgrimage party. Party E contained 79 pilgrims and family members, 2 nurses, and 2 escort officers. Counting crew, escort officers, and third-class passengers, the liner had 795 people aboard when it left Hoboken harbor. The large ship had its own print shop, and Grace kept a copy of the directory of cabin-class passengers for her scrapbook. Grace and the mothers had the run of the ship as the captain's special guests.

"The third class passengers had a grand time," she joked. "Their quarters were smaller and not as grand as those in Cabin Class. I think I should have been sick because the dining room was not ventilated as well as ours and was quite smelly."[30]

The ocean voyage itself was delightful. Grace and the mothers felt they would be seasick and often ate little at dinner. However, Grace recorded no seasickness among the party and was pleasantly surprised how smooth the trip was. Days were spent in deck chairs on the sunny side of the ship, with afternoon tea served to the mothers on deck. "Our eight days on the ocean were delightful," Grace wrote.

> We saw sea gulls nearly every day and several black porpoises and one day some flying fish.... The color of the water depends upon the sky; some days it was blue and others green. There were white caps nearly every day but the water was not rough.[31]

At the halfway point on the voyage, United States Lines held a memorial service at which Rev. Duane Wevill officiated. This service featured the casting of a memorial wreath at sea. Mrs. Emma Hyde from Chicago, the oldest mother in Party E, did the honors. The ceremony included the second oldest mother, Mrs. Sophia Sehrt, throwing a sealed bottle overboard. The bottle contained the names of the all pilgrims in the party. The announcement for this ceremony was called the "casting of the Hydrographic Drift Bottle on the Ocean." Following the ceremony, Captain Moore gave each mother a small bronze medallion courtesy of United States Lines.

Captain Moore and the entire crew were uniformly kind and solicitous toward the mothers. The pilgrims received a tour of the engine room, and the crew even provided a white cloth on which the ladies could wipe their hands. Grace reported the crew all spoke at least two languages, and the baggage master spoke eight. German-speaking travelers were not uncommon. One pilgrim in the party (not Mrs. Ziegler) spoke fluent German to the crew members.

"We were surprised by the sailors who looked like they were nice and not at all hard," she wrote. "One day, I asked the deck steward if he, like all sailors, had a girl in every port, and he refused to answer me. That proved he was guilty," Grace concluded.[32]

Grace recalled an amusing shipboard incident involving European royalty.

> We had a Polish count with us, but he was not so popular with the passengers. Someone told me he had been an automobile salesman in New York. If that were true, he must not have sold any cars lately, as his pants were so shiny. One night he strode up in front of all the mothers and took the front seat in the movie which we had on deck every night. The deck steward asked him to leave. One mother told me, "Aren't we swell; even the nobility have to get out of our way."[33]

Party E aboard the *S.S. President Harding* reached Europe on Wednesday, July 13. The ship's first stop was Cobb, Ireland. Grace thought the landscape, with its rolling hills and low hedges, a beautiful one. A small tender came close by to pick up passengers and mail. As the small boat left, a bugler played "Come Back to Erin" and other Irish tunes. The ship passed by England the following morning and reached Le Havre on the northwest coast of France on Bastille Day, July 14. After the ship docked at Le Havre, the mothers' luggage was brought off before that of any other passenger. French officials whisked the pilgrims through customs, and they quickly boarded their special train bound for Paris.

Grace reported how different the French trains were from those in America.

> The aisle is on one side and you are warned that it is dangerous to lean out. Our compartment had six comfortable seats in it, three on each side so we faced each other.... Instead of going over hills, the tracks tunnel through them so that about every five minutes we would go through a dark tunnel.[34]

On board the train, Grace and her fellow party members got their first taste of French food. Americans found the food quite different, if not unpleasant. All existing letters, diaries, and accounts, Grace's included, all remark on French food, and most specifically French coffee. Grace's account was no different.

At dinner, she wrote,

> The forks were so large that one of the mother's sons who was at my table remarked that in the states we pitched hay with that kind. We had omelets, thick-

ened pea soup, veal and potato salad, chocolate ice cream, waffles, and apricots. It cost me nearly a dollar.[35]

The meal would have been free for Louise and the other mothers, but Grace and other relatives and companions would have had to pay the full price.

After the party arrived in Paris, it was divided according to which cemetery each pilgrim was to visit. The Zieglers joined the other members of the Meuse-Argonne group and were taken to the Hotel D'Iena. There were 39 members in this group. After a brief rest and church service on July 15, all of Party E regrouped for a ceremony on Saturday, July 16, at the Arc de Triomphe. This stop was mandatory for each party and may be viewed as the official start of Party E's pilgrimage. Mary P. Clemer of Virginia laid a wreath on behalf of the party at the French Tomb of the Unknown Soldier. Following this brief ceremony, the mothers were taken to the Restaurant Laurent for a formal reception and tea. Several French and American dignitaries spoke. On Sunday, July 17, members of the party attended church in the morning and visited the gardens at St. Germain de Laye in Paris.

On Monday, July 18, Grace and her mother left Paris for Verdun, approximately 125 miles east of Paris. The trip was leisurely and included two scenic stops. The Quartermaster Corps included such diversions in the belief that a constant focus on grief and loss would have been too great a strain for some pilgrims. Grace's diary here read more like that of a tourist than a pilgrim on the way to her dead brother's grave.

The party stopped at Meaux for tea. Here the group encountered a French funeral party, and Grace remarked how two black horses drew the hearse while the mourners walked on behind. The party's second stop of the day was for lunch at Chalon-sur-Marne. "It was here at Chalon where the French Unknown soldier was selected and also the American Unknown," Grace reported. "It is one of the oldest towns north of Rome."[36]

Wartime sites and memories were part of all pilgrimage tours. The army showed the women important battlefields, cemeteries, and other points of interest along the way. On the way to Verdun, the party "went over the Marne River where General Galliene [Gallieni] and his taxicab army of 2,000 strong held back the Germans."[37] Grace was referring to the 1914 battle when the French used every available vehicle, including hundreds of Paris cabs, to rush its troops to the front.

> The bridge has been destroyed three times, in 1767, 1860, and 1914, each time to keep the Germans from advancing. We went over the Sacred Road where 3,000

French were slaughtered trying to get to the fort at Verdun. The Germans lost 4,000 men at the same time.[38]

By the end of the day, the party had arrived at Verdun. Grace and her mother stayed at the Bellevue Hotel, the proprietor of which had been at the Waldorf Astoria in New York City for 12 years, Grace noted.

Verdun, 18 miles from the Meuse-Argonne Cemetery, was the base of operations for the next three days for the Zieglers. Three cemetery visits took place on Tuesday, Wednesday, and Thursday, July 19–21. Grace recorded the party took a different bus route to the cemetery each day so the pilgrims could visit all the battlefield sites in the vicinity. "Each bus load of mothers had a nurse, an American guide, and an officer. They counted us every time we got out or in the bus. They always counted me as half and blamed me for everything that happened, even when it rained or when we ran out of gas," Grace joked.[39]

Gold Star mother firsthand accounts are very matter-of-fact and somewhat reserved. They revealed little (if any) emotions and feelings they experience at the grave of a loved one. Grace's account was no different. Her traveler's eye for detail was as sharp as ever, but she did not share with her audience the experience at her brother Fred's grave.

Grace and Louise Ziegler visit the grave of Fred Ziegler. Louise Ziegler visited the grave of her son, Private Fred Ziegler, in the Meuse-Argonne Cemetery in 1932. Her daughter Grace accompanied her on the pilgrimage. Although the government provided funds only for the mothers to make the trip, it assisted in making arrangements for family members such as Grace, who paid their own way to France. (Courtesy Ed Bliss.)

"The graves are on the southern slope of the hill and opposite is the caretaker's house," she wrote.

> The crosses are of Italian white marble set in a huge cement slab. Men wash them with soap and water. They are always cutting the grass. Small trees line all the paths and make the whole sight more beautiful. On the chapel is engraved the names of all the unknown soldiers buried in this cemetery. The Jewish soldiers are marked with marble stones in the Star of David instead of the cross.[40]

The Meuse-Argonne Cemetery, which Grace and Louise Ziegler visited, was the largest American cemetery in Europe, a distinction it still holds today. The cemetery occupies 130 acres and contains 14,246 American war dead. Graves represent virtually every American division that took part in the war. The graves are arranged in eight rectangular plots, each of which holds approximately 1,500 bodies.

To today's eye, the cemetery is a leafy oasis in the rolling French countryside. To Grace, Louise, and their fellow pilgrims, it probably had something of an unfinished appearance; the cemetery's permanent improvements were only just finished in 1931.

At the cemetery, Grace's descriptive account continued. "Each mother was given a wreath of real roses to place on her son's grave and then the photographer took her picture. The Government gave her two pictures and a negative," Grace wrote.[41]

Once the mothers had finished their cemetery visits and left the Verdun area, the party took a leisurely two-day trip back to Paris. Grace was especially interested in the French countryside and its small villages and cottages.

> The animals live in one end of the house and the people in the other. The streets are so narrow our guide used to say if we had one more coat of paint we never would have gotten past.... It is against the law to run over a goose but not a chicken. No matter how poor the home there were always lace curtains."[42]

French food was always a popular topic for pilgrims, and Grace was no exception. She remarked on the wine-producing region around Reims. (She failed to record if anyone in her party sampled the local wines. Even though it was still Prohibition back home, the mothers were free to order a drink if they chose to do so.) More than one American woman feared horse meat would be on their menu. Grace's party saw no reason to worry, but Grace learned to spot the bronze horse head outside a butcher shop to show horse meat was for sale inside.

She described the differences between French and American shopping. "There are no flies as the climate is too cool for the eggs to hatch. Hence, there are no screens or doors to the shops," she noticed. "They buy their stuff each day from one day to the next as they have never heard of ice, and things do not keep. How they keep their meat in the shops from day to day, I have no idea."[43] Next to French coffee, which the mothers singularly disliked, French bread posed the greatest challenge. Grace noticed how some loaves were so large they were baked with a hole in the middle, so shoppers could wear them on their arms as baskets. "Bread is never wrapped in France. We saw children carrying home bread a yard long and about as thick as their arms, and hard! A lot of mothers cracked their false teeth on it."[44]

After their visit the French countryside, the pilgrims returned to Paris and the same hotel in which they had stayed before on the evening of July 23. Grace and her mother settled in to their same room and found several days' worth of mail waiting for them. (The army made every effort to receive mail for the pilgrims and deliver it to them prior to their departure from France.) The women skipped church but had an evening sightseeing bus trip through Paris.

"We saw all the famous night cafes in full tilt with many people dining out in the streets," Grace wrote. "The Eiffel Tower is so beautiful at night. It is used to advertise a car which is similar to our Fords," Grace noted, referring to a large neon sign that used to occupy virtually the entire height of the tower.[45]

Monday July 25 found the pilgrims making stops at two separate churches. In the morning at Notre Dame, Grace noticed three particular stained glass windows. "In the front hang the hats of the cardinals who have died; they hang there until they drop with age. We visited the treasure room where the diamonds and precious stones were kept. It was very musty and damp there" she wrote.[46]

On Tuesday, July 26, the pilgrims made two stops. In the morning, the party visited the Louvre Museum. Grace dispensed with this stop in one sentence: "We saw most of the famous paintings and statutes."[47] They visited Napoleon's tomb in the afternoon, a site included for most every pilgrim party. Grace described the tomb, with its two kinds of marble and a burnished gold altar. Near the tomb, she noticed several carriages, the first car to cross the Sahara, and one of the cabs from the wartime taxicab army.

On Wednesday, July 27, the women made a visit to the Lafayette Escadrille memorial. This unit fought for France but included Americans who enlisted in this elite aviation outfit before the United States officially entered the war. Some of these fliers came from prominent families, and the monument itself, Grace observed, was "erected by the families of those wealthy American boys who owned their planes as early as 1914 in the French air forces."[48]

The monument's columns list the names of the men in the unit, and 68 of them (not all of whom were American) are buried inside its gray marble crypts. Stained-glass windows depict the primary battles the Escadrille fought. The Escadrille's monument was built with private funds and is not under the care of the American Battle Monuments Commission. Without scheduled maintenance and repair, the crypt today has fallen into disrepair. Water damage has buckled the floor and dangerously weakened the foundation.[49]

Party E's visit to the Lafayette Escadrille's memorial is especially ironic. Mothers of Escadrille fliers were prohibited from participating in the organized pilgrimages. The men who died did so while fighting for France, not for the United States. Therefore, under the pilgrimage statute, their mothers were ineligible. The statute provided for trips only for those mothers whose sons were part of the American naval and military forces.

Yet another provision in the original pilgrimage act would have barred the mothers of the fliers, because their sons were not buried in one of the officially designated American cemeteries. Subsequent legislation removed this barrier; however, the ban on mothers whose sons had died fighting for the Allies but not for America remained. Many of the mothers were wealthy, as Grace wrote, and a number of them did make private pilgrimages to the memorial at their own expense. However, not all of them could afford to do so, and Congress heard pleas for special dispensation for mothers of the Lafayette Escadrille flyers all throughout the 1920s.

After leaving the Lafayette Escadrille memorial, the party ate lunch in Suresnes at a restaurant called the Beautiful Bicycle. Grace did not record if the party stopped at the nearby Suresnes American cemetery after lunch. They did visit the palace at Versailles. Grace wrote, "there were beautiful oil paintings on the walls, and the building had marble floors."[50] The party saw the Hall of Mirrors and the table on which the Treaty of Versailles was signed.

After the Cluny Museum and Seine boat ride on July 28, Party E spent its last day in France on Friday, July 29. The escorts took the women shopping. "Everything is high there except leather and wool yarn," Grace recalled. "Gloves are very reasonable. After I began to understand French money, all the Mothers dragged me shopping with them. I had a grand time."[51]

The party checked out of its hotel in the early afternoon. Party E sailed for home on Saturday, July 30. "We were in the same [train] compartment as before. It was a five-hour train ride and the trains there are just as dirty as ours. The countryside from Paris to Cherbourg is not as pretty as we had gone through previously," Grace Wrote.[52]

Most pilgrim parties, of course, took the round trip from Cherbourg to Paris. Grace thought the harbor at Cherbourg a scenic one. Her party waited an hour for its liner, the *S.S. Leviathan*, because it was late arriving from Southampton. At Cherbourg, unlike at Le Havre, the party boarded a small tender to take it from the dock out to the waiting liner.

Before she left France, Grace had some special words of kindness for her military and civilian escorts. "We hated to tell our officers and nurses goodbye," she wrote. "They had shown us every courtesy and service and had made our stay in France so pleasant. We had the same [Army] officers and nurses we had on the *Harding*."[53]

The *S.S. Leviathan* was a liner with an interesting past. It was built in Germany for the Kaiser's personal use. Grace learned how one of the crewmen served the Kaiser on the ship's maiden voyage in 1914. She marveled at the liner's size. It was 950 feet long and weighed almost 60,000 tons. The main dining room held 300 people, and the ship even had a large swimming pool, filled with sea water.

> On the promenade deck, is a modernistic night club where talkies and dances are held every night. There is also a grand salon where tea concerts are held every day and the guests can play cards or write. There is also a library and bar room on deck.[54]

The return trip took six days, instead of the eight days to Europe. There were no wreath-laying or formal receptions planned for the pilgrims on this final leg of the voyage. Among their fellow passengers, two celebrities traveled with Party E: pilots James Mattern and Bennett Griffin. The two had attempted (but failed) to break the record for an around-the-world flight. Their exploits would have been front-page news to all the ship's passengers. The pair left the United States on July 5, only to abandon their trip in Russia because of mechanical problems. Grace reported that five navy pilots staged a flyover salute to Mattern and Griffin once the ship reached New York Harbor.[55]

As German-born Louise Ziegler sailed for America on a German-built luxury liner, she may have felt disappointed at not being able to visit her German homeland in July 1932. Had she done so, she would have been an unwitting witness to history in the making. July 1932 was a very turbulent and bloody month, and not just for the Bonus Army in the United States.

Germany was in a state of extreme political violence as it prepared for parliamentary elections on July 31. Adolf Hitler and his National Socialist Party was on the verge of winning more seats than any other German party in the voting. Eighty-six Germans, including 36 Nazis, were among those killed in violent street clashes in July alone.[56] By the end of the year, Hitler was knocking on the door of the German establishment, and he became chancellor of the nation early the next year. What Louise and Grace Ziegler would have seen firsthand, in other words, would have been the creation of World War II from the ashes of World War I.

Yet again, neither tension in the United States nor in Germany was of any concern to Louise and Grace as their liner docked in America on August 5. The party spent the night in the same hotel as on its first stop in New York, the Commodore. After dinner that evening, the escort officers had planned one more bit of sight-seeing. The women were bused across the new George Washington Bridge to New Jersey and returned via tunnel under the Hudson River. On Saturday morning, Grace and her mother squeezed in a bit of shopping. They caught the train back for home at 6:15 and arrived back home in Durand on Sunday, August 7. "We were gone just under five weeks," Grace's newspaper account concluded.[57]

Back at Home

Grace's good nature made an impact on her fellow pilgrims. Army escorts and pilgrims alike were both equally grateful for her lighthearted, helpful presence during Party E's trip. One of the escort officers recorded this fact in his liaison report once the party returned to New York City. His brief note read:

> Miss Katherine [sic] Ziegler who was traveling with her mother, Mrs. Louise Ziegler, was very helpful because of her cheerfulness and the voluntary assistance that she gave many of the pilgrims in various ways. A poem was written about her by one of the mothers.[58]

Mrs. A. F. Moseley, traveling with her daughter Lily, wrote the poem of tribute to which the escort officer referred. It was a poem of thanks written for Grace on the voyage to Europe. The ship's staff printed a copy for members of the party, and Grace saved it in her scrapbook. The poem was dedicated to Miss Grace Ziegler, July 6–July 14, 1932.[59]

Grace sent a thank-you note back to the army on her return. Her handwritten note, dated August 16, 1932, is preserved in Fred's burial file at the National Archives. Her note was addressed to Captain R. E. Shannon. It read:

> My mother, Mrs. Louise Ziegler, and I wish to thank the War Department for all the wonderful kindness and care she received during the Pilgrimage with Party

E. We are so happy we have made the trip. The War Dept. has certainly picked wonderful men for taking care of the mothers. No one could have been more wonderful to us than Capt. Barr, Lieut. Hammond, or Mr. Connelly. I want to thank you also for all the courtesy and promptness with which you answered my numerous letters.[60]

The Quartermaster General, Maj. Gen. J. L. DeWitt responded with his own letter to Grace, dated August 29. His letter was very complimentary, thanking Grace for her note, "It is indeed gratifying to know that the trip was entirely satisfactory and the officers of the Army rendered such courteous and efficient service," DeWitt's letter read in part.

> The Quartermaster Corps is proud of the honor bestowed upon it by being charged with the conduct of these pilgrimages, and has expended every effort that those making the journey have a comfortable and pleasant trip. I feel, however, that the task has been materially lightened by the wonderful spirit of cooperation and consideration shown by the mothers and widows.[61]

DeWitt could well have added "sisters," because Grace's cheerful good nature surely lightened the task of Party E's escort officers.

The Zieglers' trip and Grace's diary are both remarkable and very typical at the same time. Pilgrims enjoyed their trips and each others' company. The army did a good job as tour guides. The trips achieved their objective in a humane and personal way; no woman would have finished her trip and felt as if the army and her government did not care about her.

At the same time, the women's true feelings are unknown, or perhaps more accurately, unknowable. Louise Ziegler, the Gold Star Mother of the pair, remains something of an enigma. Our view of her and her pilgrimage comes from her daughter's diary, rather than from her own account. We don't know what she thought of the trip or what emotions she felt as she visited her son's grave for three days in July. What is more certain, however, is Grace's account and what it tells us of her as a person.

Grace Ziegler emerges as someone who is easily likable. She was bright, kind, and helpful. She was also simply a terrific daughter to her mother. In an era when few people traveled overseas, it probably comes as no surprise her account is more travelogue than inner dialogue. Her hometown audience most likely knew one of the Zieglers, and they were probably eager to read her account of what happened in France. They were keenly interested in the pilgrims' progress in Europe. Her diary, along with her scrapbook, photo album, and family recollections form the largest, most detailed account of any pilgrimage yet uncovered or published. If one wants to know what it was like to go on a Gold Star mother pilgrimage, one should read what Grace had to say.

Grace, as we have seen, returned to Illinois, married, and led a productive life as wife, daughter, and member of her community. She returned at the end of her life to tiny Durand. It is the type of small town where today one finds a farm implement dealer across the street from a sign proclaiming "Worms 24 Hours." Durand is tied to the land, as these twin symbols of farming and fishing reveal. Grace and her husband hosted several European foreign exchange students in their home. At least one was German, and Grace and Edward Thoren traveled to Germany to visit the student's family. She returned to France on at least two occasions to visit Fred's grave.[62]

Her close ties with Germany refute, I believe, one of the more traditional criticisms leveled at the pilgrims and their trips. Some view the trips as an exercise in nationalism, a way to show that our nation was better than any other. The pilgrims knew better, Grace included. Her close ties with what was formerly a bitter enemy showed the pilgrims could forgive and forget. The nation that had killed her brother in battle also was the same one that sent a young student to her home for a typical American school year. Her experiences also attach a face and name to America's changing alliances during the 20th century, which saw Germany end the century as a close ally but against whom the United States fought two world wars.

8

Party A

When Mrs. Amy L. Evans of Nebraska knelt at her son's grave in the Suresnes American Cemetery on May 18, 1930, it marked both an ending and a beginning in the remarkable pilgrimage story. In visiting Samuel Evans's grave, Mrs. Evans was the first Gold Star mother to kneel at her son's cross during an organized pilgrimage. She became the first of over 6,500 mothers and widows to decorate a grave during the four years of the pilgrimages. Her visit also marked the end of over a decade of public and private efforts to make the pilgrimages a reality. Party A, as this first group of women in the spring of 1930 was designated, is a fascinating microcosm of the pilgrimage movement.

Party A deserves our close study and attention. Virtually everything that happened on any pilgrim party happened to the members of this first group. Moreover, Party A delivered several unique and intriguing stories and episodes that made the pilgrimages of continuing interest. No one knew exactly what to expect as the 234 women from 15 different states made their way to New York City in early May 1930. Travelers came from every part of the nation. More women came from Ohio than from any other state. (Mrs. Hoover's drawing earlier in the year put Nebraska first, and many women from that state were present.) The party included women whose backgrounds ranged from farm widow to socialite. Party A was no more of a VIP group than the last party of 1933, but the press tirelessly logged its voyages, squabbles, and cemetery visits. This, then, is the day-by-day story of Party A, 1930.

Day by Day

The women for Party A came from all across the nation in early May. They traveled from tiny Red Cloud, Nebraska, and from Manhattan, too.

Mrs. Evans, for instance, left tiny Sutherland, Nebraska, by train on the morning of May 3. She arrived in New York City two days later. Army records duly noted her train trip would take exactly 56 hours, 36 minutes. Dozens of other pilgrims also made their prearranged train trips to New York; Party A received its official welcome at City Hall in New York City on May 7.

Although other parties always received some form of Manhattan welcome, Party A's was the largest, grandest, and most well-publicized. Seven busloads of pilgrims arrived at City Hall shortly before 3 P.M. A color guard stood at attention as each mother, carrying a small American flag, took her place in the city's Aldermanic Chamber. Maj. William F. Deegan, chair of the reception committee, served as master of ceremonies; acting Mayor McKee welcomed the party officially. Striking a chord that would be sounded in dozens of speeches over the next few years, McKee said, "Bereavement's accolade has raised you to dignity conferred on no others in this nation: a dignity beyond that attained by princes and kings and one that makes us proud to honor you."[1] Tributes to motherhood surely were a part of Party A's story, and McKee hit this note as well. "If America was great in the World War, it was because of your boys," he told them. He bid the group farewell by saying "you go now and take your sad station beside one of those white crosses and commune again with him you loved so well. And as you kneel beside his grave and offer up your prayers, know there shall ascend ... the prayers of a grateful nation."[2]

Mathilda Burling also attended the City Hall ceremony for Party A. Mother Burling, as she was widely known, was a driving force in the organized pilgrimage movement and served as the president of the Gold Star Mothers association. Her only son, George, was killed in the war at age 17; she sailed with Party B, leaving for Europe later in the month. Some wanted Mrs. Burling to have VIP status and attend Party A. The government decided, wisely, that all parties and pilgrims would receive equal treatment, however.

After the ceremonies, the party made its way to Hoboken Harbor. United States Lines organized another brief ceremony. Army Chief of Staff and war veteran Gen. Charles P. Summerall presided over this second bon voyage. He observed the pilgrims were leaving 13 years to the day and from the same pier that Gen. Pershing and the first contingent of American troops left for Europe in 1917. "It is fitting, therefore, that these members of a new Expeditionary Force of Peace should sail from the same pier," observed one of the military escort officers assigned to Party A.[3] The notion of the pilgrimages as a peace mission is not just one person's opinion; Gold Star mothers and their supporters believed they were right up until the start of World War II.

Sailing on the *S.S. Orduna* back in 1917, that initial group of doughboys contained some of America's bravest sons, many of whom did not return to the United States, Gen. Summerall reminded the mothers. In closing, Summerall read a telegram from the acting Secretary of War. The telegram exhorted the pilgrims to

> go, therefore, not in sorrow but in pride. You leave on this pilgrimage not only as those who were dearest to the men who gave their all for the perpetuation of our democracy. You go also as those who are most worthy to express the gratitude and the eternal memory of our country.[4]

Here again was a soon-to-be familiar theme.

Many viewed the pilgrims as those most worthy to mourn the nation's dead. Although the women certainly had the right to mourn their dead sons and husbands, they probably didn't welcome the role thrust on them as surrogate mourners for the entire country. This dichotomy, between the pilgrims' personal needs and views of observers, organizers, and outsiders, began in earnest with Party A and persists to this day.

The pilgrims' ship, the *S.S. America*, with Captain George Fried at the helm, made its way safely out of Hoboken Harbor after the speeches. Two fireboats escorted the ship, and both of them shot streams of water high in the air as a tribute. Soon after, more than 100 aircraft flew overhead to honor the pilgrims. This formation was one of the larger peacetime collections of aircraft up to that time, and it was certainly the largest aerial formation any of the pilgrims had ever witnessed. As the *S.S. America* put New York City behind her, Captain Fried "signaled a last farewell with the deep note of the *America*'s whistle."[5]

Fried spent his career at sea and was one of the most noteworthy captains of his day. His story contained the type of historical coincidences and famous personalities that continue to make the pilgrimages such a compelling event. Fried directed two dangerous sea rescues during the 1920s while the captain of two separate vessels. The first was a 1926 rescue of the crew of a British freighter in the north Atlantic. The second rescue, in 1929, earned him a ticker-tape parade in New York City, reported to rival the one Charles Lindbergh received for crossing the Atlantic. The public was aware enough of these events the phrase "Captain Fried of rescue fame" found its way into articles describing Party A's voyage.

Moreover, Captain Fried was familiar with this liner. Fried's first ship after the war was none other than the *S.S. America*. Ironically, the ship was originally a German vessel, the *Amerika*. It was seized while at anchor in the United States during the war and later used as a troop ship and later still as a liner for United States Lines. In short, the pilgrims were in the capable, no-nonsense hands of Captain George Fried.

On the transatlantic voyage, the women discovered service on the *S.S. America* was first-class indeed. It was surely a level of luxury far beyond what all but a few of the women had experienced before. The pilgrims and their escort officers traveled as first-class or cabin-class passengers. Cabin-class passengers could enjoy a daily tea, as well as frequent concerts and even motion pictures on their voyage. Food service was opulent. Dinner each day featured its own printed menu and included hors d'oeuvres, soups, fish, entrees, roasts, vegetables, salads, and desserts.

Public interest waxed and waned in the pilgrimages for four years. The press chronicled every step of Party A's pilgrimage, and stories ran on the front page of the *New York Times* and many other newspapers nationwide. From the very first story about Party A through the last voyage of 1933, the pilgrimages enjoyed nothing but positive press coverage — with one very noteworthy exception.

When the *S.S. America* docked in France after an apparently smooth voyage, a reporter from the *Chicago Tribune Paris Edition* filed a story that ran in the paper's May 17 edition. Unseen in the United States, the piece, "Dissension United with Tragedy Roils War Mothers' Trip," was written by special correspondent Grace Robinson. The article seemed to confirm the army's worst fears about the entire pilgrimage experience, medical care, and the women's relations with each other chief among them. Robinson reported a "frail, sweet" Ohio mother became "mentally deranged" during the voyage and remained under a doctor's care. Escort officer Capt. Dorris Hanes downplayed the episode. "She is just an elderly woman who has temporarily lost her memory," Haines asserted. Unnamed sources, however, told Robinson the woman would not be allowed to see her son's grave, for fear of further impairment.[6]

Such patient care strained the caregivers. The ship's doctor, Anson Ingels, was so exhausted by caring for the pilgrims that he resigned. Dr. Ingels told Robinson, "I will never go through such an arduous time again." However, not all of his stress was pilgrim-related. Robinson reported that a Czech passenger committed suicide by slitting his throat with a razor.[7] Fried withheld any and all unpleasant news from the press and passengers until the ship docked in France, although Robinson groaned about the censorship. No members of Party A died on the pilgrimage, but this was not the type of frenzied start the organizers wanted.

Furthermore, Robinson uncovered rifts among the pilgrims themselves. The army had hoped to minimize these types of disagreements through its careful planning. Parties contained women from just a small number of states. However, pilgrim parties were always a diverse lot. Through today's eyes, we would see segregated Party A as a homogenous group of older white women. However, it contained mothers over 80 and war widows young enough, of course, to be the Gold Star mothers' own daughters.

Party A included at least two soldiers' sisters, who served *in loco parentis* for their younger brothers. This was not an uncommon situation, and for purposes of pilgrimage regulations, sisters such as Mary Kelly were considered mothers and fully entitled to a European trip. Party A included women from both the North and South. Because many of them were born before the Civil War, the press did not know what to expect when these mothers got together.

All these underlying differences came to a head when the pilgrims decided among themselves who was to lay a ceremonial wreath at the Arc de Triomphe once the party reached Paris. It became customary for the oldest woman on board to be the honor pilgrim and perform this duty. The honor pilgrim was usually the first one off the ship when it docked. However, this practice had yet to become a tradition. Mrs. Sarah Thompson of New York City was chosen to lay the wreath in Paris. Pilgrims from New Jersey presented Mrs. Minnie Throckmorton of Nebraska a ceremonial wreath because she was considered the first woman to join the National Gold Star Mothers association. "During the voyage, the busybodies got into action and told Mrs. Throckmorton she had no right to lay the wreath and the honor should go to a New Jersey woman," Robinson reported.

Another group of New Jersey pilgrims put forth their own candidate: Mary Kelly. However, this selection caused an equal uproar, because Kelly was a sister, not a mother. A wreath eventually appeared in Mrs. Throckmorton's cabin with a note: "Gold Star Mother, do your duty."[8]

The bickering did not deter Mrs. Throckmorton. She told Robinson, "I have come to France to decorate my son's grave and not to fight over honors. Anybody can have that wreath that wants it. I think it would be better if somebody tossed it overboard."[9] The wreath matter was still unsettled when a special meeting of all the pilgrims in Party A was convened. Two mothers, one from Washington, DC, and one from Nebraska, walked out of the meeting, but Capt. Dorris Hanes, ever the diplomat, coaxed them back into the gathering.[10]

Minnie Throckmorton from tiny Red Cloud, Nebraska, and Sarah Thompson from Manhattan could not have been more unlike each other, at least on a superficial level. Mrs. Thompson was a prominent New York City woman whose husband, John Means Thompson, was a successful businessman with offices on Madison Avenue. Mr. Thompson served as a lieutenant colonel in the New York National Guard and had ties with many active-duty and retired military officers. Mr. Thompson served on the General Staff of a patriotic organization called the Military Order of the World War. The Thompson's son, Lt. Hugh Thompson, was an officer with the noted 96th Aero Squadron.

Lt. Thompson flew as an observer in a two-seater aircraft. He and his pilot, Lt. Charles P. Anderson, were involved in action on the St. Mihiel front. In mid–September 1918, Thompson's unit was concentrating its bombing runs on Conflans-en-Jarnisy, a German command center. Action was heavy, and Thompson's plane was scheduled for two missions on September 16.

The first mission included 25 American planes and left its aerodrome at 6:05 A.M. The day was breezy with good visibility. All the planes from Thompson's flight reached their objectives, dropping approximately 2,000 pounds of bombs on the Germans. Thompson's aircraft left at 5 P.M. to bomb Conflans-en-Jarnisy on its second sortie. The aircraft encountered heavy German resistance. Anti-aircraft fire was described as "active and accurate," and the Americans reported seeing 17 enemy aircraft in the skies. Four of the 96th Aero Squadron's aircraft did not return; one of them belonged to Lt. Charles P. Anderson and Lt. Hugh S. Thompson. Both men were reported as killed in action.[11]

Meanwhile, Minnie Throckmorton was a Nebraska widow, whose only child, Pvt. John Throckmorton, died of his wounds the day after the armistice, November 12, 1918. She told the army she and her late husband were grief-stricken over their son's death. Left to her own devices, Mrs. Thompson had difficulty learning of her son's final resting place five years after the war. She wrote a letter to the Graves Registration Service dated August 5, 1923, for assistance in finding out details about her son's burial. Her letter read in part:

> Private John W. Throckmorton, Co. G, 128th Infantry, laid down his life Nov. 12, 1918 for his country and his father Wesley Throckmorton passed on one year ago on the 14th of July leaving me all alone in our little home. Just waiting till the master calls but some way I want to know just where my boy is resting in France. Will you please oblige?[12]

Her letter showed that despite the army's best efforts, information on the final resting place of all World War I dead did not reach the family. (It was typical GRS practice to let families know the permanent burial location of soldiers once they were reburied in France. It is unclear why Mrs. Throckmorton was not so notified.)

Yet the two women, one from Nebraska and one from New York City, shared several common bonds. First and foremost, both had lost sons in the war and had yet to visit their graves. They shared another bond as well: both Throckmorton and Thompson were buried in graves marked with the wrong names. Thompson was first buried in a temporary grave, with a marker that read "Lt. Harry S. Thompson, Lt. O.H.S." To their credit, GRS staff noticed the error quickly and rectified it at once. This mistake was especially easy to correct, because Thompson, Hugh or Harry, had not yet had his grave marked with a permanent marble cross. The GRS sent a memo dated May 27, 1920, for the "Correction in Stenciling on Grave Marker." The marker was changed to the correct name, Lt. Hugh S. Thompson, 1st Lieut.[13] This mistake, unfortunately, was not the last one that troubled Thompson's family.

When Lt. Hugh S. Thompson was disinterred and reburied in the permanent St. Mihiel cemetery, his parents received a post card from the army informing them of the final resting place of one Lt. Hugh A. Thompson. The mistake, in one sense, would have been understandable. There was a Lt. Hugh A. Thompson. He was also a flyer in the AEF, and he, too, was from New York. John Means Thompson wrote a letter to Maj. R. L. Foster of the Army's Quartermaster Corps on January 7, 1924, to complain about this mistake. Mr. Thompson felt any expression of sorrow by the government "seems a mockery when such mistakes regarding record cards are allowed to occur."[14]

The letter went straight to the heart of an issue that affected millions of parents of war soldiers worldwide. Parents waited months or even years in some cases for word of their sons' deaths. Many hundreds of thousands of soldiers on both sides simply vanished in battle and were never accounted for. For many of these parents, final word never came at all. For the Thompsons, this letter raised other questions. Was their son actually dead? Was his body ever really found? Perhaps he was buried in someone else's grave?

"It is most harrowing to a parent to receive such erroneous information," Mr. Thompson's letter continued.

> For many months there has been a lingering fear in my mind that there might have been a mistake in the removing and re-interring of my son's remains.... Is there any way that you can assure me that there has been no mistake in the re-interment? If so, will you send me the proper card? Without this assurance, I do not care even to know the location of his grave."

His letter concluded by requesting the address of Lt. Hugh A. Thompson's parents, so he could contact them directly.[15]

Foster replied to the Thompson family at once in his own letter dated

January 10. Mr. Thompson seemed satisfied with this quick response. In a final letter back to the army, Mr. Thompson allowed

> it is a great comfort to know that there is no possible doubt as to the identity of my son's body, also to know he was buried in uniform.... If you could but know the agony I suffered between October 15, 1918, when I first heard of the possibility of my son's death and the confirming news by the Red Cross on December 15th.[16]

Mrs. Throckmorton's son, John, was buried in a grave marked with a cross that read "John M. Crock, Pvt. 1419693 USA." Private Throckmorton was buried in the grave with this wrong name until he was disinterred for reburial on October 17, 1921. There is no clear explanation in Throckmorton's burial file why this mistake occurred. The army's records of his disinterment noted the corroded tag on the body read Private Throckmorton. The army corrected its records, and the body now buried in the grave marked Private John Throckmorton is indeed Mrs. Minnie Throckmorton's only child.

Mrs. Throckmorton and Mrs. Thompson probably never spoke to each other about the wreath episode on board Party A's trip abroad. There is no evidence to suggest the women knew each other's story of loss either. In any event, after Party A returned safely to the United States, Mrs. Throckmorton shared her thoughts on the entire wreath-laying episode with the army. She suggested the

> captain of each division [escort officer] place the wreath for his special division upon the grave of the unknown soldier at the Arc de Triomphe if any is to be placed ... and to have the sailor boys drop the wreath overboard to the memory of their lost at sea which would do away with all the petty jealousies and so much hard feelings among the gold star mothers. If flowers are plentiful, let each one of the pilgrims drop one flower as they pass around so as not step on the sacred place [of the tomb].[17]

The army did learn from the mistakes it made during Party A's pilgrimage, and it changed several procedures as a direct result.

All the mothers, in fact, were ready to put any controversy aside and begin their pilgrimage in earnest as they reached French soil. In fact, other newspapers picked up on the controversy the *Paris Edition* had uncovered and sought the pilgrims' comments. Kentucky mother Blanche Hill, for one, disliked "any attempt to make statements about dissatisfaction among us. We may encounter minor difficulties but we are more than united in making this pilgrimage one to be remembered."[18]

Now in France

Perhaps the press and the army both learned their lesson with this shipboard controversy; there were no more scandalous or unpatriotic articles published in any newspapers after Party A reached France. Controversy or not, Party A made a triumphant and cheerful landing in Cherbourg, France on May 16, 1930. The *S.S. America* dropped anchor outside the harbor shortly after 3 P.M. The mothers, here referred to as "soberly dressed white-haired women," boarded a series of tenders and landed in short order at Cherbourg's Gare Maritime. The mothers and all their homespun charm were on full display for the assembled media. "Goodbye and goodbye again," one mother told a steward as she left the ship, patting the young man's hand for good measure. "You've been such a sweet boy to look after me these past nine days."[19]

Seventy-five-year-old Mrs. Lindsay from Cincinnati was the first pilgrim off the gangplank. Mrs. Thompson and the youngest widow on board, Felipa Crespin from Nebraska, were next off the ship. The pilgrims filed into the customhouse, not for the usual inspection but for a hearty welcoming ceremony. (The army had coordinated with French officials to speed pilgrims through the normally tedious customs procedures.) Once inside, polite "handshakes changed to kisses, not the French doubled-cheeked muggings but good, resounding Ohio pop-smackers."[20]

For their part, the crew of the *S.S. America* grew quite fond of its special passengers. Emma Weidlich, a shipboard stewardess, stated that "far less attention was required by these women who were used to caring for themselves than by the average tourists who were accustomed to and demanded service."[21]

The mothers boarded a special "boat train" to take them into Paris. On this train trip pilgrims of all parties encountered their first taste of French food, trains, travel, and customs. Without a doubt, they knew they were no longer in the United States, and this was especially true for the dozens of women in Party A who had never even been out of their home states, let alone visited a foreign country. French beverages always presented the pilgrims a special challenge. "I'm SO thirsty," one mother exclaimed when she was offered a bottle of mineral water in the dining car. "But I was afraid to drink that. It's jumping so. I thought it must be wine. I was told I would have to drink wine in France, but I just can't."[22] Familiar coffee, the preferred beverage of the day, was little better. French coffee was far too strong and bitter for American' tastes. In one dining car, thirsty pilgrims bypassed the coffee entirely, leaving 47 full cups of coffee at 47 place settings.

Strong coffee notwithstanding, Party A made its way to Paris. The party was divided into smaller groups at this time, based on what cemetery each woman was to visit. Mrs. Anna Norris, in the Meuse-Argonne group, stayed at the Hotel Ambassador in Paris, while Aisne-Marne pilgrim Mary Jane Pennington stayed in the Hotel de Paris, for example. Groups stayed in several first-class hotels in Paris, in fact. Saturday, May 17 was the party's first full day in the French capital, and the pilgrims made their official appearance at the Arc de Triomphe. Gen. John Pershing, American ambassador to France Walter Edge, and a number of other French and American dignitaries welcomed the women. An enormous crowd of French well-wishers, numbering over 10,000, turned out to meet the Americans. Twelve years after the armistice, the war was still a central focus of French life, as indeed it was for most Europeans.

The French population had nothing but respect, praise, and admiration, not just for the Gold Star mothers but for most Americans in general. "Every man's head was bared from the moment the mothers arrived until their departure," the *New York Times* reported.[23] Back in an era when men of all walks of life had their heads covered by a hat or cap, removing one's hat was a gesture of respect. This seemingly small gesture showed the solemn, reverent, and patriotic nature of the pilgrims' reception not only in Paris but all throughout France.

Party A provided, of course, the first opportunity for the dignitaries to meet the travelers. Walter Edge served as U.S. ambassador to France from 1929 to 1933, essentially during the entire run of the pilgrimages. He and his wife were often on hand to welcome the pilgrims to Paris. Edge often took the opportunity to address the pilgrims and sound the now-familiar themes of motherhood and patriotism.

> You, mothers, instilled into these young men the principles for which they laid down their lives; you taught them the fundamentals of loyalty and courage and truth and vision; you with the fortitude which mothers throughout the ages have mustered held your heads high as you bid them goodbye,"

Edge told a later group of pilgrims in a speech typical of his customary remarks.[24]

Listening to speeches and laying the wreath at the French Tomb of the Unknown soldier both became obligatory activities for all future pilgrim parties. Shipboard controversy aside, Mrs. Sarah Thompson of New York City did indeed lay the first official wreath on behalf of Party A. Nevertheless, all women deemed eligible to decorate the tomb were allowed to do so. Mary Kelly laid her wreath on behalf of the New Jersey women, and Minnie Throckmorton did indeed do her duty and laid her wreath on behalf of the Nebraska delegation. Finally, Annie Marks from Florida placed a bronze wreath on behalf of the Daughters of the American Confederacy.

Following Saturday's ceremonies, the army divided Party A into two groups. The larger of the two enjoyed two days of Paris sight-seeing and shopping. The Quartermaster Corps built these rest periods into the pilgrimages for a reason. They wanted not so much to make the pilgrimages into a grand vacation as to separate periods of grief. Visits to tourist staples such as the place at Versailles, Les Invalides, and other Parisian landmarks entertained the women, although the government was always quick to affirm the sacred nature of the pilgrimage experience.

The pilgrims were astounded by their first few days in France. "What strikes me most about Paris is the difference of everything from what we are used to in America," an Indiana mother remarked. "Houses, streets, the way people move, even the way they dress, are difficult to get accustomed to. At times I can hardly get my breath, the change is so great."[25]

Even those familiar with European travel found the pilgrimage experience quite a change. New York City's Mrs. Thompson said she was impressed with the

> splendid manner in which our visit has been arranged. All has gone so smoothly. It is a great problem to handle the first contingent of Gold Star mothers, yet those in charge seem to have been most successful. Paris is not new to me, yet this occasion makes everything appear in an entirely different light.[26]

Mrs. Thompson and her group saw the sights. The smaller of the two groups prepared for its cemetery visit. The 16 mothers in this group (sometimes reported as 18 in different news accounts) were bound for Suresnes Cemetery, on the outskirts of Paris. For this vanguard of pilgrims, their trip started on May 18. Army Capt. William F. Dalton and interpreter C. Cherie took the women by bus to scenic Suresnes. Pilgrims such as Mrs. Evans and the 15 others "passed a quiet day of meditation in the cemetery, sitting on the grass near the white crosses or basking in the sunlight on the benches. The birds in the trees on the hill just beyond twittered little chants of sympathy."[27]

Press accounts, starting with this first one, pictured nature in sympathy with the pilgrims as they moved about the battlefields and cemeteries, trying to lend its own type of comfort to the pilgrims in anyway possible. Cemetery superintendent James Duncan delighted the women by informing them they would be permitted to have a few words or a brief passage engraved on the backs of their loved ones' markers, at their own expense.

Mrs. Evans was the first pilgrim to reach her son's grave. The *Paris Edition* reported she was the first to reach her own plot of holy ground. She placed an American flag on the grave. For more than an hour, she remained on her knees in prayer."[28]

Because Mrs. Evans was reported as the first woman to visit her son's grave, it is worth examining the details of her son's death in more detail. Army Private Samuel Evans, 338th Field Artillery, 88th Division, died of cerebrospinal meningitis on November 3, 1918. He was buried the next day, just one week before the armistice, in a temporary AEF cemetery in Talence, France. Along with thousands of other bodies, Private Evans was disinterred and reburied in one of the eight permanent American cemeteries in Europe.

Thousands of Americans in the AEF died not of wounds in battle but of disease. Many were victims of the worldwide influenza epidemic or complications related to it. Suresnes held an especially large number of men who died from illness, although many battle casualties are buried here as well. Evans's body rests in Block A, Row 1, Grave 7 at Suresnes.

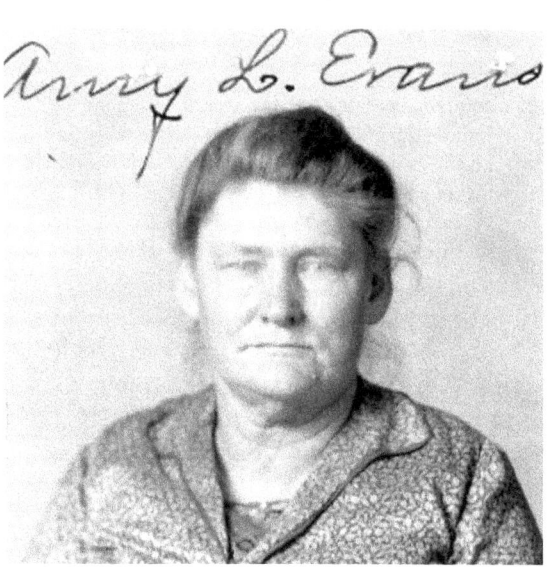

Amy Evans was the first mother to visit her son's grave during a pilgrimage. Mrs. Amy Evans from Red Cloud, Nebraska, traveled with Party A (1930), and decorated the grave of her son, Private Samuel Evans, in the Suresnes American Cemetery outside Paris. (National Archives, Samuel Evans Burial File, RG 92.)

The cemetery visit for Mrs. Evans and her fellow pilgrims set the tone for all subsequent graveside visits. The army's plan avoided pomp and spectacle. Rather, the escorts, nurses, interpreters, and even reporters let the mothers experience their grief and loss with as much dignity, privacy, and space as possible. (For many subsequent parties, the press did not actually accompany the mothers to the cemeteries, as it did for all portions of Party A. This was especially true for pilgrimages in 1932 and 1933.) "Although plainly shaken with grief at first," the *New York Times* reported, "and with many of them sobbing, they soon recovered their composure and pride for their soldier dead restored their spirits."[29]

Pilgrims and visitors alike always remarked on the well-kept and peaceful nature of the cemeteries. Many had been recently completed; in fact, final work continued on some as the pilgrimages progressed. Nevertheless, Suresnes and the other cemeteries very much impressed women from Party A. Katherine Brockman from Cleveland told Helen Akin from the *Paris Edition* that

> it is such a comfort to know that he rests in such a beautiful place. I've seen it many times in moving pictures and have stayed to see the [news] reels over twice, but I didn't realize it was so beautiful with these hawthorn trees, catalpas, and laburnum shrubs. I'm so grateful to these dear men who have taken such good care of the graves.[30]

The pilgrims wanted to see for themselves the graves were orderly and well maintained. Today we would consider proper care as a given, but it was a cause for real concern as Party A sailed in 1930. Reports about makeshift cemeteries with missing markers had filtered back to anguished parents. There was no real cause for concern, however. Even the temporary cemeteries were well cared for, and the permanent ones were in 1930 and remain today as beautiful as when Mrs. Brockman first saw them.

The remaining pilgrims, all except the Suresnes women, were now further subdivided into groups based on which cemetery they were to visit. Groups for the Meuse-Argonne, Oise-Aisne, Somme, St. Mihiel, and the Aisne-Marne Cemeteries left Paris on buses in the early morning of May 20. Eighteen women each headed to the Somme and St. Mihiel Cemeteries. Forty were bused to the Oise-Aisne Cemetery, and the largest group, 140 strong, headed for the largest American cemetery, the Meuse-Argonne. Each bus trip took the better part of a day and took a scenic route with planned stops for sight-seeing, battlefield viewing, and even having tea in the French countryside. (Suresnes pilgrims such as Mrs. Evans spent their entire trip in and around Paris; they were scheduled to visit the cemetery on as many as six separate days.)

These stops along the way, again, were carefully planned. The army wanted to make the pilgrimage experience more than simply a one-day stop at the boy's grave. Therefore, each pilgrim received a detailed itinerary for her trip. For most women, this schedule called for cemetery visits over three successive days. After the visits were done, the individual groups would reassemble as the full party in Paris prior to sailing back to the United States.

Despite the highly organized nature of the pilgrimages, many impromptu and unexpected stops took place. This was especially true right from the beginning with Party A. On two consecutive days in late May, several busloads of pilgrims drove by the isolated grave of Lt. Quentin Roosevelt. The young oak did indeed lie where he fell, in a remote corner of the French countryside. The grave lies "in a lonely wheat field" about two miles from the French village of Nesles. The grave was clearly visible from the road, and the mothers wanted to stop and see it. Muddy, wet weather on May 23 prevented the pilgrims from reaching the gravesite. Nevertheless, pilgrims on the next day "would not be content until they had stood beside the tomb of the hero and bravely trudged through the mud."[31] Quentin Roosevelt was a household name at the time, and all women would have recalled his exploits while his father was in the White House.

Perhaps the most remarkable and striking moment of any pilgrimage happened on Party A. It took place in full view of the press. The drama unfolded on May 22 when a contingent of approximately 20 pilgrims and their escorts visited St. Mihiel Cemetery. Here the pilgrims encountered German Gen. Otto von Gessler, War Minister from 1920 to 1923. Ten officers accompanied the general, all dressed in civilian clothes. Gen. von Gessler and his staff had just finished inspecting a nearby German war cemetery when he stopped by St. Mihiel and requested permission to enter. Permission was granted. After a brief visit, his party was preparing to leave when the busload of pilgrims arrived. The *New York Times* reported Gen. von Gessler and the other German visitors made "a quick glance at the placard on the bus hood ... [then] the Germans lined up stiffly at attention as though a military command had been uttered."[32] The mothers got off their bus, quite unaware of who these visitors were.

The attendant press delighted in the exchanges that followed. French escort officers tried to keep the press and the mothers away from the Germans. Nevertheless, the Germans posed for a picture and chatted with the pilgrims and the press before departing. Reporter Edmond L. Taylor of the *Paris Edition* observed:

> Standing at full attention according to the rigid Prussian drill regulations, the visitors with their cropped hair and heavy Teutonic faces seemed curiously awkward and unnatural, especially with the pudgy little French officer fluttering nervously at their flanks.[33]

Reporters even had the chance to interview one of von Gessler's aides, Col. Kell. Described as a warrior with a scarred face, Kell paused to pay tribute to the fallen Americans buried at St. Mihiel. Kell recounted his first encounter with doughboys during the war. "When those vigorous, fresh troops came sweeping toward us, we knew we were finished. I never saw anything so terrible in my life as these battles around St. Mihiel," Kell said.

> Our machine guns mowed down American troops by the hundreds, but they kept on coming. Hardened by four years of war, we were sickened with pity because of the horrible butchery, and we also began to know fear, because we realized no amount of butchery would stop that advancing wave.[34]

Von Gessler and his entourage were especially complimentary of the American cemetery. "How beautiful it is here," he told reporters. "I wish we had something like this." Weatherbeaten black crosses marked graves at nearby German cemeteries. The general approved of St. Mihiel, with "all these white marble crosses, these neat gravel walks, this lovely grass."[35] With these comments, the Germans left the cemetery and the American pilgrims behind. Unfortunately, we have no comments from the pilgrims themselves on this somewhat surreal encounter.

Another one of Party A's special stories also had a German connection. She was Ohio pilgrim Katherine Schmitt. Born in Germany, Mrs. Schmitt gave birth to 15 children, 9 of whom remained in her native land. Mrs. Schmitt immigrated to the United States and became an American citizen. After the war, in 1922, Mrs. Schmitt traveled from her home in Grove City, Ohio, to visit relatives in Germany. She did not visit France. However, State Department records indicated a European trip, a trip that, the Quartermaster Corps concluded, most likely included a trip to her son Franz Schmitt's grave. Mrs. Schmitt received her invitation to sail with Party A in a letter dated March 19, 1930. Nevertheless, she received a separate letter from the Quartermaster Corps on April 10, revoking her invitation. (At this time, a prior, private pilgrimage disqualified a woman from a government-sponsored trip.)

Mrs. Schmitt enlisted the aid of the American Legion post in Columbus, Ohio. The legion drafted a quick response to the army. The reply stated that although Mrs. Schmitt had indeed visited Europe, she had definitely not traveled to France and had certainly not visited Franz's grave. The last-ditch plea worked, and Mrs. Schmitt was allowed to sail with Party A. (By the time Party A actually sailed, Congress revised the statute, allowing women who already made a European trip or even a cemetery visit the chance to go on a government pilgrimage.)

Mrs. Schmitt was especially glad to arrive in Europe, because the pilgrimage gave her a chance to see some of her family from Germany whom she hadn't seen in eight years. Newspaper accounts reported her daughter and husband had traveled to Paris from Germany to visit. She was especially interested in seeing them, but her army escort officer kept her with her party and its strict itinerary. "They came to Paris last night," she told a reporter, "but I can't be with them except when I get permission from Captain [William F.] Dalton and I have to stay with the party."[36] It was not reported, in fact, if she was allowed to see her relatives. However, she did say her son Franz loved flowers, and several friends in the United States gave her money to buy extra flowers to decorate his grave.

Several women traveled with Party A at their own expense. Most were ineligible for a pilgrimage because of technicalities in the pilgrimage act. The press, at least, reported these legal considerations as technicalities; in reality, certain provisions in the legislation excluded a number of women. One example was Massachusetts mother Tillie Duncan. She traveled with Party A at her own expense, on an itinerary arranged for her by a private tour operator. Her son, an American, had fought and died for the Allies in the war. However, he fought and died with Canadian forces before the United States entered the war. Since her son was not serving with the American armed forces at the time of his death, Mrs. Duncan was not eligible for a government-sponsored pilgrimage. Another woman traveling on her own with Party A was Mrs. Michael Galloway of Chicago. The press reported how she "was cheated of her trip from the Government because her son fell with the British Legion in Africa."[37]

There would be no congressional reprieve for Mrs. Galloway and Mrs. Duncan as there had been for Mrs. Schmitt. Despite the many changes it made in the initial pilgrimage act, Congress never changed the provision which prohibited mothers of sons who died fighting under a foreign — albeit friendly — flag from taking part in an organized trip.

The Objective

If the press chronicled Party A's highlights and sidelights, it left the women alone at the graves of their husbands and sons. Beginning with Party A and carrying on throughout the pilgrimages, both the press and the army left the women alone to grieve and to find peace in America's European cemeteries, just as they had done at Suresnes from the very beginning. No one knew what to expect as Mrs. Evans and other members of Party A fanned out across France to decorate the graves. Would there be hysteria? Would women be overcome by ailments and heart attacks at the graves of their sons? Would there be recrimination against the government, perhaps directed toward the army's escort officers? The answers to these questions were "no" in each case, but the officers and pilgrims both had to experience pilgrimages such as Party A to learn for themselves.

The pilgrims were strong women who were very unlikely to cause trouble. They wanted to see their sons' and husbands' graves. One such woman was Cincinnati mother Anna Norris. She had traveled with Party A to decorate the Meuse-Argonne grave of her son, Alexander Norris. Mrs. Norris's group was slated to visit the cemetery during successive days, May 20–25. She suffered from severe rheumatism in her right shoulder and required medical treatment two different days. On May 23, army records noted she was "much improved over yesterday but suffering today. Insists on going to Cemetery."[38] The women all insisted on going to the cemetery, and the officers and attendants of Party A made this fully possible.

Mrs. Norris was not the only health concern. As Party A continued its pilgrimage, illness began to take its toll on the women. Stress, the advanced age of many of the women, and the unseasonably cold and wet weather were all contributing factors. Anna Platt from Florida suffered a mild heart attack at her son's grave. Unable to make the rest of trip, doctors ordered her to bed to rest. The press found Mrs. Platt in front of a roaring fire, complaining of cold feet. "She seemed very weak and her eyes were still red from the emotion of the farewell to the grave she had been so afraid she would not be able to make."

"I don't care now," she told reporters accompanying Party A. "I'll never be able to make the trip again but I've seen the place where my son lies and I know he's resting. Nothing else matters."[39]

Other pilgrims concerned the escort officers, too. Mary Reynolds from Ohio suffered acute angina pectoris. Although she survived the cemetery visit, doctors were so concerned about her health they notified her next-of-kin about the severity of her condition. Florence Williams, also from Ohio, was one of a number of women caught in a sudden downpour at the Meuse-Argonne Cemetery. She caught pneumonia, and an army doctor remained with her in a Verdun hotel while the rest of the party returned to Paris. As with Mrs. Reynolds, Mrs. Williams's condition was so serious that doctors advised her daughter in Ohio that her mother was "sinking rapidly."

Mrs. Reynolds and Mrs. Williams each survived, although both remained in France while the rest of Party A sailed for the United States on May 29. That no one died during Party A was considered a good showing; the army feared the strain of the trip would be too much for the pilgrims to bear.

One man who was in an excellent position to observe Party A was one of its escort officers, Capt. John J. Noll. Noll accompanied the pilgrims to France and escorted a party to the Somme Cemetery. He wrote of his trip in an article for *American Legion* magazine on his return. "When the women first got to cemetery," Noll recalled, all was again simplicity. There was no ceremony—no speechmaking. Quietly each mother or widow was shown the grave they sought. Here was the end of the long trail. Here was the spot that had been in each woman's heart for twelve long years. Here rested her dead. Carefully and reverently the wreaths and flowers were placed before the cross—with them, an American flag from home.[40]

They must have thought it was the mothers themselves who were trying to make their sons proud of them. Noll and his fellow officers saw no hysteria, heard no antigovernment rhetoric. What they saw instead was the first clue as to the healing nature of a war grave pilgrimage.

Noll and the other escorts noted how delighted and at peace the mothers and widows seemed after their cemetery visits. He noted it was difficult for the pilgrims to say goodbye to the cemetery,

> but most of the women left with thankfulness that the graves of their boys were being so carefully tended by the Government. Gratitude toward that Government, gratitude for the opportunity of visiting their dead, gratitude for the splendid courtesies extended to them by everyone connected with the pilgrimage was uppermost in their hearts.[41]

The pilgrims were grateful for their experience. One woman wrote the army after her return to praise the escort officers. She felt "all our attendants were men well-fitted for their places and by their care and tenderness for us made the trip perfect. The Lord must have led in every selection and every bit of planning for our pilgrimage."[42]

Party A satisfied itself the graves were maintained and the cemeteries well cared for. An Ohio woman was more than satisfied with her pilgrimage. "Now that I know how fine Bill's resting place is," she said, "I'm ready to go back home."[43]

For their part, the army escorts were grateful toward the first group of pilgrims. Army nurse Capt. Blanche Rulon accompanied Party A and had overall responsibility for pilgrims' nursing care. The pilgrims' strength, stamina, and resilience did not fail to impress Rulon. She praised

> the remarkable manner in which these elderly women have held up under the long journey and the way in which they always are ready to smile, no matter how tired they are. They have been simply splendid, better than I possibly could have expected. I am sure this first visit will be more than successful.[44]

Party A said good-bye to the cemeteries in late May, and the individual parties reformed in Paris. The pilgrims of Party A had two days in the French capital for sight-seeing and shopping before the boat train to Cherbourg on May 29. Mrs. Mary Jane Pennington, for instance, returned to

Paris from the Aisne-Marne Cemetery on May 25. Her sight-seeing included a scheduled trip to Versailles on May 28.

By this time, the pilgrimages were now in full swing. Party B had already been in Europe long enough to visit England and Belgium. Mathilda Burling sailed with Party B, and her itinerary scheduled her first day at her son's grave on the same day Party A sailed for the United States. Party A was a success. The army's arrangements and personnel worked effectively, and the women held up much better than could have been imagined. For Amy Evans, Minnie Throckmorton, Sarah Thompson, and all the others, the pilgrimages were everything they could have expected and more.

9

The Pilgrimage Experience

"I only want to see my boy's grave. That's what I came for. I don't care about anything else," Ida Lyons from New York told the *Paris Edition* during her Party B pilgrimage visit in 1930.[1] Mrs. Lyons understood the essence of the pilgrimage experience and captured it in three short sentences. Yet a more complete understanding of the meaning and nature of pilgrimages requires more space.

This final chapter will examine the results of the pilgrimage experience. We shall hear from participants, observers, and organizers of the trips, as well as from those who have studied pilgrimages from a scholarly point of view. Pilgrimages are not history; today a dedicated group of Vietnam veterans continues to take Vietnam Gold Star mothers to Asia for a closer look at where their sons fought and died.

The pilgrimages began as a learning experience for all involved. When the trips began, no one knew exactly how the women would react. Maj. Gen. J. L. DeWitt set much of this tone himself when he delivered his speech to the first group of escort officers in 1930. He realized the average age of the pilgrims would exceed 65 years and allowed that virtually all of them would be in an environment with which they were completely unfamiliar. In fact, he expected the worst. "Many of them will become hysterical, I have no doubt, upon the least provocation."[2] Few became hysterical. It was sometimes the men accompanying the pilgrims that had a much harder time with the experience.

Covering Party A, one veteran photographer found the experience too emotional to witness. He observed Party A decorating graves at the Meuse-Argonne Cemetery, and it was too much for him. The hands of the unidentified photographer shook so much on the visit he was unable to do his job. When he realized the task was too much for him, he walked off the job. "'To hell with this business,' he exploded. 'I won't do it. I won't do it. They can send someone else.'"[3]

Pilgrimages in Context

Coming to understand the Gold Star mother pilgrimages means coming to understand pilgrimages in general. War grave pilgrimages began before the first Gold Star mother took her first step on French soil, and they continue to this day around the world. What distinguishes a pilgrimage from ordinary travel? Can a trip contain elements of both tourism and pilgrimage? Did the Gold Star mother pilgrimages deserve the label "pilgrimage?"

Those who have studied pilgrimages in depth report several elements that differentiate pilgrimages from ordinary travel. First and foremost, participants consider a pilgrimage a sacred voyage with a specific purpose in mind. When Mrs. Fox declared she came to Europe only to see her boy's grave, we can be assured she's on a pilgrimage. Some tourism is unavoidable, but tourists are not pilgrims, although some pilgrims can be tourists. An element of risk is expected; making a pilgrimage means making a sacrifice. Unexplained phenomena and spiritual coincidence are common. Pilgrims could be expected to form close bonds with each other, certainly closer than one would expect among a group of tourists. Most important, reaching the pilgrimage's objective often resulted in an emotionally charged catharsis, followed by a feeling of peace and serenity. The Gold Star mother pilgrimages of the 1930s exhibited all these characteristics. The nature of a pilgrimage experience meant risk was

Margaret Slagle decorates the grave of her son, Cpl. Alfred Slagle, Somme Cemetery, 1930. The objective of the pilgrimages was to get the soldier's widow or mother to the cemetery to visit his grave. The government gave each pilgrim flowers to decorate the grave. (Courtesy Margaret Ramsey, granddaughter of Margaret Slagle.)

involved. One had to make a sacrifice to go on such a trip. It need not be a financial one, because all pilgrims were guests of the government. DeWitt's prediction of hysteria fit the pattern. The army's fears of dozens of grief-stricken mothers dying in Europe were understandable but proved to be unfounded. Instead, the pilgrimage destination of Paris itself proved all the risk the pilgrims would encounter.

By 1930, the so-called Lost Generation made Paris its official home. Many American artists and writers were disillusioned with the war and its aftermath. They sought the freedom of Paris and its café society to help them forget the folks back home. Although there is no evidence Paris nightlife was ever a serious temptation for the mothers, the women knew this indeed was a different world. Prohibition was the law of the land back home, but the mothers could enjoy alcohol in Paris if they wished.

"But oh my, I have got so much to tell all my home folk when I get there. I'm so glad to know they've been praying for me," North Carolina pilgrim Sarah Dyson wrote home.

> But oh my, the devil is loose goin' up and seeking whom he may devour — the old as well as the young. Oh, the shocking things that are goin' on now one can't imagine until they get out over the world. Just to think of all the carousin' I've seen on this trip.[4]

Mrs. Dyson traveled in summer 1930 to make the pilgrimage to the grave of her son, Don Williams. Mrs. Dyson kept a scrapbook of her trip and wrote letters to the folks back home. Dyson's family has preserved her scrapbook and has drawn inspiration from it. (Families who have these types of records are very lucky; many have been thrown out, and one even finds pilgrimage memorabilia for sale today on eBay.)

Lynne Payne Cable, one of her descendants, wrote a play based on Dyson's pilgrimage as a master's thesis in English at East Tennessee State University in 1993. Her script, *Gold Stars and Purple Hearts*, is a good one. Cable combines her own understanding of the pilgrimage experience with Dyson's words and letters. We see Dyson bringing some dirt from the hills of home to sprinkle on Don's grave. She also carries some French soil back from Don's grave. In the end, Mrs. Dyson finds the pilgrimage to be of great comfort. She feels the government did not need to treat the women to fancy meals and luxury hotels. "I needed the dirt of your body," she says aloud at Don's grave. "This is just somethin' that I'll never be able to explain. They think I'm goin' home happier because of all the money they've spent. There's no need for me to try an' explain why my heart is at peace."[5] Putting a mother's heart at peace were what the pilgrimages were all about.

Yet the Lost Generation and American expatriates did not want to be reminded of any wholesome, sentimental, or familiar part of the pilgrims' world. While some of their fellow citizens were more than willing to entertain the mothers and listen to their stories, as Tommie Edwards and Noble Sissle had done so graciously, still more were content to let the pilgrims' world fade into the past. Recall Fitzgerald's Dick Diver, who was content to close the curtains on the pilgrims in *Tender Is the Night*. Perhaps this is the greatest risk the Gold Star mothers faced: Everyone would have lost interest when it came time for them to mourn.

The nature of a true pilgrimage meant unusual, fantastic, or even supernatural events were likely to occur. These type of events underscored the notion the trips were no mere holiday. Party A's encounter with German Gen. Gessler and his entourage in May 1930 remains the most memorable example. Yet it is not the only one. Brooks Wooten from Shellman, Georgia, accompanied Gladys Wooten on her pilgrimage in 1931 with Party Q. Young Brooks was 6 when he went to France, and the trip made a lifelong impression on him. He kept a diary of his trip, and his widow told me he recalled it fondly his whole life. During Party Q's visit to the French Tomb of the Unknown Soldier, Brooks noticed something out of the ordinary. The Eternal Flame, which burned continuously, miraculously went out in the pilgrims' presence.[6]

Brooks Wooten's supernatural recollection was in fact perfectly natural in the context of war graves pilgrimages, however. "Stories of miraculous coincidences emphasized that the [pilgrimage] journey was out of the ordinary, a spiritual experience," David Lloyd observed in his book on war graves pilgrimages, *Battlefield Tourism*.[7]

Another pilgrim, Illinois mother Sophia Miller, had her own tale of extraordinary coincidences. She went to Europe in 1931 to visit her son Earl's grave at St. Mihiel. In retelling her pilgrimage story, she invoked the powers of mysticism and numerology. In her account, in *Gold Star Mothers of Illinois*, Mrs. Miller recounted that her son was 23 at the time of his death. She traveled on the #3 bus in New York City and had three roommates on the voyage to France. In Paris, Mrs. Miller and her party stayed three days and nights at the Hotel D'Ieana. The number 13 took on a special significance once she arrived in Verdun. She stayed in room 13 at the hotel. The next day at St. Mihiel, Mrs. Miller found her son buried in row 13, grave 13. Mrs. Miller realized it had been 13 years since the armistice, and the letter m, from Earl's last name, was the 13th letter of the alphabet.

Today one is left to ponder the meaning of these coincidences, Sophia Miller thought them significant and perhaps even comforting. There is no doubt, however, about the circumstances surrounding Earl Miller's death in the war. "A shrapnel hit my son; he died at first aid. He was the only one that day. They all ducked, but alas it took him," Mrs. Miller wrote.[8]

Unusual episodes are not confined to the pilgrims themselves. The folks back home in wartime saw their share of unusual coincidences and unexplained events. One of these episodes centered on the death of a Wisconsin war soldier, Clarence G. Olson. Shortly after he shipped out for France, his fiancée back home contracted polio. When the woman learned of her beloved's death overseas, she is reported to have jumped out of her wheelchair and run downstairs.[9]

Meetings and reunions with long-lost family members also characterized the pilgrimage experience. Although these visits were neither miraculous nor mystical, they did underscore the strong ties Americans of the World War I generation had with Europe, both allies and enemies alike. A number of mothers had been born in Europe, especially Germany. Several of them made side trips, at their own expense, to visit friends and relatives in Germany during their pilgrimages. Others had German relatives travel to France to meet them.

The case of Mrs. Emilie Kennedy of Germantown, Pennsylvania, is the most well documented and most remarkable. Furthermore, Mrs. Kennedy's pilgrimage contained some especially extraordinary moments. It is all the more remarkable because she made a pilgrimage for a son who died before he reached Europe and found a son who had never left.

Mrs. Kennedy traveled with Party D, 1931, to visit the grave of her son, Private John A. Kennedy. Private Kennedy, aged 22, died onboard a troop ship on October 13, 1918, from complications of the worldwide influenza epidemic. He was buried at sea before even setting foot in Europe. Leaving Germantown on the morning of May 25, she arrived precisely one hour, and 50 minutes later in Jersey City, New Jersey. Mrs. Kennedy reached New York City and then sailed for Europe onboard the *S. S. President Roosevelt* on May 27. She arrived with her party in Europe on June 4. The party also visited Brookwood cemetery outside London prior to sailing back to the United States on June 18. The party reached New York City on June 26. She traveled alone on her pilgrimage, although she had requested permission to bring a relative with her. Permission was granted, but she decided against bringing a companion.

But Private Kennedy was not Mrs. Kennedy's only child. He was a child of a second, American marriage. Mrs. Kennedy was pleasantly surprised by a son from her first marriage when her ship docked in France. Herman Weitmuller fought for Germany during the war and had not seen his mother for 25 years. (Misspellings of the names of pilgrims and their families were common in contemporary press accounts. Mrs. Kennedy's first name was listed variously as Emil, Emily, or Emalie. Her German son's last name was reported as Weismuller, Weidmuller, or Weitmuller. According to the burial records in the National Archives, Emilie is the correct first name. There is no definitive record of her son's name.)

Weitmuller had contacted both his mother and pilgrimage officials in advance so he could meet her aboard the ship in Cherbourg. "I went on the boat and a lady walked around with me, calling my mother's name," he told an American reporter. "I had a very strange feeling. I was holding her photograph, and I looked at each face, wondering whether or not that might be she. When I found her we were both very happy. It is like not having a mother for 32 years and then having a real one come to life."[10]

The press described Weitmuller as a "stocky, good-humored Bavarian with wide features and frank eyes"[11] Pilgrimage officials were uncomfortable with his presence, however, and forced him to wait at his mother's hotel while she participated in wreath-laying ceremonies at the Arc de Triomphe. He passed time chatting with the press in the hotel lobby. He talked with Don Brown from the *Paris Edition* until he spotted a modestly dressed old lady walking through the smart-looking crowd in a far corner of the lobby. He leapt from his chair, nearly turning it over, and ran through the astonished crowd with surprising agility. He threw one arm around the old lady and nearly whirled her around, crying "mutter, mutter!"[12] Mrs. Kennedy was so delighted to see her son she began speaking in her native German tongue.

Herman took his mother on a side trip to Germany at his own expense; he was an employee of the German national railroad. (Side trips, at pilgrims' own expense, were not uncommon. Mrs. Kennedy was one of six pilgrims to leave Party D at various times for side trips with relatives and friends.) She rejoined her party in Paris safe and sound on June 11. She and her party saw the sights, including Napoleon's Tomb and the Colonial Exposition.

Mrs. Kennedy's was not the only such meeting of long-lost German and American relatives. Elizabeth Streiber, a 71-year old Cleveland pilgrim, traveled to Europe with Party F in 1931. Her sister, Anna Fraubel from Essen, Germany, came to France to visit. The sisters had not seen each other in 57 years, the press reported. Walter Streiber was killed in the Meuse-Argonne campaign while serving with the 5th Division. His cousin, Mrs. Fraubel's son, was killed with German forces fighting the Russians on the eastern front. Reporters couldn't help but comment on the numerological coincidences of the sisters' meeting. Mrs. Fraubel's son served with the 57th German infantry, a figure that matched the number of years the sisters had been apart.[13]

The recollections of two Illinois pilgrims further reinforce the spiritual side of the pilgrimages. Agnes Joos from Morris, Illinois, remembered the visit to her son William's grave in the Somme cemetery. "[The Somme] seems a very fitting place for the body of our boy to be laid to rest. The spirit, of course, is not there. We have a stone in Morris Cemetery in his honor and I feel that the spirit is often with us there," she recalled.[14]

Fannie B. Patient made her pilgrimage in July 1930 to visit the grave of her son, Marine Private James R. Patient. Mrs. Patient visited the Aisne-Marne Cemetery along with 17 other women in her party. She appreciated the army's efforts to provide a camp chair and flowers for each mother in her group. "Our military escorts were grand to us," Mrs. Patient remembered. "Everything was planned for our comfort from the time we left our homes until we were safely home again."[15]

With typical Gold Star mother reticence, Mrs. Patient devoted only one sentence of her brief account, published in *Gold Star Mothers of Illinois*, to her experience at the gravesite itself. "I had several thrills, but the greatest of all was when I stood at my son's grave and sensed he was there in his spirit body."[16] The Gold Star mothers pilgrimages were all about saying good-bye and obtaining closure. Feeling the presence of a loved one's spirit body was the province of a pilgrimage alone.

Before the pilgrimages began, guidebooks reminded travelers that a visit to a European cemetery was not simply a vacation or cultural experience. It was a pilgrimage, carried out in the spirit of the Crusaders in the Middle Ages. "So too, in reverence and in memory of the deeds of their countrymen, are our people to-day visiting the American battlefields of France and Belgium, on a pilgrimage to a new Holy Land, made theirs by the sacrifices of their kindred."[17] The guidebook, *America in Battle*, continued:

> It is in the spirit of reverence, not curiosity that the visitor should approach the battlefields to visit the scenes of one of the greatest tragedies in the history of mankind — scenes of sacrifice made and sufferings endured not only by the hosts that fought and died there, but also by the civilian population — old men, helpless women and little children whom the ravages of war engulfed. Let him remember that he is going into an atmosphere of holiness pervaded by the spirits of the heroic dead. Let him approach the battlefields, therefore, in the same reverential attitude that he would enter a place of worship.[18]

Those who have studied war graves pilgrimages and see the Gold Star mothers' experiences are not surprised by their deeply spiritual nature. "Implicit in the act of making a pilgrimage was an instinctive spiritualism which expressed itself in the belief that it was possible to get closer to the spirit and even the spirits of the dead by visiting sites associated with the war," historian David Lloyd observed.[19]

Release

Yet by far the most distinguishing characteristic of a pilgrimage is the emotional catharsis. The pilgrimages worked; the women felt far better for having gone on their trips. Hysteria and nervous breakdowns were almost nonexistent. What the escort officers and the pilgrims themselves experienced was relief, gratitude, and healing. Part of the reason was fear and apprehension. Many women were concerned about finding makeshift graves in unkempt cemeteries. The cemeteries were beautiful, as all observers noted. The beauty of the surroundings certainly soothed many a mother's broken heart. Yet it took more than shrubbery and fresh marble crosses to account for the entire experience.

The army's careful planning deserved at least partial credit. In the final analysis, the pilgrimages were very personal in nature. Ceremony, pomp, and circumstance at the cemeteries were kept to a minimum. The emphasis was squarely on personal loss and healing. Mitch Yockelson from the National Archives observed the "War Department also was very concerned that while this was a special trip they organized, the true purpose, the true meaning, was not going to be clouded, and the women had a chance to mourn and to see the graves on their own."[20] The true meaning emerged as it did in virtually all war grave pilgrimages.

The journeys gave the mothers a tangible way to say good-bye. By not bringing the body back home, the mother had no plot to tend in the hometown cemetery. "Visiting the grave, or the name on the memorial, substitutes for the missing funeral," observed Tony Walter.

> At a funeral, the physicality of the coffin is crucial: it brings home, almost unbearably, that what has died is no ethereal memory, but a living human of the flesh — a son who laughed, a brother who excelled in sports, a husband who made love. That is why the soldier's name carved into the stone, his physical remains under the pilgrim's feet, is so important to those who could not attend a funeral.[21]

The pilgrimage experiences lead to a tremendous release, catharsis, and full sense of well-being for the mothers. This experience is not solely the province of the Gold Star mothers either. A British tour guide observed the same phenomenon after the pilgrims in her group had made their graveside visit. She remarked, "The moment they've had their cemetery visit — right! it's knees up time! And they dance down the coach, singing."[22] Although no Gold Star mothers danced on their buses, their sense of relief and peace was real.

Gold Star mothers at their hotel in France. Parties of pilgrims formed cohesive groups, much like their sons had done with their buddies in battle. The smiling faces and relaxed appearance of the women probably meant they had already decorated their sons' graves. The pilgrimage experience brought a feeling of relief and peace to the mothers and widows. (Courtesy Janet Payne. Her grandmother Sarah Dyson is tenth from left.)

But before the joy, there were tears. Cemetery caretakers were in a good position to assist the pilgrims and observe their behavior. One caretaker, John Blaine at Flanders Field Cemetery in Belgium, had formed a definite impression as to the effects of a graveside visit. Blaine told the press,

> I have welcomed many a Gold Star Mother ... here in the past years. I know that for an hour or more they want to stay quietly beside the grave. I hope the Gold Star mothers [who visit Flanders Field] tomorrow will cry. Tears are consoling. I dread Mothers who don't cry. Those Mothers stand speechless and tearless at the grave of their sons I have sometimes carried as though lifeless from the cemetery after a few minutes.[23]

The Gold Star mothers knew this sense of relief. Virginia Bateman Hopkins from Tyrone, Pennsylvania, took time after her 1930 pilgrimage to write to President Hoover to thank the government for her trip to her husband's grave.

> The trip was so delightfully conducted that much of the sadness was lost by the ability of our leaders to divert our thoughts as soon as we would leave a cemetery. In many ways I dreaded the trip but our Captain Lambert kept us so active that we had very little time to be introspective. Thus the old ache was erased by new scenes, interesting side trips to places of interest and renown, and — as I said above — excellent leadership.... I am not able to express in words what is in my heart.[24]

The pilgrimages succeeded not because they herded the women across France in a frantic rush, but because they achieved a proper balance between mourning and travel.

Laura Stevens from tiny Bend, Oregon, visited her son Percy Stevens's grave on her pilgrimage. Percy was lost when his troopship the *S.S. Tuscania* was torpedoed. He was buried in the Brookwood Cemetery outside London. Mrs. Stevens was born in Norway, and her pilgrimage was her first trip back to Europe. Mrs. Stevens was an adventurous pilgrim, eager to travel in Europe. As her grandson William Stevens Prince recalled,

> Granny had heard that in London you could ride as far as you want to on a bus for a penny. So she rode, until she got lost, way out into the country someplace, and a conductor took her under his wing, and sent her back on another bus to the center of town. So that was a very positive experience for her.[25]

Despite the tourism involved, Laura Stevens never forgot the purpose of her pilgrimage to England. Prince recalled his grandmother's reaction when she came back from Europe. "Granny was happy she'd gone. All the mothers were, I think, happy they'd gone," he said.[26]

Witness to History

As in so many other cases with the pilgrimages, we are left today with others' accounts, observations, and interpretations. The Gold Star mothers themselves left relatively few written diaries, letters, or other published accounts. American officials in Europe provided us with some of the most detailed accounts of the mothers and what they experienced in Europe. One of them was U.S. ambassador to Great Britain Charles Dawes.

Charles Gates Dawes was born in Ohio and served as an officer in World War I. He was vice president from 1925 to 1929 and also something of an amateur musician. He co wrote the pop standard "It's All in the Game," a song covered by dozens of artists from the Four Tops to Donny

Osmond. In his position as ambassador, Dawes observed Americans from all walks of life visiting Britain and was also able to form his own ideas on the meaning of the pilgrimages. In late May 1930, Dawes welcomed members of Party B, traveling with veterans from the 27th Division, to London. He met many of the pilgrims and introduced them to British dignitaries. In his diary, Dawes wrote:

> I was very proud of the simple and unaffected way in which these fine and natural American women conducted themselves, and I could not but think how majestic was their naturalness as contrasted with some of their countrywomen who besiege me with requests to be presented at Court.[27]

Evidently, the British shared Dawes's assessment. "While standing near Lord Plumer, some one told us that one of the mothers present had lost two sons in the 27th Division. I told him that I would find her and present her to him. His answer was a request to go with me 'to be presented to her.'"[28]

Ambassador Dawes shared much the same sentiment during a speech at Cambridge University on June 5, 1930.

> As American Ambassador, I come frequently in contact with certain traveled Britons and Americans who are continual purveyors of the trivial and irritating in international relationship. But recently we have had in London a body of American travelers representing a cross-section of the American people, the bone and sinew of the American people, the proud attitude of the American people — a body of travelers not self-invited, with their minds occupied by thoughts of society reports or fashionable dressmakers, but mothers invited by the government of the United States to make their first and last visit to the graves of their sons in France.[29]

Dawes's comments remind us that overseas travel in the 1920s and 1930s was strictly the province of the privileged and well-to-do, the sort of people for whom society reports and fashionable dressmakers would have been a part of daily life. The pilgrimages provided a level playing field.

Yet Dawes was not the only American official to observe the pilgrims in Europe and report what he saw. Walter E. Edge served as U.S. ambassador to France from 1929 to 1933. He attended many receptions, and his office provided assistance to pilgrimage officers.

> The courageous women who crossed the seas to pay their silent and deeply poignant tribute at the grave of a son or a husband have profoundly impressed us with their brave dignity and their chivalrous simplicity of their sorrow. The

spirit in which they have come gives us some little insight into the greatness of their sacrifice and our only hope is they return to their homes reassured that their boys are being well cared for which must be partial compensation for their suffering.[30]

As much as dignitaries such as Dawes and Edge may have come to know the pilgrims, most viewed the mothers not so much as individuals but as icons representing some form of the American ideal. Notions of motherhood and nationalism were heaped on the shoulders of women who wanted simply to mourn at their husbands' or sons' graves. At another reception for the pilgrims, Edge declared,

> You, Mothers, instilled into these young men the principles for which they laid down their lives; you taught them the fundamentals of loyalty and courage of truth and vision; you with the fortitude which mothers have throughout the ages have mustered held your heads up high as you bid them "goodbye." Today you have not only the satisfaction of knowing that your sons lie honored here with thousands of their brave comrades but the assurance that they will live as a solemn inspiration to those of us who follow and to the generations to come.[31]

In Their Own Words

To understand the pilgrimage experience, we would ideally turn to the words and stories the pilgrims themselves left behind. No one other than a Gold Star mother or widow could begin to explain the experience of traveling to a foreign country to visit a loved one's grave. Some accounts do come down to us. Joyce Kilmer's mother's account, excerpted in Chapter 4, is the longest one, the only book written by a Gold Star mother about her pilgrimage experience. A few diaries and assorted letters surface occasionally, sometimes even for sale on eBay, sometimes in long-forgotten or even defunct rural newspapers.

Eva Trowbridge, from Williston, North Dakota, recorded her pilgrimage in a lengthy column for her hometown newspaper, the *Williams County Farmer Press*. Published in the July 31, 1930, edition, Mrs. Trowbridge's account read more like a travelogue than the tale of a mourning heart. Mrs. Trowbridge boarded the Empire Builder train for the East Coast on May 31, 1930. She found the ocean crossing agreeable. "The sea was very calm and the ship was beautifully decorated with flowers. Everyone was so kind to us everywhere we went. There was some kind of entertainment every night on the ship, and the band played several selections at every meal," she wrote.[32] Mrs. Trowbridge marveled at the well-organized pilgrimage.

She noted how army officers tracked every piece of luggage. She appreciated how each pilgrim received a different color badge on the train trip into Paris. The different badges signified the separate pilgrimage hotels in use. Mrs. Trowbridge's badge was blue, indicating her inclusion in the Aisne-Marne group of pilgrims.

Her description at the cemetery was very matter-of-fact. "Friday morning, June 17, at 9:30 we were taken in the bus to the cemetery for the first time," she wrote.

> There was a chair at each grave and we were given a large wreath of flowers to put on the grave. The photographer took our pictures at the grave and gave us each two pictures. The cemetery is beautiful: it is all perfectly level and kept up with the greatest care. It is just like a well-kept lawn. The crosses are large and are made of perfectly white marble. They are in rows any way you look. I think there are 1200 buried in this cemetery. The crosses have the name, company and division, and the state the boys are from.[33]

Although all pilgrims visited the cemeteries on several days, Mrs. Trowbridge wrote only of this one visit in her article.

Mrs. Trowbridge and her party did some shopping, saw some sights (including the Louvre), and sailed for home via Ireland on June 27. The party had time to visit Coney Island after arriving in New York City on July 5. Mrs. Trowbridge caught the midnight train on July 6 heading back to Williston. "It was a glorious trip from start to finish," she remembered. "Everything was planned so well by the government as to care and courteous treatment. We were looked after all the time to see that we were comfortable, to see we were provided for and taken care of at the table. They were always counting us and taking the roll so as not to miss anyone. We did not need to take every trip unless we wanted to, but I never missed any."[34]

Mrs. Trowbridge had a marvelous trip, one that surely would have soothed her in her loss. Hers is one of the longer published accounts, and even at that it just scratches the surface of personal loss, grief, and healing. Perhaps the gratitude is a window to the catharsis and healing. Mothers like Mrs. Trowbridge finished their pilgrimages with a grateful attitude toward the government, so one may conclude that any overt feelings of bitterness, loss, and suffering were gone.

Yet it was Henrietta Haug's efforts on the eve of World War II to collect and preserve Gold Star mothers accounts that today offers us the best understanding in the pilgrims' own words. Her book, *Gold Star Mothers of Illinois*, was published in 1941. It contained some of the most detailed pilgrimage accounts available, and any understanding of the pilgrimage experience must include these stories. Haug's remarkable book included probably one of the longest, detailed, and most evocative accounts of a pilgrim's experience, and it is worth examining in length.

The account belonged to Mary A. Mann from Antioch, Illinois. Mrs. Mann was born in Chicago in 1876. Her son, Willard J. Mann, was also born in Chicago and was 22 years old when he entered military service on October 4, 1917. Willard Mann served with the 33rd Division's 131st Infantry. He was killed in battle near Chipilly, France, on August 9, 1918.

Mrs. Mann began her pilgrimage on the morning of May 19, 1930, by train. She arrived in Chicago in just under two hours and waited for several other pilgrims to arrive at the station before they all caught a train for the East Coast that evening. Mrs. Mann and her fellow members of Party D reached New York City the following morning and checked into the Hotel Roosevelt. The party left the hotel early in the morning of May 21 for Hoboken Harbor in New Jersey. Mrs. Mann noted with interest that many pilgrims had flowers or telegrams waiting for them as they boarded the *S.S. George Washington*. Although she received no such bon voyage present herself, she was not disappointed. "I did not envy anyone but could not help but admire the thoughtfulness of the [American] Legion Posts who sent messages of cheer," she recorded in her diary.[35]

Mrs. Mann's ocean crossing was eventful. The voyage began smoothly enough. The liner pulled away from the pier so steadily, in fact, Mrs. Mann said she could scarcely tell her trip had begun. Several mothers became violently ill when the ship encountered fog and choppy seas. Two women fell in the heavy weather; one broke a few ribs, the other a wrist. A steward even told Mrs. Mann one mother went insane on the trip and ended up in care of relatives in Germany. The Gold Star mother had high praise for all the staff. Bad weather forced the party to postpone its arrival in Cherbourg by a day. The party spent their last evening on the liner anchored in the harbor. The fog horn disturbed the pilgrims; Mrs. Mann was able to sleep only between "toots" of the horn.[36]

Despite the rough weather, Mrs. Mann enjoyed her voyage. Crackers and bouillon were served every morning and tea and cakes in the afternoon. An orchestra played during meal times, and she enjoyed watching passengers dance to the music. The ship's captain presented each pilgrim with a

> beautiful bronze medal bearing a miniature of the steamship *George Washington*, Statue of Liberty and the Eiffel Tower and an 18-carat gold star on one side and the inscription "Gold Star Pilgrimage to the battlefields of the World War, United States Lines" on the reverse side.[37]

The party finally landed on May 30. As the party left the liner, passengers remaining on board waved good-bye and sang "God Be With You 'till We Meet Again" to the departing pilgrims. Mrs. Mann considered this a truly "beautiful and impressive" gesture.

Once on French soil, her account read more like any typical pilgrim's diary. This is to say, it read like a travelogue of someone who had never been abroad before. She delighted in the unusual trees and flowers, and she remarked on the houses with their distinctive red tile roofs. She observed no large fields of grain, typical of the Illinois countryside back home; instead, she enjoyed the dense patchwork of brightly colored flowers on the boat train to Paris. Mrs. Mann and her fellow members of Party D shared a compartment on the six-hour train ride to Paris. She got her first taste of French food on the trip. She remarked on the bottled, sparkling mineral water but failed to mention if she tried the strong French coffee, which most pilgrims disliked intensely.

Once in Paris, Mrs. Mann and her fellow members of Party D engaged in the now-traditional wreath-laying at the Arc de Triomphe. A Detroit mother, selected as the party's honor pilgrim, laid the wreath. Ambassador Edge hosted a tea for the ladies. Mrs. Mann recalled how "after a social hour all departed feeling kindly toward those who were responsible for such fine entertainment."[38] The party engaged in some afternoon sightseeing and returned to its hotel prior to departure for the cemeteries. Escort officers told the women to pack just the essentials for their cemetery visits; their Paris hotels would store the rest until their return.

As she recounted her preparations to visit the cemetery, Mrs. Mann took time to praise those escorting the party. Capt. John McReynolds was the Somme group's escort officer. Robert J. Neal, a former-serviceman, served as their interpreter. Two nurses, Miss Handley and Miss Thompson, tended to the party. Mrs. Mann reserved special words of kindness for the party's official host and hostess, Maj. Floyd B. Carlock and Marjorie Nelson, respectively. (Both men were career army officers; each served during World War II. Floyd Carlock, born in Ohio, received the Purple Heart for injuries suffered during World War I.)

The escorts, in turn, evidently praised Mrs. Mann and her fellow pilgrims. "Our group was a congenial bunch," Mrs. Mann wrote. "Caused so little trouble that the word preceded us, and was conveyed to the cemeteries, that the 'Sunshine Group' was on its way. Of course we were justly proud to learn of this."[39] She attributed these kind words to Maj. Carlock and Miss Nelson.

On June 1, Mrs. Mann joined 29 other pilgrims, plus escort officers and nurses, on their trip to the Somme Cemetery. On the way to St.

9. The Pilgrimage Experience　　　　　　　　　　　　　　　193

Quentin, their rural French base of operations during their cemetery visits, the women saw the countryside and some battlefield sites. The party passed the area near Chantilly, where the railroad car in which the armistice was signed was on display. This journey outside Paris revealed Mrs. Mann's sharp eye for detail and her direct writing style. About this trip, she wrote,

> our trip from Paris starting June 1 took us through some beautiful country; roads all along were lined with beautiful shade trees in most places, double rows of trees on each side of the road. In places where the trees had been destroyed during the war, new ones had been planted; by being well cared for they were making splendid growth.[40]

What came next differentiates Mrs. Mann's diary from all other pilgrimage accounts. She described the visit to her son's grave in detail. She began by observing the grounds of the lovely Somme Cemetery.

> The scenery in and around this Somme Cemetery is all that could be desired. Margins of shrubbery, trees and flowers, beds of graveled driveways, flowers everywhere blooming in season, beds of pansies, forget-me-nots, daisies and baby breath bordered with foliage of all colors and dwarf varieties of flowers blooming profusely, being among the decoration seen.[41]

Mrs. Mann and the rest of her Somme Party visited the cemetery on two separate days. Once there on the first day, she wrote,

> We marched silently and reverently to the final resting place of our beloved sons. *The day was one of the most beautiful and impressive of my life.* Bright sunshine, deep blue sky and a few snow-white fleecy clouds moved gracefully above us, as if to shelter us, underneath our feet a velvety carpet of green.[42]

Once at the graveside, Mrs. Mann continued her narrative, paying special attention to the flowering wreaths each pilgrim received.

> The first day at the cemetery, each mother was provided with a beautiful wreath of flowers, composed of roses, carnations, daisies and ferns, a gift from our Government. This was the most beautiful and consoling feature and one appreciated by each mother, who carried the wreath and placed it upon the grave of her *hero, as no one but a mother could do.*[43]

Her passage at the graveside was noteworthy because she considered decorating her son's grave at the Somme as a special, sacred event reserved for a mother alone. Anyone can bring flowers, but only a mother could place a wreath on the grave of her personal hero. The differences between a pilgrim and tourist could not be more clearly defined.

Mrs. Mann and her group visited the cemetery for a second and final day on June 3. They decorated the sons' graves with floral arrangements donated by a French women's group. "Willard's row is 15, Grave 4, Block D," she said of her final visit. "The time for our stay at the cemetery having expired, we departed after taking a last look at the lovely spot herein our beloved sons sleep in peace. Their resting place will abide and their names be honored through all ages."[44]

Mrs. Mann and the rest of the Somme pilgrims left on June 4 to make their way back to Paris, pausing for stops both scenic and instructive. Stops included Vimy Ridge battlefield, site of Canada's war triumph, and an unreconstructed German trench complex. Escort officers were careful to shield the pilgrims from any lingering dangers, but they were unable to protect them from the pain of memories. "Everywhere about were scenes of destruction, the horror of which kind nature has in a measure obliterated. Leaving these scenes of horror we moved on through Albert to Amiens; somewhere near where Willard fought and was killed, August 9, 1918."[45]

The party returned to Paris on June 7 but had little time for shopping, Mrs. Mann lamented. The party saw Napoleon's Tomb, Marshal Foch's burial site, and the Eiffel Tower, which she felt was especially lovely in the evening. The train ride back to Cherbourg gave Mrs. Mann a final chance to indulge in her horticultural observations. "There had been little or no rain in the meantime and vegetation had suffered. So things along the line had lost some of the beauty about which we raved so in France."[46]

The ship ride home was memorable. The mothers' liner, the *S. S. George Washington*, impressed them with its beauty and good food. However, a fire broke out onboard. Mrs. Mann noted with some satisfaction how the "fire laddies took care of the situation and soon had the fire extinguished to the delight of all aboard."[47] Troubles did not end with the fire. The ship was stuck on a sandbar for several hours in sight of the harbor in the United States. She finally arrived in Hoboken Harbor on June 19, spent the night at the Hotel McAlpin, and reached Antioch, Illinois, by rail on the evening of June 20.

If one were to have asked Mrs. Mann if she thought the trips were worthwhile, she would not have hesitated in her reply.

> This Pilgrimage ... stands out as one of the greatest achievements of our honored and beloved Nation. I extend my deepest and most heartfelt thanks to all who made it possible to stand in silence and alone at the grave of my beloved son, Willard J. Mann, whose life was one of unselfish devotion to justice and right, and in death were reflected the same noble characteristics.[48]

Gold Star Mothers Go Hollywood

The Gold Star mother pilgrimages were so widely reported and in the public eye they became the subject of a Hollywood movie in 1933. *Pilgrimage*, directed by John Ford, set such a high standard for realism that parts of the film looked almost like a contemporary newsreel account. The film captured all the essential elements of a pilgrimage, especially catharsis, but also reminded the viewer that not all mothers and sons had idealized relationships. (Lynne Cable hinted at such family dynamics in her play *Gold Stars and Purple Hearts*.) Ford's story of an Arkansas family was a different voice in this regard.

Pilgrimage told the story of the fictional Jessop family from Three Cedars, Arkansas. Hannah Jessop was living with her son Jim when the war broke out. Mrs. Jessop (played by Henrietta Crosman) kept Jim under her thumb, belittling him for talking of enlistment. Jim (Norman Foster) fell in love with a neighbor girl, Mary (Marian Nixon). Mrs. Jessop disapproved of the relationship and threatened to disown Jim if he married the girl. When Jim announced his plans to get married, Mrs. Jessop hurried to the local draft board to declare Jim's services were no longer needed on the family farm and that he was eligible for the draft. Jim was drafted and sent to the front, but not before he and Mary had a chance for a parting roll in the hay. While Jim was at war, Mary gave birth to their son, Jimmy. Mrs. Jessop wanted nothing to do with the child, especially because Jim and Mary were not married. Meanwhile, Jim was killed in battle the day before the war ended.

Pilgrimage then leaps ahead 10 years. We find little Jimmy protecting himself from schoolyard bullies who taunt him by saying his parents weren't married when he was born. Mrs. Jessop still hated Mary and Jimmy and wanted nothing to do with them. The pilgrimages were big news, but Mrs. Jessop was reluctant to go. She plainly did not want to dredge up memories of her son and the war. The mayor of the small town finally convinced her to go on the trip and began to make plans for her pilgrimage.

Pilgrimage offered a very realistic look at the Gold Star mother experiences. Ford's crew built an entire Arkansas village in the Hollywood hills, along with a replica French village, Arc de Triomphe, and Tomb of the Unknown Soldier. The crew wanted to find a way to age Jim's dog, Jerry, while still using the same dog as little Jimmy's pet. Rather than simply get an older dog of the same breed, Ford and his crew substituted the bark of an older dog on the film's soundtrack for the puppy's happy bark. They also attached small weights to the dog's paws to make him walk like an older pet.[49]

Interactions between the pilgrims and the escorts were equally realistic. An army nurse and escort officers passed out badges to the women as their party was set to sail. The mothers shown represent all walks of American life (except the African American element.) A German woman spoke almost no English, and an Italian pilgrim took her family to the railroad station. Pilgrims boarded their ship amid bands and banners. One man saw the party and declares, "that's more American than a whole day of speeches." Mrs. Jessop met a backwoods Southern woman, Mrs. Hatfield, who shared her cabin. Mrs. Hatfield lost three sons in the war, but she would have rather lost them in war than in an ongoing feud with the neighbors back home. She smoked a pipe at dinner and recommended some of her homebrew white lightning to a seasick nurse.

The early stages of the pilgrimage transformed Mrs. Jessop. Her bitterness began to fade. She even accepted a bouquet of flowers from Mary and Jimmy to place on Jim's grave. As she boarded the liner, a weeping mother gave her a pathetic little flower in a dirty little pot. She said her boy is still missing after the war, and she was not allowed to go on a pilgrimage. (Technically, this was not true by the time of Ford's film.) Mrs. Jessop took the flower willingly and even began to tend it on her voyage to France. Once in France, she mingled with the other mothers and planned to make her visit to Jim's grave.

However, Mrs. Jessop underwent an unusual and largely unexplained transition in the middle sections of *Pilgrimage*. Rather than coming to terms with the death of her son, she refused at the last minute her cemetery visit with her fellow pilgrims. Instead, she began to wander the streets of Paris aimlessly. As she crossed a bridge, she noticed a disheveled young man looking over the railing. The young man was clearly on the verge of suicide before she intervened. Rather miraculously, he invited her back to his flat and she fixed him breakfast. We learn the young man is Gary Worth (played by Maurice Murphy). Gary's fiancée, Suzanne (Heather Angel), arrived. Mrs. Jessop learned Gary's mother is opposed to their marriage. Mrs. Jessop visited Mrs. Worth (columnist Hedda Hopper). Mrs. Jessop delivered a speech directed as much directed toward herself as to Mrs. Worth. She said nothing should ever come between a mother and her son, certainly not a boy's choice of a wife. Mrs. Worth was quickly convinced to bless Gary's wedding to Suzanne. Mrs. Jessop herself was transformed. She took her own advice, put aside her own bitterness, and decorated Jim's grave. She returned to the United States with the rest of her party and arrived back home in Arkansas at peace with her life.

Pilgrimage is a remarkable film for several reasons. First, it offers the only contemporary look at the pilgrims and their times. Ford re-created many scenes just as they would have looked to the participants themselves. The film also put the pilgrimages back into the public eye. By 1933, the last year of the pilgrimages, the press stopped reporting on the trips and the public had stopped caring.

The film is also noteworthy because it portrayed the healing power of the pilgrimage experience. Granted, Mrs. Jessop must come to Gary Worth's rescue first, but her transformation is just as complete as any other pilgrim's. She returned to Arkansas, embraced Mary and Jimmy, and felt much better about her life in general. The film also touches on a topic that simply did not emerge in any other venue for the pilgrimages: family strife and hard feelings. Surely, all 6,500 pilgrims did not have storybook relationships with the sons or husbands. Many women may have felt guilt, along with their sense of loss. How many and to what degree we'll simply never know. Nevertheless, Ford's *Pilgrimage* remains an intriguing and entertaining footnote in pilgrimage history.

The film was very popular and well received. Critics praised its ability to tell a story without resorting to two hours of pure sentimentality. "This is a fable that could drip with maudlin tears in any one of a score of sentimental scenes. It is a triumph for Miss Crossman and for Mr. Ford that *Pilgrimage* achieves delicacy and tact where those commendable qualities seem beyond reach" the *New York Times* reported.[50] Nevertheless, the film did make its emotional impact on audiences. The *Times* noted, "Audiences are stifling their sobs and crying softly into their handkerchiefs twice a day."[51] Like the pilgrimages themselves, *Pilgrimage* is now largely forgotten. It has aired in the past few years on cable television in late-night time slots. For its contemporary audience, however, Ford's film succeeded in keeping the pilgrimages in the public eye.

Pilgrims Under Fire

The pilgrimages were largely free from controversy. Aside from the somewhat scandalous story in the *Paris Edition* that chronicled Party A's arrival in Europe and scattered letters to the editor, most Americans were content to let the pilgrims have their trips and mourn their dead. As the Depression wore on, this sentiment began to change. With Hitler's rise to power in Europe, not even the most patriotic observer declared we had made the world safe for democracy. Beyond that, traditional values of motherhood were under attack in the culture; some saw the mothers in very unflattering light.

A 1935 article in the new men's magazine *Esquire* remains to this day the harshest, most vitriolic attack on the pilgrimages and the pilgrims.

The article, "Gold Star Mother," by Philip Stevenson, portrays the Gold Star mothers as cows. Mrs. Holstein and Mrs. Guernsey attend a meeting, while another mother recounts the inspirational remarks of Mr. Bramah in France. Stevenson belittles their matronly, small-town language. The mothers remark on their "morvelous" visit overseas and the "poitry" of death. A speech concludes with an "I thankya." The piece is tongue-in-cheek, but it is no less bitter for being so. Just in case the reader didn't get it, "satire" appeared under the byline.

The reader learns all about Mr. Bramah. Delivering a speech to her fellow pilgrims, a mother recalls,

> Mr. Bramah for instance he was the one that made the Speech of Welcome. I just want to tell you ladies, it was a morvelous speech and Mr. Bramah was sure morvelous looking, too, so big and strong in spite of a slight hump in his back, a regular bull neck and what shoulders! I guess some of us couldn't help but making kind of cow eyes at him sort of![52]

Stevenson uses capitalization, Speech of Welcome, to mock the solemn nature of the pilgrimages. One also reads of the Spirit of Giving, Over There, and Life is the Survival of the Fittest.

Stevenson is harsh on the mothers because they have reared their sons (calves?) to be led to the slaughter. The mothers see nothing wrong with having their sons die in battle. In fact, they see it as part of life itself. We learn

> most of us had sort of the shivers when we saw where Our Boys had died and blood was actually spilled and all. But then, I guess I can say that not a one of us forgot she was a Gold Star Mother. We all just realized that those terrible things have to be and We Mothers have just got to be mothers and expect those things because that's just the way life is, isn't it?[53]

But Stevenson's mothers saw very little blood. On the contrary, their sons' deaths were quick, clean, and painless. "Death is clean and kind! I thought Death is merciful!" the speaker declares. "And for the first time I realized the Great Wisdom behind it all. I saw life as hard and cruel. What did those dear young creatures have ahead of them but sorrow and longing and old age? After all, they couldn't *all* be a Bramah, one Bramah goes a long way."[54]

Calling their sons "creatures" sets the stage for what comes next. Stevenson sets up the soldiers as so many cattle to be slaughtered.

> Our Dear Boys, with their morvelous big soft eyes, and their sturdy young legs, and their dear little budding horns, and — oh! all the rest of it. But I can't,

I just simply can't describe it. They never stopped, but only whimpered a little for their mothers, and marched straight ahead of them, their eyes open, to make the Supreme Sacrifice before their Maker. And when the twenty-pound sledge fell and their front legs collapsed and the blood spurted I thought: How morvelous![55]

Yet the mothers had sacrificed, too. The cows in the herd, however, had no strong objections according to Stevenson's view. The mother's account concludes:

And now I've found the word I've been looking for all this time. The very exact word to make you feel what we all felt there in the Valley of the Departed. Morvelous. That's just what it was: just simply *morvelous*! And so I make my resolution: Never again would I object to having a calf of mine taken away from me in the name of Humanity. No never, because I realized: It had all been Well Worth While.[56]

One suspects Stevenson's attack is not so much against the mothers as against the nationalistic mindset that led to their sons' deaths. Stevenson and many others from the interwar generation realized how futile the war had been. Most Gold Star mothers would have agreed. Although they were proud of their sons and husbands, the pilgrims were unlikely to declare the war a "morvelous" experience. One imagines 1935 is as soon after the war as Stevenson's article could have been published. Most Americans would not have accepted his piece, even labeled as satire, after the war or even during the pilgrimages themselves. In any event, "Gold Star Mothers" remains the most concerted attack not just on the pilgrimages but on the pilgrims themselves.

In a broader context, Stevenson's article signals a larger cultural change in the attitude toward women. Rebecca Jo Plant states:

It indicates there is this kind of hostility rising towards maternal figures, and I'm sure that the economy has a lot to do with that. It also has to do, however, with cultural change as a whole, away from the kind of idealization of women in general, not just mothers, but a growing skepticism as feminine influence as a positive force.[57]

The Pilgrimages Continue

The pilgrimage experience is not dead. It continues today with the Vietnam-era generation of Gold Star mothers. The emotional impact and effects of the pilgrimage experience today are really no different than they were some 70 years ago. Today's pilgrims overcome the obstacles

Promotional poster for the PBS documentary *Gold Star Mothers: Pilgrimage of Remembrance.* The documentary premiered in Urbana, Illinois, on Memorial Day 2003. It aired nationwide on many PBS stations during 2004. The author served as co producer. (WILL-TV, University of Illinois at Urbana-Champaign.)

of foreign travel, unusual food, and unfamiliar sights. They share the experience with other women who know just what they feel, as no one else can. The women also report the same feelings of relief, catharsis, and acceptance the World War I Gold Star mothers and widows experienced.

Private groups with private funds conduct today's pilgrimages. A group of Vietnam veterans runs Operation Gold Star. The veterans belong to the Dusters, Quads, and Searchlights, an association composed of air defense artillery men from the Vietnam War. Through Operation Gold Star, the Dusters have made two separate trips to Vietnam to date; the first one was in July 2002. They raise all funds privately and provide each mother with her own all-expenses-paid trip. Veterans traveling at their own expense accompany the mothers. Organizers attempt to have at least one veteran in each party who served in roughly the same area of Vietnam as the sons. (America did not build permanent cemeteries in Vietnam. All recovered bodies were returned to the United States. Only those whose remains have never been found still rest in Vietnam.)

The absence of a grave seems not to have lessened the pilgrimage experience at all. Just being close by was all that mattered for Michigan mother Valerie May. "And by then, that time is gone," she said, recalling the Vietnam War.

> So it just helped to go where you were breathing not the same air, but at least where he was. And by walking his footsteps. We had our picture taken of our footsteps in the sand where they'd been, and we had services at the site, nearest to what we figure, where our sons died.[58]

Bodies had already been returned to the United States and families held burial ceremonies years before Operation Gold Star began. Nevertheless, families always held out hope for their loved ones to return. Mary Wheeler believed the same thing before her pilgrimage to Vietnam. "I always felt that he was going to knock on the door, and he'd be there," she told Alison Davis Wood in her interview for *Gold Star Mothers: Pilgrimage of Remembrance*. "The trip to Vietnam helped me realize that's not going to happen, and I was extremely proud of him. I really almost hated those people [the North Vietnamese], and I know I wasn't brought up to hate, but I really think in my heart that I did hate them."[59]

Mrs. Wheeler found the pilgrimage experience to be difficult at first. "When we got out and saw the places where they [their sons] were, and we each went to the place where our son was killed and we held a memorial service for a few minutes, it was rough," she said.

> But then afterwards we got back on our bus, and were on our way, and were able to get over it. I always said I wanted to walk where he walked his last few days on earth. And for me it was closure. I was able to say, yes, I know he's he not coming home. I learned to love those people.[60]

Mary Wheeler's comments are a perfect summary of the pilgrimage experience, an experience that seems unchanged from World War I to the present.

10

Conclusion

On Thursday, August 24, 1933, the final group of Gold Star mothers and widows docked in New York harbor. The 166 women in this last party brought the total number of pilgrims transported to 6,654. Gone was the fanfare and adulation from earlier trips; their return was uneventful. The pilgrims spent a final night in New York City before catching separate trains to return home. In just a few short days, the pilgrimages were over.

With is customary military precision, the Quartermaster Corps tallied the scope of the trips. Forty-seven separate parties of pilgrims were transported a total of 3,800,000 miles during four years. Only four died on the trips—less than 10 percent of the original forecasted amount. Not one piece of baggage was lost along the way. Yet the trips succeeded not because of superior logistics but for the hearts they soothed and the minds they calmed.

Even today, the Gold Star mothers and widows pilgrimages of the 1930s are endlessly fascinating. The pilgrimages raise more questions than they answer. They combine large-scale issues, such as war and national identity, with personal loss, grief, and mourning. Were the pilgrimages the story of national elites manipulating the loss of mothers and widows for its own ends? Or were they simply a government's kind gesture that enabled thousands of grieving mothers to find some peace in their golden years? Did the pilgrimages fix women in their place as fit only to mourn their soldier dead? Or did the trips actually reveal to the military and the media thousands of strong women who were not the least bit hysterical during their cemetery visits?

One finds no easy answers to these questions today. My goal is to let readers make up their own minds regarding the pilgrimages and their place in history. My hope in writing this book has been to let the participants

10. Conclusion

speak for themselves through surviving diaries, letters, and other eyewitness accounts.

Making cemetery visits certainly did not originate after World War I. However, comrades and family members made unprecedented numbers of battlefield and cemetery visits after the war ended. Veterans groups such as the American Legion and war mothers and widows from all nations toured the battlefields and paused in war cemeteries. Even today, tour operators offer World War I packages, complete with battlefield and cemetery visits.

Allies of the United States saw the need for war grave pilgrimages and encouraged them at every turn. However, England, Canada, Australia, and New Zealand never seriously considered government-sponsored trips for its war mothers and widows. The distances were too large, and the costs were too great. Only the United States could muster the resources to send its war widows and mothers on all-expenses-paid pilgrimage after the war. Although the United States may not have won the war single-handedly, it did emerge as the world's only true superpower after World War I. Perhaps the pilgrimages may be viewed as America's coming out party on the world stage.

Yet the notion of a winning side in World War I is somewhat illusory. Commonsense wisdom today tells us World War I did little but kill millions and sow the seeds for an even more destructive World War II some 20 years later. There was no question millions of American doughboys helped turn the tide in World War I. Did those Gold Star mothers who survived to the beginning of World War II wonder what their dead sons had actually won in the trenches of France?

Yet by 1933, the Gold Star pilgrimages had largely left the popular imagination. By that time, the trips were relegated to short columns in the women's or society pages of newspapers—when they were reported at all. The *Paris Edition* ran front-page stories each day during Party A's visit in 1930. A one-column-inch blurb chronicled the last party's departure from Cherbourg harbor in 1933. By 1933, the parties were smaller, frailer, older, and frankly less newsworthy.

A sea change had occurred during the last five years, from the first approval by Congress of the pilgrimage bill in 1929 through the return of the final group in 1933. Twin forces of growing Nazi aggression in Germany and worldwide economic depression began to obscure the pilgrimages, much like a wall of smoke enveloped a war battlefield. The year 1933 was, in many ways, the depth of the Great Depression. Millions were out of work, and money concerns were the beginning of the end of the expatriate world of Paris's Left Bank.

By 1933, Germany, in the mind of many Americans, was not just the foe from World War I, it was also the home to a curious fellow named Hitler. The Allies had lost interest in policing Germany aggression; in 1933, the final Allied troops were withdrawn from the Rhine River bridgeheads. This end to the famous Watch on the Rhine preceded Hitler's rise to power. Press coverage of the trips began the ominous foreshadowing by placing pilgrimage stories next to those about Hitler's Germany. The *New York Times* reported a 1931 controversy about Nazis visiting a German cemetery in France. Another article in the *Times* commented on the unsolved disappearance of Polish intellectuals in Germany.

Perhaps the most ironic press juxtaposition took place with the last pilgrim party in 1933. The *New York Times* edition of August 18, 1933, reported that the last group of pilgrims had left France for their return to New York. "Last Gold Star Mothers Sail Home From France" signaled a retreat into America's then-typical isolationism. "The twenty or more officers who have been sent over annually to take care of these pilgrimages and the regular service that has been maintained here will now be disbanded," the article noted. "It is understood, also, that there will be a general decrease in United States Army personnel engaged in post-war work here."[1] The fact that American military personnel would return by the millions to Europe during World War II was years in the future.

Right next to this article on the final pilgrimage, the *Times* reported on a new German development. The article, "Publisher Scored for Hitler's Book," reported Houghton Mifflin had agreed to distribute Hitler's *Mein Kampf* in the United States. Jewish groups denounced the decision. One opponent was quoted as saying,

> They would do well to print the text in red, as symbolic of the blood that has dripped from Nazi bludgeons in the Third Reich, and to enclose its title page in a black border for the death-knell of civilization which this obsessed demagogue and his cohort of thugs have brought to the Germany of old.[2]

By 1933, many in Germany were already opposed to Hitler's new Reich. Some in America may have been aware of what was happening to the Germany of old, but most were too concerned with domestic problems at home to care.

This pilgrimage achievement was especially noteworthy given the Great Depression. Worldwide economic calamity was the second of two forces that forced the pilgrimages from the front pages. By the time the first pilgrimage party sailed in 1930, the country had begun its worst economic downturn in history. By 1933, the final year of the pilgrimages, the Depression was at its worst. Millions were out of work, and little relief was

10. Conclusion

Meuse-Argonne Cemetery today. The Meuse-Argonne American Cemetery is the largest American cemetery from any war located on foreign soil. More than 14,000 Americans are buried on its grounds. Today's cemeteries, with their mature trees and landscaped grounds, appear different than the newly constructed cemeteries the pilgrims visited. (American Battle Monuments Commission, Arlington, VA.)

in sight. Early that year, President Franklin Roosevelt took office, after beating incumbent Herbert Hoover in the 1932 election. Even these changes couldn't stop the pilgrimages. They concluded in 1933 as scheduled.

There is no record of any official discussion of stopping the pilgrimages for economic reasons once they began. The Quartermaster Corps' careful planning is a big reason. The trips, once under way, were remarkably free from incident and controversy. Moreover, the Corps' planning brought the trips in under budget, a big plus during the Depression.

Beyond the depths of the Depression and the rise of Hitler, the trips resonate for other reasons. The Gold Star mother pilgrimages remind us that historical eras do not begin and end neatly. The old doesn't necessarily replace the new; rather, these things coexist at the same time and even in the same place. Expatriate Paris is a good illustration. American artists, writers, musicians, and others sought refuge from the United States in Paris after World War I. Yet these same expatriates witnessed mothers and widows visiting Paris to mourn the loss of their sons and husbands. Moreover, many were quick to proclaim religion dead after the War. In Paris, however, pilgrims attended church services, said prayers, and drew on God for support during difficult cemetery visits. Religion was dead, in other words, for some but not for all.

Yet the Gold Star mothers, for me at least, remain a purely personal (not political) phenomenon. Most people who knew a mother or widow would want to do whatever was possible to help her say good-bye to her boy on foreign soil. The Gold Star mothers who were able to go on pilgrimages—or today's mothers who visit sick soldiers—are strong, admirable people.

Others think the same way. One Vietnam veteran put it this way on behalf of fellow veterans, but anyone who has come to know Gold Star Mothers, pilgrims or not, probably feels the same way. "I feel a reverence among vets for Gold Star moms," he said. "I tell you, when one of them walks by, it almost makes a drunk man sober. Hell, I don't know what it is. There's something about them."[3] I could not agree more.

Notes

Chapter 1

1. Exact numbers on the pilgrimages is somewhat hard to obtain. Press stories may report the total number of pilgrims who sail on the voyage or who return with their party. A one-page "Consolidated Report 1930 Pilgrimage War Mothers and Widows" listed 3,653 pilgrims sailing but reported 3,658 women actually began a pilgrimage on one of the 20 parties to sail the first year. The report may be found in the National Archives in Record Group 92, Quartermaster Corps, Box 47, W-198.

2. William Stevens Prince, *Crusade & Pilgrimage* (N.p.: Oregon Historical Society Press, 1986), 73.

3. Woodrow Wilson to Dr. Anna Howard Shaw, May 16, 1918, in Arthur S. Link, ed., *The Papers of Woodrow Wilson*, vol. 48 (Princeton: Princeton University Press, 1985), 28. See also p. 111 and 117 in same volume.

4. G. Kurt Piehler interview in Knoxville, Tennessee, June 24, 2001.

5. American Gold Star Mothers, *History* (Washington, DC: American Gold Star Mothers, 1970), 6.

6. *World Almanac* (New York: Press Publishing, 1919), 637.

7. Al Brown, Thomas Hoier, and Bernie Grossman, "There's a Service Flag Flying at Our House" (New York: J. Morris Music, 1917).

8. Theodore Morse and Casper Nathan, "When a Blue Star Turns to Gold" (New York: Leo Feist, 1918).

9. Nathan Conney, J. Edward Woolley, and Paul L. Specht, "The Heavens Are a Mother's Service Flag" (Reading, PA: Monarch Music, 1919).

10. American Gold Star Mothers, *History*, 1.

11. Valerie May interview in Knoxville, Tennessee, June 24, 2001.

12. May interview.

13. Teresa Davis interview in Knoxville, Tennessee, June 24, 2001.

14. G. Kurt Piehler interview in Knoxville, Tennessee, June 24, 2001.

15. Robert Ginsburg, "This, Too, Is America," *American Legion* 15 (November 1933), 16.

16. Louis C. Wilson, "The War Mother Goes Over There," *Quartermaster Review* (May–June 1930), 25.

17. Eva Trowbridge, "Williston Gold Star Mother Tells of Trip to Grave of Son in France," *Williams County (North Dakota) Farmer Press* (July 31, 1930), 5.

18. Menu on board the *S.S. President Harding*, July 1932. In Grace Ziegler's pilgrimage scrapbook.

19. Trowbridge, p. 5.

20. Anne Somers House, "War Mothers Hear Pershing Eulogize Songs at Memorial," *Chicago Tribune Paris Edition* (June 2, 1930), 3.

21. "The War Mother Goes Over There," p. 23.

22. Henrietta L. Haug, ed. *Gold Star Mothers of Illinois* (Brussels, IL.: N.p., 1941), 132.

23. *Ibid.*, 181.

24. "The War Mother Goes Over There," p. 25.

25. Rebecca Jo Plant interview in Nashville, Tennessee, March 12, 2002.
26. Haug, p. 55.
27. Haug, p. 132.
28. "Gold Star Mothers," *L'Intranigeant* (August 14, 1930), 185. In Col. Richard Ellis scrapbook, RG 92, entry 1908.
29. *Chicago Tribune Paris Edition* (July 8, 1930), in Col. Richard T. Ellis scrapbook, National Archives, RG 92, Entry 1908, 138.
30. *Ibid.*, 138.
31. Trowbridge, 5.

Chapter 2

1. David F. Trask, *The A.E.F. and Coalition Warmaking 1917–1918* (Lawrence: University Press of Kansas, 1993), 5.
2. *Ibid.*, 4.
3. John Keegan, *The First World War* (New York: Vintage Books, 1998), 372.
4. Leonard P. Ayres, *The War with Germany: A Statistical Summary* (Washington, DC: Government Printing Office, 1919), 56.
5. Paul Fussell, *The Great War and Modern Memory* (London: Oxford University Press, 1975), 153.
6. Charles C. Krulak, "Through the Wheat to the Beaches Beyond: The Lasting Impact of the Battle for Belleau Wood," *Marine Corps Gazette* (July 1998), 13.
7. Ayres, *The War with Germany*, 21.
8. William S. Prince interview in Bend, Oregon, December 18, 1999.
9. Francis P. Duffy, *Father Duffy's Story* (New York: George H. Doran, 1919), 68.
10. Kermit Roosevelt, ed., *Quentin Roosevelt: A Sketch with Letters* (New York: Charles Scribner's Sons, 1921), 151.
11. Edward M. Coffman interview in Lexington, Kentucky, July 23, 2001.
12. *Ibid.*
13. Henrietta L. Haug, ed., *Gold Star Mothers of Illinois* (Brussels, IL: N.p., 1941), 143.
14. Louis Hein, undated affidavit, in Alexander Norris GRS Burial file, RG 92.
15. Thomas Kane, undated affidavit, in Edward Pennington GRS Burial file, RG 92.
16. *The World Almanac* (New York: World Almanac Books, 2001), 209.
17. Coffman interview.
18. Erna Risch, *Quartermaster Support of the Army: A History of the Corps 1775–1939* (Washington, DC: Government Printing Office, 1989), 691.
19. *Ibid.*, 690.
20. *Ibid.*, 691.
21. James A. Moss and Harry S. Howland, *America in Battle* (Menasha, WI: Geo. Banta Publishing, 1920), 586–587.
22. Oscar Haug GRS Burial file, RG 92.
23. Winifred Lancy interview in Knoxville, Tennessee, June 24, 2001.
24. Stephen Graham, *The Challenge of the Dead* (London: Cassell & Company, 1921), 124.
25. *Ibid.*, 126.
26. "French Pleas to Let Our Dead Rest," *Literary Digest* 65 (April 17, 1920), 45.
27. *Ibid.*, 45.
28. "Returning Our Dead from France," *Literary Digest* 64 (January 3, 1920), 35.
29. *Ibid.*, 34.
30. Charles Henry Brent, "Forever Overseas," *The World's Work* 43 (December 1921), 136.
31. "Roosevelt Objects to Removal of Son," *New York Times* (November 18, 1918), 11.
32. U.S. Congress. House Committee on Military Affairs, *To Authorize Mothers of Deceased World War Veterans Buried in Europe to Visit the Graves: Hearings before the Committee on Military Affairs*, 68th Cong., 1st sess., 1924, 20.
33. *Ibid.*, 21.
34. *Ibid.*, 3–4.
35. *Ibid.*
36. Haug, *Gold Star Mothers of Illinois*, 40.
37. *Ibid.*
38. G. Kurt Piehler interview in Knoxville, Tennessee, June 24, 2001.
39. *Ibid.*
40. American Battle Monuments Commission, *Annual Report Fiscal Year 1926* (Washington, DC: Government Printing Office, 1926), 17.
41. *Ibid.*
42. Risch, *Quartermaster Support*, 695.
43. Piehler interview.
44. Coffman interview.
45. Chris Rosing interview in Cincinnati, February 2, 2002.
46. Elizabeth S. Grossman, "Architecture for a Public Client: The Monuments and Chapels of the American Battle Monuments Commission," *Journal of the American Society of Architectural Historians* 43 (May 1984), 142.
47. *American Armies and Battlefields in Europe* (Washington, DC: Government Printing Office, 1938, 1992), 465.

48. *Ibid.*, 138.
49. Coffman interview.

Chapter 3

1. James J. Hudson, *Hostile Skies: A Combat History of the American Air Service in World War I* (Syracuse, NY: Syracuse University Press, 1968), 97.
2. *Ibid.*, 246.
3. *Ibid.*
4. U.S. Congress, House, Committee on Military Affairs, *To Authorize Mothers and Unmarried Widows of Deceased World War Veterans Buried in Europe to Visit the Graves*, 70th Cong., 1st Sess., January 27, 1928, 27 (hereafter cited as *1928 House Hearing*).
5. U.S. Congress, Senate, Committee on Military Affairs, *To Authorize Mothers and Widows of Deceased World War Veterans Buried in Europe to Visit the Graves*, 71st Cong., 2nd Sess., May 14, 1928, 13 (hereafter cited as the *1928 Senate Hearing*).
6. U.S. Congress, House, Committee on Military Affairs, *To Authorize Mothers of Deceased War Veterans Buried in Europe to Visit the Graves*, 68th Cong., 1st Sess., February 19, 1924, 12–13. (hereafter cited as the *1924 Hearing*).
7. *Ibid.*, 15.
8. *Ibid.*, 19.
9. *Ibid.*, 20.
10. *Ibid.*, 1.
11. *Ibid.*, 11.
12. *Ibid.*, 10.
13. *Ibid.*, 18.
14. *Ibid.*, 21.
15. *Ibid.*, 15.
16. *Congressional Record*, 71st Cong., 2nd Sess., 72, pt. 6, April 9, 1930, 6765.
17. *1924 Hearing*, 29.
18. *Ibid.*, 23.
19. American Red Cross Website, www.redcross.org, October 1, 2002.
20. *1928 Senate Hearing*, 5.
21. *1928 House Hearing*, 2.
22. *1928 Senate Hearing*, 8.
23. *Ibid.*, 23.
24. *Ibid.*
25. *Proceedings of the Tenth National Convention of the American Legion, San Antonio, Texas, October 8–11, 1928*, 70th Cong., 2nd Sess., H.Doc 388, Serial Set 9010, 47.
26. *1928 Senate Hearing*, 3.
27. *Ibid.*
28. *Ibid.*, 19.
29. *Ibid.*, 19–20.
30. *1928 House Hearing*, 20–21.
31. *Ibid.*, 26.
32. *1928 Senate Hearing*, 10.
33. *Ibid.*, 27.
34. Alison Davis Wood, discussion with the author, after Ms. Wood's interviews with the Gold Star mothers in Knoxville, Tennessee, 2001.
35. Rebecca Jo Plant interview, Nashville, Tennessee, March 18, 2002.
36. G. Kurt Piehler interview, Knoxville, Tennessee, June 24, 2001.
37. *1928 House Hearing*, 23.
38. *1928 Senate Hearing*, 24.
39. *Ibid.*, 7.
40. *Ibid.*
41. *Ibid.*, 22.
42. *Ibid.*, 17.
43. *Ibid.*, 25, covering the entire exchange between Senators Bingham and Wagner.
44. *1928 House Hearing*, 24.
45. *Ibid.*, 21.
46. *Ibid.*
47. *Ibid.*, 22.
48. William S. Prince interview, Bend, Oregon, December 17, 1999.
49. *Congressional Record*, 71st Cong., 2nd Sess., 72 pt. 4, February 17, 1930, 3804.
50. *1928 Senate Hearing*, 9.
51. *1928 House Hearing*, 21.
52. *Ibid.*, 27.
53. *1928 Senate Hearing*, 13.
54. *1928 House Hearing*, 27.
55. Public Law 70–272.
56. *Ibid.*
57. *Ibid.*
58. U.S. Congress, House, Subcommittee on Appropriations, *Expenses of Pilgrimages to American Cemeteries in Europe*, 71st Cong., 2nd Sess., January 21, 1930, 10.
59. *Ibid.*, 4.
60. *Ibid.*, 7.
61. U.S. Congress, House, Committee on Military Affairs, *To Authorize Mothers of Deceased World War Veterans Buried in Europe to Visit the Graves*, 71st Cong., 2nd Sess., December 17, 1929, 1 (hereafter cited as *1929 Hearing*).
62. *Ibid.*, 2.
63. *Congressional Record*, 71st Cong., 2nd Sess., February 17, 1930, 72 pt. 4, 3803.
64. Public Law 71–227.
65. *1929 Hearing*, 10.
66. "Asks Trip for Fathers," *New York Times*, February 14, 1930, 15.

67. *1928 Senate Hearing*, 18.
68. *Chicago Tribune Paris Edition*, May 30, 1930, 10.
69. *1928 House Hearing*, 25.
70. *Ibid.*, 27.
71. *Ibid.*, 29.
72. *Ibid.*, 28.
73. Letter to the editor, *New York Times*, January 17, 1933, 8.
74. Letter to the editor, *New York Times*, January 22, 1933, sect. 4, 5.
75. Letter to the editor, *New York Times*, February 8, 1930, 14.
76. Letter to the editor, *New York Times*, April 18, 1932, 14.
77. Mrs. C. D. DuBois to President Herbert Hoover, March 17, 1930, in Presidential Personal Files, Gold Star Mothers 1929–1931, Herbert Hoover Presidential Library.

Chapter 4

1. U.S. Congress, House, Committee on Military Affairs, *To Authorize Mothers of Deceased War Veterans Buried in Europe to Visit the Graves*, 68th Cong., 1st Sess., Hearing February 19, 1924, 33.
2. E. B. Garey, O. O. Ellis, and R. V. D. Magoffin, *American Guide Book to France and its Battlefields* (New York: Macmillan, 1920), 48.
3. *Ibid.*, 48.
4. *Ibid.*, 49.
5. "The Pilgrimage Story Chapter X," *American War Mother*, July 1932, 8.
6. *Ibid.*
7. *Ibid.*
8. *Ibid.*
9. "Gold Star Mothers' Tour," *New York Times*, March 15, 1925, 16.
10. U.S. Congress, House, "Proceedings of the Tenth National Convention of the American Legion," 70th Cong., 2nd Sess., 1929, H. Doc. 70-388 (Serial 9010), 245.
11. *Ibid.*, 244.
12. "Bon Voyage" (advertisement), *American Legion Monthly*, September 1927, 7.
13. American Legion Tenth National Convention Report, 250.
14. *Ibid.*, 251.
15. Philip Von Blon and Marquis James, "The A.E.F. Comes Home," *American Legion Monthly*, December 1927, 39.
16. American Legion Tenth National Convention Report, 254.
17. "Times Star Offers to Send Gold Star Mothers to France," *Cincinnati Times-Star*, May 25, 1927, 8.
18. *Ibid.*
19. *Ibid.*
20. Blon and James, "The A.E.F. Comes Home," 72.
21. *Ibid.*, 30.
22. *Ibid.*
23. David W. Lloyd, *Battlefield Tourism: Pilgrimage and Commemoration of the Great War in Britain, Australia and Canada, 1919–1939* (Oxford: Berg, 1998), 107.
24. *Ibid.*, 160.
25. "Gold Star Mothers and Vets Miss King on Visit to Belgian Capital and Palace," *Chicago Tribune, Paris Edition*, May 30, 1930, 1.
26. Francis P. Duffy, *Father Duffy's Story* (New York: George H. Doran, 1919), 16.
27. *Ibid.*
28. *Ibid.*, 336.
28. *Ibid.*, 338.
30. *Ibid.*, 69.
31. *Ibid.*, 96.
32. *Ibid.*, 97.
33. *Ibid.*
34. Lt. Col. William J. Donovan, affidavit dated October 11, 1918, Joyce Kilmer GRS File, RG 92, National Archives.
35. Kenton Kilmer, *Memories of My Father, Joyce Kilmer* (New Brunswick, NJ: Joyce Kilmer Centennial Commission, 1993), 119–120.
36. Annie Kilburn Kilmer, *Memories of My Son, Sergeant Joyce Kilmer* (New Brunswick, NJ: Brentano's, 1920), 13.
37. Annie K. Kilmer, reply to War Department letter dated October 7, 1929, Joyce Kilmer GRS File, RG 92, National Archives.
38. Annie Kilburn Kilmer, *Leaves from My Life* (New York: Frye, 1925), 130–31.
39. F. B. Kilmer to War Department, October 18, 1920, Joyce Kilmer GRS File, RG 92, National Archives.
40. Kilmer, *Memories of My Son*, 12.
41. *Ibid.*
42. *Ibid.*, 15.
43. James J. Hudson, *Hostile Skies: A Combat History of the American Air Service in World War I* (Syracuse: Syracuse University Press, 1968), 97.
44. Kermit Roosevelt, ed., *Quentin Roosevelt, A Sketch with Letters* (New York: Charles Scribner's Sons, 1921), 163–64.
45. *Ibid.*, 164.
46. *Ibid.*, 121.
47. *Ibid.*, 175–76.

48. *Ibid.*, 168.
49. *Ibid.*, 172.
50. *Ibid.*, 175–76.
51. *Ibid.*, 177.
52. *Ibid.*, 165.
53. Edward J. Renehan Jr., *The Lion's Pride: Theodore Roosevelt and His Family in Peace and War* (New York: Oxford University Press, 1998), 198.
54. "Roosevelt Objects to Removal of Son," *New York Times* November 18, 1918, 11.
55. Sylvia Jukes Morris, *Edith Kermit Roosevelt. Portrait of a First Lady* (New York: Coward, McCann & Geoghegan, 1980), 442.
56. U.S. Congress, Senate, Committee on Military Affairs, *To Authorize Mothers and Unmarried Widows of Deceased World War Veterans Buried in Europe to Visit the Graves*, 70th Cong., 2nd Sess., Hearing May 14, 1928, 2.
57. In Kermit Roosevelt, ed., Quentin Roosevelt: A Sketch with letters (New York: Charles Scribner's Sons, 1921).
58. U.S. Congress, House, Committee on Military Affairs, *To Authorize Mothers and Unmarried Widows of Deceased World War Veterans Buried in Europe to Visit the Graves*, 70th Cong., 1st Sess., Hearing January 27, 1928, 26.
59. U.S. Congress, House, Committee on Military Affairs, *To Authorize Mothers of Deceased World War Veterans Buried in Europe to Visit the Graves*, 71st Cong., 2nd Sess., Hearing December 17, 1929, 19.
60. "War Mothers Turn to Field of Battle," *New York Times*, May 24, 1930, 17.

Chapter 5

1. G. Kurt Piehler interview, Knoxville, Tennessee, June 24, 2001.
2. Connie Potter interview, Washington, DC, December 9, 1999.
3. U.S. Congress, House, Subcommittee on Appropriations, *Expenses of Pilgrimages to American Cemeteries in Europe*, 71st Cong., 2nd Sess., 1930, 2.
4. *Ibid.*, 6.
5. *Ibid.*
6. A. D. Hughes, "Pilgrims," *Quartermaster Review* (May–June 1931), 31.
7. John J. Noll, "Crosses," *American Legion* (September 1930), 14.
8. Major John T. Harris to Mrs. Anna Norris, June 29, 1929, Alexander Norris GRS File, RG 92, National Archives.
9. Major John T. Harris to Mrs. Anna Norris, October 7, 1929, Alexander Norris GRS File, RG 92, National Archives.
10. "Medals Used to Identify Gold Star Pilgrims," *New York Times*, April 23, 1930, 23.
11. Captain A. D. Hughes to Mrs. Anna Norris, March 20, 1930, Alexander Norris GRS File, RG 92, National Archives.
12. *Pilgrimage Regulations* (Washington, DC: Government Printing Office, 1930), 3.
13. War Department to Mrs. Anna Norris, April 21, 1930, Alexander Norris GRS File, RG 92, National Archives.
14. 22 CFR 51.62.
15. Captain A. D. Hughes to Mrs. Anna Norris, March 20, 1930, Alexander Norris GRS File, RG 92, National Archives.
16. Paul Fussell, *The Great War and Modern Memory* (London: Oxford University Press, 1975), 186.
17. Henrietta Haug to War Department, May 6, 1930, Oscar Haug GRS File, RG 92, National Archives.
18. Captain A. D. Hughes to Mrs. Henrietta Haug, May 13, 1930, Oscar Haug GRS File, RG 92, National Archives.
19. William John Thomas and Naomi Thomas to the Quartermaster General, April 28, 1930, William I. Penry GRS File, RG 92, National Archives.
20. Captain A. D. Hughes to Mrs. Andrew Reid, May 2, 1930, Howell L. Reid GRS File, RG 92, National Archives.
21. *Ibid.*
22. Mrs. Nina Reid to War Department, May 6, 1930, Howell L. Reid GRS File, RG 92, National Archives.
23. Maj. Gen. Fred W. Sladen to Maj. Gen. John L. DeWitt, May 7, 1930, Howell L. Reid GRS File, RG 92, National Archives.
24. Mrs. Nina Reid to the Quartermaster General, June 17, 1930, Howell L. Reid GRS File, RG 92, National Archives.
25. Mr. E. E. Bleckley to Maj. John T. Harris, July 8, 1929, Erwin Bleckley GRS File, RG 92, National Archives.
26. W. A. Ayres to Maj. John T. Harris, July 11, 1929, Erwin Bleckley GRS File, RG 92, National Archives.
27. Maj. General B. F. Cheatham to W. A. Ayres, July 18, 1929, Erwin Bleckley GRS File, RG 92, National Archives.
28. Party O Itinerary, Meuse-Argonne Group, 1932, Erwin Bleckley GRS File, RG 92, National Archives.
29. Darle McGough affidavit, undated,

Roy Moran GRS File, RG 92, National Archives.

30. Charles E. Moran to Starr Cadwallader, November 6, 1919, Roy Moran GRS File, RG 92, National Archives.

31. Report of Disinterment and Reburial, September 21, 1921, Roy Moran GRS File, RG 92, National Archives.

32. Hughes, "Pilgrims," 35.

33. Speech by Maj. Gen. John L. DeWitt, April 15, 1930, in Col. Richard T. Ellis Scrapbook, RG 92, Entry 1908, National Archives, 3.

34. Robert Ginsburgh, "This Too Is America," *American Legion Monthly* (November 1933), 50.

35. Mrs. E. H. I. Robinson to Col. Richard T. Ellis, September 3, 1931, Col. Richard T. Ellis Scrapbook, RG 92, Entry 1908, National Archives, 1–2.

36. "Last War Mothers Start Return Trip," *New York Times*, September 23, 1930, 5.

37. DeWitt speech, 1.

38. *Ibid.*, 2.

39. *Ibid.*, 3

40. *Ibid.*

41. Edward Coffman interview, Lexington, Kentucky, July 23, 2001.

42. *New York Daily News*, in Col. Richard T. Ellis Scrapbook, RG 92, Entry 1908, National Archives, 12.

43. *Ibid.*

44. *Ibid.*

45. DeWitt speech, 2.

46. Ginsburgh, "This Too Is America," 51.

47. Ann Wolf, telephone interview with the author, June 28, 2002.

48. Marvin Fletcher interview, Athens, Ohio, July 24, 2001.

49. Dellah Mae Miller to the Army Quartermaster General, August 22, 1932, RG 92, Entry 1904, Box 50, Folder 201.22, National Archives.

Chapter 6

1. U.S. War Department, *Pilgrimage Regulations* (Washington, DC: Government Printing Office, 1930), 4.

2. Marvin Fletcher interview, Athens, Ohio, July 24, 2001.

3. Edward "Mac" Coffman interview, Lexington, Kentucky, July 23, 2001.

4. "Capital Rebuffs Gold Star Negroes," *New York Times*, May 30, 1930, 21.

5. *Ibid.*

6. "Government Goes Jim Crow," *The World Tomorrow* (August 1930), 325.

7. "Black Stars and Gold," *The Nation* (July 23, 1930), 85.

8. *Ibid.*, 86.

9. *Ibid.*

10. Tom Canty to George Akerson, May 30, 1930, Herbert Hoover Presidential Library Presidential Papers, Subject File: Gold Star Mothers.

11. Maurice Spencer to Herbert Hoover, February 19, 1930, Herbert Hoover Presidential Library Presidential Papers, Subject File: Gold Star Mothers.

12. "Gold Star Mothers," *L'Intransigeant* (August 14, 1930) in Col. Richard T. Ellis Scrapbook, National Archives RG 92, Entry 1908, p. 185.

13. Chatham Unit, American Legion Auxiliary, Savannah, Georgia, to Herbert Hoover, May 31, 1930, Herbert Hoover Presidential Library Presidential Papers, Subject File: Gold Star Mothers.

14. Donald J. Lisio, *Hoover, Blacks & Lily-Whites: A Study of Southern Strategies* (Chapel Hill: University of North Carolina Press, 1985), 235.

15. Barbara Ransby interview, Chicago, Illinois, March 27, 2003.

16. Coffman interview.

17. Elnora Davis McLendon to the author, June 26, 2000.

18. Marvin Fletcher interview, Athens, Ohio, July 24, 2001.

19. "Gold Star Negroes Guests Here Today," *New York Times* (July 11, 1930), 10.

20. *Ibid.*

21. "Negroes Assail Bias at Fete at City Hall," *New York Times* (July 12, 1930), 30.

22. *Ibid.*

23. "Report, Liaison Officer, Party L," Benjamin O. Davis in Benjamin O. Davis, Sr. Papers, Military History Institute, Papers: Official Correspondence, 1930–1940, July 12, 1930, 1.

24. *Ibid.*

25. *Ibid.*, 2.

26. "Arrival in France of Colored Mothers," *Le Matin* (July 22, 1930), in Col. Richard T. Ellis scrapbook, National Archives RG 92, Entry 1908, 153.

27. "Negro Mothers Will Go Friday to Visit Graves: Gold Star Group Will Return for Fried Chicken Dinner," *Chicago Tribune, Paris Edition* (July 23, 1930), 3.

28. "Negro Mothers See Hot Show,"

Chicago Tribune, Paris Edition (July 31, 1930), 8.
29. *Ibid.*
30. "Report, Liaison Officer, Party L," 2.
31. *Ibid.*
32. *Ibid.*, 3.
33. *Ibid.*
34. *Ibid.*, 4.
35. "Praises Gold Star Trip," *New York Times* (August 8, 1930), 34.
36. "Report, Liaison Officer, Party L," 3–4.
37. Connie Potter, "World War I Gold Star Mothers Pilgrimages, Part II," *Prologue* 31 (Fall 1999), 215.
38. *Ibid.*
39. "Farewell Ceremony for Gold Star Mothers on Board SS *American Farmer*, Pier 4, Hoboken, NJ, 3 p.m., May 29, 1931." In Benjamin O. Davis Sr. Papers, Military History Institute, Papers: Official Correspondence, 1930–1940, 1.
40. *Ibid.*, 1–2.
41. "Greeted by Sissle Band at Station," *Chicago Tribune, Paris Edition* (June 8, 1931), 1.
42. "Edge and Pershing Speak at Reception," *Chicago Tribune, Paris Edition* (June 9, 1931), 2.
43. *Ibid.*
44. Will Barber, "Paris Enraptures Negro Gold Stars and Not Perhaps," *Chicago Tribune, Paris Edition* (June 10, 1931), 1, 5.
45. *Ibid.*
46. *Ibid.*
47. *Ibid.*
48. Waverley Root, *The Paris Edition: The Autobiography of Waverley Root 1927–1934* (San Francisco: North Point Press, 1987), 75.
49. "Negro Gold Stars Enjoy Vaudeville by Their Own Folk," *Chicago Tribune, Paris Edition* (June 20, 1931), 2.
50. *Ibid.*
51. *Ibid.*
52. F. Scott Fitzgerald, *Tender Is the Night* (New York: Charles Scribner's Sons, 1933), 100–101.
53. Barbara Ransby interview, Chicago, Illinois, March 27, 2003.
54. "Consolidated Report Steamship Liaison, East and West Voyages, Party K," Benjamin O. Davis Sr. Papers. Military History Institute, Papers: Official Correspondence, August 10, 1931, 2.
55. *Ibid.*
56. "Last Negro Group of 1931 Gold Star Pilgrims Arrives," *Chicago Tribune, Paris Edition* (July 20, 1931), 2.
57. "Negro Gold Star Mothers in France," *New York Times* (June 20, 1932), 7.
58. Barber, "Paris Enraptures Negro Gold Stars," 5.
59. *Ibid.*, 1, 5.
60. Benjamin O. Davis Jr., *Benjamin O. Davis, Jr.: American* (Washington, DC: Smithsonian Institution Press, 1991), 43.

Chapter 7

1. Grace Ziegler's scrapbook contains the clippings of her published diary. Grace's nephew, Ed Bliss of Durand, Illinois, had her scrapbook and kindly let me examine it. Grace has written page numbers in the book. All subsequent references to her article are marked "Diary." Diary, 8.
2. Mr. Bliss also has in his possession Grace's photo album, with captions in her writing. All subsequent references to the unpaginated album are marked "Photo Album." Photo Album.
3. U.S. Army, *American Military History* (Washington, DC: Government Printing Office, 1989), 413.
4. Rebecca Jo Plant interview, Nashville, Tennessee, March 18, 2002.
5. Fred Ziegler to Tressa Ziegler, April 5, 1918.
6. Fred Ziegler to Tressa Ziegler, April 27, 1918.
7. Fred Ziegler to Tressa Ziegler May 15, 1918.
8. U.S. Secretary of War, *Report of the Secretary of War to the President* (Washington, DC: Government Printing Office, 1926), 200.
9. Edward M. Coffman, *The War to End All Wars* (Madison: University of Wisconsin Press, 1986), 326.
10. Fred Ziegler to Tressa Ziegler, June 28, 1918.
11. Fred Ziegler to Tressa Ziegler, July 29, 1918.
12. Fred Ziegler to Tressa Ziegler, September 12, 1918.
13. Coffman, *War to End All Wars*, 326–27.
14. Fred Ziegler to Tressa Ziegler, October 3, 1918.
15. *Ibid.*
16. *Ibid.*
17. The Graves Registration Service burial files contain information on Gold Star mothers and widows. They are part of

Record Group 92 at the National Archives in College Park, Maryland. The records are filed under the name of the soldier who died. The file for Fred M. Ziegler contains information on his service and death, along with correspondence for Louise and Grace Ziegler's pilgrimage. This quote comes from an affidavit of Pvt. John Hanses, October 14, 1918, Ziegler GRS File, RG 92.
18. Disinterment, Preparation, Shipment and Reburial of Body report, Ziegler GRS File, RG 92.
19. *Ibid.*
20. War Department to Louise Ziegler, November 7, 1918, Ziegler GRS File, RG 92.
21. Lt. Col. G. G. Bartlett, to Louise Ziegler, May 18, 1932, Ziegler GRS File, RG 92.
22. Frank Lowden to Louise Ziegler, November 29, 1918.
23. Lt. Col G. G. Bartlett to Louise Ziegler, May 18, 1932, Ziegler GRS File, RG 92.
24. American Express Travel Department, *A Message to Friends and Relatives of Gold Star Mothers* (New York: American Express Travel Department, 1931), [5].
25. Louise Ziegler identification card, Ziegler GRS File, RG 92.
26. Fred and Ed Bliss interview, Durand, Illinois, May 11, 2002.
27. Diary, 1.
28. *Ibid.*
29. Diary, 2.
30. *Ibid.*
31. Diary, 3.
32. Diary, 2.
33. Diary, 3.
34. Diary, 4.
35. *Ibid.*
36. *Ibid.*
37. Diary, 5.
38. *Ibid.*
39. *Ibid.*
40. Diary, 6.
41. Diary, 5.
42. Diary, 6.
43. *Ibid.*
44. *Ibid.*
45. *Ibid.*
46. Diary, 7.
47. Diary, 8.
48. *Ibid.*
49. Steven Komarow, "WWI Markers around Europe Falling to Pieces," *USA Today*, May 25, 2001, A13.
50. Diary, 8.
51. *Ibid.*
52. *Ibid.*
53. Diary, 9.
54. *Ibid.*
55. *Ibid.*
56. William L. Shirer, *The Rise and Fall of the Third Reich* (New York: Simon and Schuster, 1960), 165.
57. Diary, 9.
58. Liaison Report, Party E, 1932, Ziegler GRS File, RG 92.
59. The poem may be found in Grace Ziegler's scrapbook.
60. Grace Ziegler, to Capt. R. E. Shannon, August 16, 1932, Ziegler GRS File, RG 92.
61. Maj. Gen. J. L. DeWitt, to Grace Ziegler, August 29, 1932, Ziegler GRS File, RG 92.
62. Fred and Ed Bliss interview, Durand, Illinois, May 11, 2002.

Chapter 8

1. "Gold Star Mothers Get City's Welcome," *New York Times*, May 7, 1930, 16.
2. *Ibid.*
3. John J. Noll, "Crosses," *American Legion Monthly* (September 1930), 15.
4. "Gold Star Mothers Get City's Welcome," 16.
5. "Gold Star Mothers Honored at Sailing," *New York Times*, May 8, 1930, 3.
6. Grace Robinson, "Dissension United with Tragedy Roils War Mothers' Trip," *Chicago Tribune, Paris Edition*, May 17, 1930, 1, 3.
7. *Ibid.*, 1.
8. *Ibid.*, 3.
9. *Ibid.*
10. *Ibid.*, 1, 3.
11. Maurer Maurer, ed. *The U.S. Air Service in World War I*, vol. 3 (Washington, DC: Government Printing Office, 1979), 625–27.
12. Minnie Throckmorton to GRS, August 5, 1923, in John Throckmorton GRS File, RG 92.
13. Correction in Stenciling on Grave Marker memo, May 27, 1920, Hugh S. Thompson GRS File, RG 92.
14. John Means Thompson to Maj. R. L. Foster, January 7, 1924, Hugh S. Thompson GRS File, RG 92.
15. *Ibid.*
16. John Means Thompson to Maj. Robert

L. Foster, January 14, 1924, Hugh S. Thompson GRS File, RG 92.

17. Minnie Throckmorton to pilgrimage escort officers, undated, John Throckmorton GRS File, RG 92.

18. "'What Strikes Me Most,' Told by Gold Star Mothers," *New York Herald, Paris Edition*, May 18, 1930, in Col. Richard T. Ellis scrapbook, Entry 1908, RG 92, 40.

19. "Dissension United with Tragedy Roils War Mothers' Trip," 1.

20. *Ibid.*, 3.

21. Noll, "Crosses," 15.

22. "Dissension United with Tragedy Roils War Mothers' Trip," 3.

23. "Gold Star Mothers Bow at Paris Tomb," *New York Times* May 18, 1930, 1.

24. Walter E. Edge, *Speeches and Public Statements* (Issoudun, France: Imprimerie Rapide du Central, 1933), 87.

25. "What Strikes Me Most," *New York Herald*, 40.

26. *Ibid.*

27. Helen L. Akin, "Sixteen Gold Star Mothers Lay Wreaths on Graves of Sons in Suresnes Cemetery," *Chicago Tribune, Paris Edition*, May 19, 1930, 2.

28. Akin, "Sixteen Gold Star Mothers," 1.

29. "17 Gold Star Mothers Pray at Graves of Sons Buried on Slopes of Mont Valerien Near Paris," *New York Times* May 19, 1930, 1.

30. Akin, "Sixteen Gold Star Mothers," 1–2.

31. "War Mothers Turn to Field of Battle," *New York Times*, May 24, 1930, 17.

32. "11 Germans Salute Gold Star Mothers," *New York Times*, May 23, 1930, 25.

33. Edmond L. Taylor, "Unexpected Drama Marks Pilgrimage of Gold Star Mothers to St. Mihiel," *Chicago Tribune, Paris Edition*, May 23, 1930, 3.

34. "11 Germans Salute Gold Star Mothers," 25.

35. Taylor, 3.

36. Akin, 2.

37. Akin, "Sixteen Gold Star Mothers," 2.

38. Medical Record, Anna Norris, May 21, 1930, in Alexander Norris GRS File, RG 92.

39. Edmond L. Taylor, "Mothers in Belleau and Oise-Aisne Bid Farewell to Graves," *Chicago Tribune, Paris Edition*, May 25, 1930, 3.

40. Noll, "Crosses," 53.

41. *Ibid.*, 54.

42. A. D. Hughes, "Pilgrims," *Quartermaster Review* (May–June 1931), 29.

43. Noll, "Crosses," 53.

44. "What Strikes Me Most," *New York Herald*, 40.

Chapter 9

1. "159 War Mothers Reach Brussels," *Chicago Tribune, Paris Edition* May 29, 1930, p. 3

2. Speech by Maj. Gen. John L. DeWitt, April 15, 1930, in Col. Richard T. Ellis scrapbook, RG 92, Entry 1908, p. 3.

3. Edmond Taylor, "Gold Star Mothers Honor Their Dead on Peaceful Hill Once Battle Torn," *Chicago Tribune, Paris Edition*, May 22, 1930, 3.

4. Lynn Cable, *Gold Stars and Purple Hearts*, master's thesis, East Tennessee State University, May 1993, 90.

5. *Ibid.*, p. 91–92.

6. Jane Wooten to John Graham, June 28, 1999.

7. David W. Lloyd *Battlefield Tourism: Pilgrimage and the Commemoration of the Great War in Britain, Australia and Canada, 1919–1939* (Oxford: Berg, 1998), 142.

8. Henrietta Haug, ed. *Gold Star Mothers of Illinois: A Collection of Notes Recording the Personal Histories of the Gold Star Mothers of Illinois* (Brussels, Illinois: N.p., 1941), 143.

9. Barbara Lepley to John Graham, April 2, 2004.

10. Don Brown, "Gold Star Mother Leaves for Bavaria with Son Who Fought in German Army," *Chicago Tribune, Paris Edition*, June 6, 1931, 1.

11. *Ibid.*

12. *Ibid.*

13. "War Mothers, Sisters, Meet after 57 Years." *New York Times* June 15, 1931, 2.

14. Haug, *Gold Star Mothers of Illinois*, 132.

15. *Ibid.*, 181.

16. *Ibid.*

17. James A. Moss and Harry S. Howland, *America in Battle: With Guide to the American Battlefields in France and Belgium* (Menasha, Wisc.: Geo. Banta, 1920), xi.

18. *Ibid.*, 493–94.

19. Lloyd, *Battlefield Tourism*, p. 5.

20. Mitch Yockelson interview, College Park, Maryland, December 10, 1999.

21. Ian Reader and Tony Walter, eds. *Pilgrimage in Popular Culture* (London: Macmillan, 1993), 77.
22. *Ibid.*, 82.
23. "Caretaker Grieves When 13 Mothers Miss Flanders Field," *Chicago Tribune, Paris Edition,* May 30, 1930, 3.
24. Virginia Bateman Hopkins to Herbert Hoover, September 10, 1930, in Presidential Papers, Secretary's File, Gold Star Mothers, 1929–1931, Herbert Hoover Presidential Library.
25. William Stevens Prince, *Crusade and Pilgrimage: A Soldier's Death, a Mother's Journey, and a Grandson's Quest* (N.p.: Oregon Historical Society Press, 1986), p. 96.
26. William Stevens Prince interview, Bend, Oregon, December 18, 1999.
27. Charles S. Dawes, *Journal as Ambassador to Great Britain* (New York: Macmillan, 1930), 210.
28. *Ibid.*
29. "Gold Star Mothers Extolled by Dawes." *New York Times* June 6, 1930, 15.
30. "Edge Pays Tribute to Gold Star Pilgrims as Courageous Women; Praises France, U.S.," *Chicago Tribune, Paris Edition,* September 11, 1930, 2.
31. Walter Edge, *Speeches and Public Statements* (Issoudon, France: Imprimerie Rapide du Central, 1933).
32. Eva Trowbridge, "Williston Gold Star Mother Tells of her Trip to Grave of Son in France," *Williams County (ND) Farmer Press,* July 31, 1930, 5.
33. *Ibid.*
34. *Ibid.*
35. Haug, *Gold Star Mothers of Illinois,* 150.
36. *Ibid.*, 151.
37. *Ibid.*, 152.
38. *Ibid.*, 153.
39. *Ibid.*, 152.
40. *Ibid.*, 154.
41. *Ibid.*, 153–54.
42. *Ibid.*, 153; emphasis in original.
43. *Ibid*; emphasis in original.
44. *Ibid.*, 154.
45. *Ibid.*
46. *Ibid.*, 156.
47. *Ibid.*, 156–57.
48. *Ibid.*, 157.
49. "Studio Problems," *New York Times,* June 25, 1933, IX, 3.
50. "The Screen," *New York Times,* July 13, 1933, 17.
51. "If You Have Tears," *New York Times,* July 16, 1933, IX, 3.
52. Philip Stevenson, "Gold Star Mother," *Esquire* (January 1935), 47.
53. *Ibid.*
54. *Ibid.*, 205.
55. *Ibid.*
56. *Ibid.*
57. Rebecca Jo Plant interview, Nashville, Tennessee, March 18, 2002.
58. Valerie May interview, Knoxville, Tennessee, June 24, 2001.
59. Mary Wheeler interview, Knoxville, Tennessee, June 24, 2001.
60. *Ibid.*

Chapter 10

1. "Last Gold Star Mothers Sail Home from France," *New York Times,* August 18, 1933, 16.
2. "Publisher Scored for Hitler's Book," *New York Times,* August 18, 1933, 16.
3. Jim Belshaw, "Gold Star Mothers," *VVA Veteran* (February/March 1999), 30.

Bibliography

American Battle Monuments Commission. *Flanders Field American Cemetery and Memorial.* Washington, DC: Government Printing Office, 1971.
_____. *Meuse-Argonne American Cemetery and Memorial.* Washington, DC: Government Printing Office, 1971.
_____. *33d Division: Summary of Operations in the World War.* Washington, DC: Government Printing Office, 1944.
American Gold Star Mothers. *History.* Washington, DC: American Gold Star Mothers, 1970.
Ayres, Leonard P. *The War with Germany: A Statistical Summary.* Washington, DC: Government Printing Office, 1919.
Baldwin, Hanson W. *World War I.* New York: Harper & Row, 1962.
Beatty, David Pearce, ed. *The Vimy Pilgrimage July 1936: From the Diary of Florence Murdock, Amherst, Nova Scotia.* Amherst, Nova Scotia: Acadian Printing, 1987.
Belshaw, Jim. "Gold Star Mothers." *VVA Veteran* (February/March 1999): 29–30.
Berton, Pierre. *Vimy.* New York: Penguin Books, 1987.
"Black Stars and Gold." *The Nation* 131 (July 23, 1930): 85–86.
Branson, N. E., and Nellie M. Dunn. "Gold Star Mother." Sedalia, Missouri: A. W. Perry's Sons, 1930.
Brent, Charles Henry. "Forever Overseas." *World's Work* 43 (December 1921): 135–37.
Brown, Al W., Thomas Hoier, and Bernie Grossman. "There's a Service Flag Flying at Our House." New York: J. Morris Music, 1917.
Budreau, Lisa M. "Mourning and the Making of a Nation: The Gold Star Mothers Pilgrimages, 1930–33." 2002, unpublished.
Cable, Lynne. "Gold Stars and Purple Hearts." Master's thesis, East Tennessee State University, 1993.
Chicago Tribune, Paris Edition. 1930–33. Commonly called the *Paris Edition.*
Clark, Mary Sine. "If They Consent to Leave Them over There." *Virginia Cavalcade* 50 (summer 2001): 134–41.
Cochran, Joseph Wilson. *Friendly Adventurers: A Chronicle of the American Church in Paris 1857–1931.* Paris: Brentano's, 1931.
Coffman, Edward. *The War to End All Wars.* Madison: University of Wisconsin Press, 1968.
Congressional Record. 1919–35.

Conney, Nathan A., J. Edward Woolley, and Paul L. Specht. "The Heavens Are a Mother's Service Flag." Reading, Penns.: Monarch Music, 1919.
Cornebise, Alfred Emile. *Art from the Trenches*. College Station: Texas A&M University Press, 1991.
Crary, Dean. "Keeping Their Tryst with God." Guide Rock, Neb.: Dean Crary, 1927.
Crowell, Benedict. *American's Munitions, 1917–1918*. Washington, DC: Government Printing Office, 1919.
Davis, Benjamin O., Jr. *Benjamin O. Davis, Jr.: American*. Washington, DC: Smithsonian Institution Press, 1991.
Davis, Benjamin O., Sr. Records kept as an escort officer during the pilgrimages are located in the Military History Institute, U.S. Army War College, Carlisle Barracks, Pennsylvania. 20 boxes of papers, "Memoir, Correspondence, and Inspection Reports."
Dawes, Charles G. *Journal as Ambassador to Great Britain*. New York: Macmillan, 1930.
Dooly, William G. Jr. *Great Weapons of World War I*. New York: Walker, 1969.
Duffy, Francis P. *Father Duffy's Story*. New York: George H. Doran, 1919.
Edge, Walter E. *Speeches and Public Statements*. Issoudun, France: Imprimerie Rapide du Central, 1933.
Fish, Hamilton. *Memoir of an American Patriot*. Washington, DC: Regnery Gateway, 1991.
Fitzgerald, F. Scott. *Tender Is the Night*. New York: Charles Scribner's Sons, 1933.
Fletcher, Marvin. *America's First Black General*. Lawrence: University Press of Kansas, 1989.
"French Pleas to Let Our Dead Rest." *Literary Digest* 65 (April 17, 1920): 45.
Fussell, Paul. *The Great War and Modern Memory*. London: Oxford University Press, 1975.
Garey, E. B., O. O. Ellis, and R. V. D. Magoffin. *American Guide Book to France and Its Battlefields*. New York: Macmillan, 1920.
Gillis, John R., ed. *Commemorations: The Politics of National Identity*. Princeton, N.J.: Princeton University Press, 1994.
Ginsburgh, Robert. "This, Too, Is America." *American Legion Magazine* 15 (November 1933): 16–19, 49–52.
"Gold Star Mothers of Nebraska Make First Voyage to France." *United States Daily* 4 (February 8, 1930): 3.
"The Government Goes Jim Crow." *World Tomorrow* 13 (August 1930): 325.
Graham, John W. "Quentin Roosevelt and the Gold Star Mothers Pilgrimages." *Over the Front* 19 (fall 2004): 222–236.
Graham, Stephen. *The Challenge of the Dead*. London: Cassell & Company, 1921.
Grossman, Elizabeth S. "Architecture for a Public Client: The Monuments and Chapels of the American Battle Monuments Commission." *Journal of the American Society of Architectural Historians* 43 (May 1984): 119–43.
Haug, Henrietta, ed. *Gold Star Mothers of Illinois*. Brussels, Ill.: N.p., 1941.
Hoover, Herbert. Presidential Subject File, Herbert Hoover Presidential Library, West Branch, Iowa.
Hornung, Charlotte. *Arizona's Frank Luke*. Phoenix: D & L Press, 1976.
Hudson, James J. *Hostile Skies: A Combat History of the American Air Service in World War I*. Syracuse: Syracuse University Press, 1968.
Hughes, A. D. "Pilgrims." *Quartermaster Review* (May–June 1931): 29–41.
Infantry in Battle, 2nd ed. Washington, DC: Infantry Journal, 1939.

Jolas, Eugene. *Man from Babel*. Andreas Kramer and Rainer Rumold, eds. New Haven: Yale University Press, 1998.
Josephy, Alvin M. Jr., ed. *The American Heritage History of World War I*. New York: American Heritage Book Publishing, 1964.
Keegan, John. *The First World War*. New York: Vintage Books, 1998.
Kennett, Lee. "The A.E.F. through French Eyes." *Military Review* 52 (November 1972): 3–11.
Kilmer, Annie Kilburn. *Leaves from My Life*. New York: Frye Publishing, 1925.
———. *Memories of My Son, Sergeant Joyce Kilmer*. New York: Brentano's, 1920.
Kilmer, Kenton. *Memories of My Father, Joyce Kilmer*. New Brunswick, NJ: Joyce Kilmer Centennial Commission, 1993.
Knapp, Michael. "World War I Service Records." *Prologue* 22 (fall 1990): 300–303.
———, and Constance Potter. "Here Rests in Honored Glory: World War I Graves Registration." *Prologue* 23 (summer 1991): 190–93.
Koch, Fred. *Flamethrowers of the German Army 1914–1945*. Atglen, Penn.: Schiffer Military History, 1997.
Krulak, Charles C. "Through the Wheat to the Beaches Beyond." *Marine Corps Gazette* 82 (July 1998): 12–17.
Lisio, Donald J. *Hoover, Blacks & Lily-Whites: A Study of Southern Strategies*. Chapel Hill: University of North Carolina Press, 1985.
Lloyd, David W. *Battlefield Tourism: Pilgrimage and Commemoration of the Great War in Britain, Australia and Canada, 1919–1939*. Oxford: Berg, 1998.
Love, Albert G. *The Medical Department of the United States in the World War*. "Statistics," pt. 2, "Medical and Casualty Statistics." Washington, DC: Government Printing Office, 1925.
Maurer, Maurer. *The U.S. Air Service in World War I*, 4 vols. Maxwell AFB, Alabama: Albert F. Simpson Historical Research Center, distributed by Government Printing Office, 1978–1979.
Morris, Sylvia Jukes. *Edith Kermit Roosevelt: Portrait of a First Lady*. New York: Coward, McCann & Geoghegan, 1980.
Morrow, John Howard. *The Great War in the Air: Military Aviation from 1909 to 1921*. Washington, DC: Smithsonian Institution Press, 1993.
Moss, James A., and Harry S. Howland. *America in Battle: With Guide to the American Battlefields in France and Belgium*. Menasha, Wisc.: Geo. Banta Publishing, 1920.
Mosse, George L. *Fallen Soldiers: Reshaping the Memory of the World Wars*. Oxford: Oxford University Press, 1990.
"Mrs. Slagle, Macon's 'Gold Star Mother,' Tells of Trip to France." *Franklin Press* (North Carolina) (October 16, 1930): 6–7.
Nathan, Casper, and Theodore Morse. "When a Blue Service Star Turns to Gold." New York: Leo. Feist, 1918.
New York Times. 1929–1933.
Noll, John J. "Crosses." *American Legion Magazine* 9 (September 1930): 14–17, 52–54.
Piehler, G. Kurt. *Remembering War the American Way*. Washington, DC: Smithsonian Institution Press, 1995.
Potter, Constance. "World War I Gold Star Mothers Pilgrimages, Part I." *Prologue* 31 (summer 1999): 140–145.
———. "World War I Gold Star Mothers Pilgrimages, Part II." *Prologue* 31 (fall 1999): 210–15.
Prince, William Stevens. *Crusade & Pilgrimage: A Soldier's Death, a Mother's Journey, & a Grandson's Quest*. N.p.: Oregon Historical Society Press, 1986.

Reader, Ian, and Tony Walter, eds. *Pilgrimage in Popular Culture.* London: Macmillan, 1993.
Renehan, Edward J. Jr. *The Lion's Pride: Theodore Roosevelt and His Family in Peace and War.* New York: Oxford University Press, 1998.
"Returning Our Dead from France." *Literary Digest* 64 (January 3, 1920): 34–35.
Risch, Erna. *Quartermaster Support of the Army: A History of the Corps 1775–1939.* Washington, DC: Government Printing Office, 1980.
Roosevelt, Kermit, ed. *Quentin Roosevelt: A Sketch with Letters.* New York: Charles Scribner's Sons, 1921.
Root, Waverley. *The Paris Edition.* San Francisco: North Point Press, 1987.
Stevenson, Philip. "Gold Star Mother." *Esquire* 4 (January, 1935): 47, 205.
Stovall, Tyler Edward. *Paris Noir: African Americans in the City of Light.* Boston: Houghton Mifflin, 1996.
Trask, David F. *The A.E.F. and Coalition Warmaking 1917–1918.* Lawrence: University Press of Kansas, 1993.
Trowbridge, Eva. "Williston Gold Star Mother Tells of Trip." *Williams County Farmer Press* (North Dakota) (July 31, 1930): 5.
United States. Army. Center of Military History. *American Armies and Battlefields of Europe.* Washington, DC: Government Printing Office, 1938, 1992.
_____. Congress. House of Representatives. *Pilgrimage for the Mothers and Widows of Soldiers, Sailors, and Marine Forces Now Interred in the Cemeteries in Europe.* 71st Congress, 2nd Session, H. Doc. 71-1404. Washington, DC: Government Printing Office, 1930.
_____. _____. _____. Committee on Appropriations. *Expenses of Pilgrimages to American Cemeteries in Europe.* 71st Congress, 1st Session, 1930. Washington, DC: Government Printing Office, 1930.
_____. _____. _____. Committee on Military Affairs. *Authorizing Mothers of Deceased World War Veterans to Visit Graves in Europe.* 68th Congress, 1st Session, H. Rept. 68-909. Washington, DC: Government Printing Office, 1924.
_____. _____. _____. _____. *To Authorize Mothers of Deceased War Veterans Buried in Europe to Visit the Graves.* Hearings held February 19, 1924. 68th Congress, 1st Session, 1924. Washington, DC: Government Printing Office, 1924.
_____. _____. _____. _____. *To Authorize Mothers of Deceased War Veterans in Europe to Visit the Graves.* Hearings held December 17, 1929. 71st Congress, 2nd Session, 1930. Washington, DC: Government Printing Office, 1930.
_____. _____. _____. _____. *Enabling Mothers and Unmarried Widows of Deceased Soldiers, Sailors, and Marines to Visit European Cemeteries.* 70th Congress, 1st Session, H. Rept. 70-543. Washington, DC: Government Printing Office, 1928.
_____. _____. Senate. Committee on Military Affairs. *To Authorize Mothers and Unmarried Widows of Deceased World War Veterans Buried in Europe to Visit the Graves.* Hearings held May 14, 1928. 70th Congress, 2nd Session, 1928. Washington, DC: Government Printing Office, 1928.
_____. War Department. *Annual Report.* Washington, DC: Government Printing Office, 1918–1933.
_____. _____. *Pilgrimage Regulations.* Washington, DC: Government Printing Office, 1930.
_____. _____. Historical Branch, War Plans Division. *Catalogue of Official A.E.F. Photographs Taken by the Signal Corps, U.S.A.* War Department Document no. 903. Washington, DC: Government Printing Office, 1919.
Venzon, Anne Cipriano, ed. *The United States in the First World War: An Encyclopedia.* New York: Garland, 1995.
Von Blon, Philip, and Marquis James. "The A.E.F. Comes Home." *American Legion Magazine* 3 (December 1927): 28–40.

Ware, Fabian. *The Immortal Heritage*. Cambridge: Cambridge University Press, 1937.
Warner, Philip. *World War One: A Narrative*. London: Cassell, 1995.
Wilson, Louis C. "The War Mother Goes 'Over There.'" *Quartermaster Review* (May–June 1930): 21–25.
Winter, Jay. *Sites of Memory, Sites of Mourning: The Great War in European Cultural History*. Cambridge: Cambridge University Press, 1995.
Wittig, Raymond, Mrs. C. Vincent Hall, and Ed Chenette. *Our Gold Star Mothers Brave and True*. Milwaukee: Kilbourn and Navratil, 1928.
Yockelson, Mitchell. "They Answered the Call: Military Service in the United States Army during World War I, 1917–1919." *Prologue* 30 (fall 1998): 228–34.

Correspondence

Ed Bliss, Durand, Illinois, letters dated May 18, 2000, and December 3, 2001.
Anne Kilmer, email to the author, July 31, 1999.
Bill Luke, Jr., email to the author, October 1999.
Elnora Davis McLendon, Arlington, Virginia, letters to the author June 8, 1999, and June 26, 2000.
Ann Wolf, Washington, DC, telephone interview, June 21 and 22, 2002.
Mrs. Brooks Wooten, Shellman, Georgia, letter to the author, November 6, 1999.
Mitch Yockelson, Washington, DC, letter to the author December 15, 1998.

Interviews

Most of these interviews were conducted during the production of the documentary *Gold Star Mothers: Pilgrimage of Remembrance*.
Bliss, Fred, and Ed Bliss. Durand, Illinois, May 11, 2002.
Budreau, Lisa. Nashville, Tennessee, June 2002.
Coffman, Edward S. Lexington, Kentucky, July 23, 2001.
Davis, Theresa. Knoxville, Tennessee, June 24, 2001.
Fletcher, Marvin. Athens, Ohio, July 24, 2001.
Lancy, Winifred. Knoxville, Tennessee, June 24, 2001.
May, Valerie. Knoxville, Tennessee, June 24, 2001.
Piehler, G. Kurt. Knoxville, Tennessee, June 24, 2001.
Plant, Rebecca Jo. Nashville, Tennessee. March 18, 2002.
Potter, Connie. Washington, DC, December 9, 1999.
Prince, William S. Bend, Oregon, December 18, 1999.
Ransby, Barbara. Chicago, Illinois, March 27, 2003.
Stevens, Jane Alden. Cincinnati, Ohio, March 27, 2002.
Walden, Iris. Knoxville, Tennessee, June 24, 2001.
Wheeler, Mary. Knoxville, Tennessee, June 24, 2001.
Yockelson, Mitch. College Park, Maryland, December 10, 1999.

In addition to these published sources, the chief source of information on the pilgrimages resides in the collection of the National Archives. Two groups of records from the Army's Quartermaster Corps are of essential in researching the pilgrimages. Record Group 92 holds the Quartermaster Corps' papers on the pilgrimages. The other set of records are the Corps' Cemeterial Burial Files kept on soldiers who died in the service. These files contain not only information on the service member's death and burial but also all correspondence of his mother's or widow's pilgrimage over a decade later.

Index

African-American Pilgrims *see* Pilgrimages, segregation
Aisne-Marne American Cemetery 42, 45, 177
Akerson, George 120
Akin, Helen 171
Allen, Henry 71
America, S.S. 161–67
America in Battle 184
American Armies and Battlefields of Europe 48
American Battle Monuments Commission 6, 9, 42–44, 48, 205
American Express Travel Department 115–16
American Farmer, S.S. 131
American Gold Star Mothers, Inc. 7, 14, 16
American Legion 57, 78, 173; *see also* Second A.E.F.
American Legion Auxiliary 121
American Legion Monthly 75, 175
American Merchant, S.S. 118, 128–30, 135
American Red Cross 56–57, 61, 65, 75–76, 78, 107
Anderson, Charles P. 164
Anderson, Sally Ann 133
Andrews, A. Piatt 69
Arc de Triomphe 20, 125
Arlington National Cemetery 41
Asheville, North Carolina 62, 133
Australian War Graves Pilgrimage 7
Ayres, W. A. 105–6

Bach, Mrs. J. S. 54
Baker, Josephine 128

Baltimore, Maryland 103–4
Bankhead, Tallulah 128
Barber, Will 133–34
Barrymore, John 147
Barrymore, Lionel 147
Bartlett, George G. 125
Bates, Harriet 8, 109
Battlefield Tourism: Pilgrimage and Commemoration of the Great War in Britain, Australia, and Canada, 1919–1939 81, 181
Bayley, Mrs. Hamilton 57
Beautiful Bicycle restaurant 154
Bechet, Sidney 128
Beery, Wallace 147
Belleau Wood 33, 45
Bellevue Hotel 151
Bend, Oregon 187
Bennettsville, South Carolina 125
Bentley, Mrs. Frederic 43
Bicknell, Ernest P. 61
Bingham, Hiram 62
Black, Loring 72
Blaine, John 186
Blake, Eubie 128
Bleckley, Erwin 6, 8, 31–32, 47, 105–7
Bleckley, Margaret Alice 105–7
Bloom, Sol 63
Blue Star Flags 14
Boechat, John A. 80
Boechat, M. F. 80
Bonus Army 139–41
Bony, France 37, 39, 47–48
Boston Post 55
Boylan, John 124
Brent, Bishop Charles Henry 38

Brick Top (Ada Smith) 127–35
Bridgeport, Connecticut 71
British Legion 67, 81, 174
Brooklyn, New York 88
Brookwood American Cemetery 42, 45, 130, 137, 187
Brown, Al "Panama" 127
Brown, Don 183
Buckley, Mrs. G. A. 131
Buffalo, New York 23, 80
Buford, Edward, Jr. 89
Burling, George 160
Burling, Mathilda "Mother" 10, 53, 60, 160
Bush, Eva 137
Butler, Samuel 49
Butler, Thomas 56, 65

Cable, Lynne Payne 180, 195
Calhoun County, Illinois 102
Camp Logan, Texas 141–42
Camp Upton, New York 142
Campbell, Hattie 134
Cantigny, France 47
Canty, Tom 120
Carlock, Floyd D. 192
Carpenter, Estella Ann 39–40
Carpenter, Jay 40
Carrington, Zelina 137
Cavell, Edith 6
Cemeteries 41–49; *see also* individual cemetery names
Cerreta, Canio 71
The Challenge of the Dead 36–37
Chalon-sur-Marne 150
Chapman, Paul W. 124, 131
Chateau-Thierry 88
Cheatham, B. F. 69, 106, 124–25, 127
Cherbourg Harbor, France 19, 23, 77, 96, 125, 155
Chicago 12, 13
Chicago Historical Society 13
Chicago Inn 126
Chicago Tribune, Paris Edition 126, 132–34, 137, 162–63, 170–71, 178, 183, 197, 203
Chocolate Dandies 128
Cincinnati, Ohio 32, 167
Clemer, Mary P. 150
Cleveland, Ohio 171
Cluny Museum 139, 154
Coffman, Edward 30–31, 33, 45, 49, 112, 117, 121, 143
Cohn, Eveline Alice 73

College Park, Maryland 83, 198
Columbus, Ohio 137, 173
Congress *see* Pilgrimages, legislation
Congressional Record 55
Conner, Joseph T. 109
Conney, Nathan A. 15
Coolidge, Calvin 18, 64
Coolidge, Hamilton 89
Copeland, Royal 58
Cotton, Fanny 127, 134
Cram & Ferguson 45
Crawford, Joan 147
Crespin, Felipa 167
Cret, Paul 44–45
Crosses (grave markers) 43–44, 64, 165
Crossman, Henrietta 195
Crusade and Pilgrimage 10, 30
Cuperly, France 74

Dalton, William F. 169, 174
Daughters of the American Confederacy 169
Davis, Benjamin O. 113, 121–22, 124–32, 135–38
Davis, Benjamin O., Jr. 138
Davis, Elnora 122
Davis, Mrs. J. L. 22
Davis, Theresa 16
Dawes, Charles Gates 187–89
Deegan, William F. 160
DeHavilland DH-4 31
Delcro, Mme. 76
Densleo, Dr. 127, 129
The Desert Song 23
DeWitt, J. L. 105, 111–13, 157, 178
Dickstein, Samuel 39, 52, 63, 124
Dingell, John 72
Diver, Dick 134–35, 181
Donovan, William J. 83
Doumerge, President 77
Downes, Sarah 133
Drayton, Teddy 127, 134
DuBois, Clara 74
DuBois, Norman 74
Duffy, Father Francis 29, 81–82
Duncan, James 76
Duncan, Tillie 174
Durand, Illinois 147, 158
Dusters, Quads, and Searchlights 10, 200
Dyson, Sarah 114, 180, 186

East Tennessee State University 180
Edge, Walter 125–27, 132, 168, 188–89
Edwards, Thelma "Tommie" 23

Eiffel Tower 20, 48, 153, 194
88th Division 170
Eisenhower, Dwight 140
Ellis, Richard T. 67, 97–98, 125, 127 130, 132
Elmore, Ohio 71
Ephraim, Robert 134
Esquire magazine 10, 197–99
Evans, Amy L. 159–60, 170–74, 177
Evans, Samuel 170
Everett, Washington 58

Father Duffy's Story 82
Fathers, on pilgrimages 71–72
Fere-en-Tardenois 47
Ferguson, Jimmy 134
5th Division 183
57th German Infantry 183
Fish, Hamilton 49, 59, 63–64
Fisher, Snow 127, 134
Fitzgerald, F. Scott 134–35, 181
Fitzpatrick, James M. 92
Fitzsimmons, William 34
Flamethrowers 28
Flanders Field American Cemetery 34, 42, 45, 186
Fletcher, Marvin 114
Ford, John 9, 195–97
42nd Division 107
Foster, Norman 195
Foster, R. L. 165–66
Four Tops 187
4th Infantry 32
Fox, Rose 109
French view of repatriation of war dead 37
Fried, George 161–62
Funeral home industry 40–41
Fussell, Paul 28, 101

Gallieni, General 150
Galloway, Mrs. Michael 174
Garbo, Greta 147
Garrett, David 59
Gee, James 90
George Washington, S.S. 77, 105, 191, 194
Germantown, Pennsylvania 182
Gessler, Otto von 172–73, 181
Gibson, William R. 66–68, 97
Ginsburgh, Robert 113–14
Goettler, Herman 31–32
"Gold Star Mother" article 197–99
Gold Star Mother's Day 10

Gold Star Mothers of Illinois 10, 102, 181, 184, 196–97
Gold Star Mothers: Pilgrimage of Remembrance 10, 16, 22, 28, 36, 49, 160, 200
Gold Star pilgrimages *see* Pilgrimages
Gold Star symbol and flag 5–6, 12–14
Gold Stars and Purple Hearts 180, 195
Gourard, Henry 125–26
Government Printing Office 48
Graham, Stephen 36–37
Grappelli, Stephane 128
Grand Hotel 147
Grave markers 43–44, 64, 165
Graves Registration Service 34–35, 41, 43, 75–76, 84, 95–101
The Great War and Modern Memory 28, 101
Griffin, Bennett 155
Grossman, Bernie 14
Grove City, Ohio 173

H.R. (House Bill) 4109 52
H.R. (House Bill) 5494 56
Haas, Mrs. Charles 59, 61
Haas, Lottie 74
Hanes, Dorris 162–63
Hanses, John 144
Harris, John 105
Haug, Henrietta 10, 102, 190–91
Haug, Oscar 6, 10, 35–36, 102
"The Heavens Are a Mother's Service Flag" 15
Heifitz, Jascha 128
Hein, Louis 32
Herrick, Myron 77
Hill, Blanche 166
Hillsdale, New York 39
Hindenburg, Paul von 27
Hindenburg Line 48
Hitler, Adolf 156, 204
Hoboken Harbor, New Jersey 19, 34, 160
Hoier, Thomas 14
Holley, Katherine Bell 130
Hoover, Herbert 69, 73, 120, 205
Hoover, Lou Henry 7
Hopkins, Virginia Bateman 186–87
Hopper, Hedda 196
Horne, Lena 128
Hotel D'Ieana 150, 181
Hotel McAlpin 194
Hotel Splendide 134
House Committee on Appropriations 66
House Committee on Military Affairs 57
Howe, George 47

Hughes, A. D. 102
Hurley, Patrick 121, 123, 140
Hyde, Emma 148

Illinois National Guard 141
"I'm Just Wild about Harry" 128
In Loco Parentis 66, 102, 108
Ingels, Dr. 162
Interstate Commerce Commission 68
Irving, Minna 92
Issoudun, France 87
"It's All in the Game" 187

Jacobson, Mrs. A. O. 109
Johnson and Johnson Co. 84
Joos, Agnes 22, 184

Kahn, Florence 70
Kane, Thomas 32
Kay, Mabel 58
Kell, Colonel 172–73
Kelly, Mary 163
Kennedy, Caroline 38, 86
Kennedy, Emilie 182–83
Kennedy, John A. 182–83
Kennedy, John, Jr. 38, 86
Kilmer, Aline 82
Kilmer, Annie Kilburn 84–86
Kilmer, Christopher 84
Kilmer, F. B. 85
Kilmer, Joyce 5, 6, 17, 24, 47, 75, 81–86, 88
Kilmer, Kenton 84
Kimbro, Louise 130
King George V of England 6, 79
Kingsbury, Elizabeth 109
Knights of Columbus 78

Lafayette Escadrille 62, 65, 153–54
La Guardia, Fiorello 6, 17, 51–53, 64–65, 72
Lambezellec Cemetery 34
Lancy, Winifred 36
Leaves from my Life 84
Leviathan, S.S. 155
Lewis, Elsie L. 73
Lindbergh, Charles 46
Lloyd, David 81, 181, 185
Lodi, California 115
Lost Battalion 31, 47
Louvre 153
Lowden, Frank 145
Lowrey, Vance 127
Lyons, Ida 178

MacArthur, Douglas 139–40

Mann, Mary A. 191–94
Mann, Willard 191, 193–94
Manson, Mrs. Gilbert 39
March, Peyton 91–92
Marks, Annie 169
Mattern, James 155
May, Valerie 15, 200–1
McCrae, John 46
McGough, Darle 107
McKee, Joseph 123, 160
McLendon, Elnora Davis 122
McReynolds, John 192
McSwain, John J. 54, 104–5
Mein Kampf 204
Memories of My Son, Sergeant Joyce Kilmer 85
Meuse-Argonne American Cemetery 21, 32, 34, 42, 46–47, 99, 105–6, 139, 141–45, 151–52, 178, 205
Mike, Kate 24
Military Order of the World War 164
Miller, Dellah Mae 115
Miller, Earl 31–32, 181
Miller, Sophia 32, 181–82
Moore, A. M. 148–49
Moore, Fred 124
Moran, Charles W. 107
Moran, Grace 107–8, 115
Moran, Lula 108
Moran, Roy 107
Morgan, Willis 126
Moroney, William J. 23
Morris, Illinois 184
Morse, Theodore 15
Moseley, Mrs. A. F. 146, 156
Moseley, Lily 146, 156
Muller, Louise *see* Ziegler, Louise
Murphy, Joseph 80–81
Murphy, Maurice 196
Mussolini, Benito 79

NAACP 18, 117, 123
Napoleon's Tomb 20, 133, 194
Nathan, Casper 15
The Nation 119
National Archives 69, 83, 98
National Association for the Advancement of Colored People 18, 117, 123
National Equal Rights League 120
Neal, Robert J. 192
Nelson, Marjorie 192
New York Times 38, 92, 126, 137, 162, 171–72, 204
Newton, Isaac 125

Newton, Laura 125
91st Division 45
95th Aero Squadron 29, 87, 89
Nixon, Marian 195
Nock, Ethel 57, 59, 64–65, 76–77, 93–94
Noll, John J. 175–76
Norris, Alexander 6, 31, 99
Norris, Anna 98–99, 175
Norton, Mary 59
Notre Dame Cathedral 153
Nouvel Hotel 109

O'Connell, David 72, 124
O'Daniel, John W. 113
Oestreich, William 71
Oise-Aisne American Cemetery 42, 47, 84, 130
110th Infantry 90
127th Infantry 32, 99
128th Infantry 184
132nd Infantry 143
166th Infantry 107
Operation Gold Star 10, 200–1
O'Ryan, John 37
Osmond, Donny 188
Ourcq River 47

"Pagan Love Song" 23
Paquet, Leo 113
Paris Edition, Chicago Tribune 126, 132–34, 137, 162–63, 170–71, 178, 183, 197, 203
Parker, Emma J. 138
Parker, Herbert 127
Party A (1930) 7, 94, 159–77; (1931) 8; (1932) 9; (1933) 9
Party B (1930) 7, 71, 188
Party C (1930) 105
Party D (1930) 191–94; (1931) 182–83
Party E (1931) 8, 132–35, 183; (1932) 9, 139–58; (1933) 9
Party H (1930) 7
Party K (1931) 8, 135–37
Party L (1930) 8, 124–30
Party O (1931) 106
Party Q (1930) 8, 130–32; (1931) 9, 181
Party T (1930) 8
Passports 101
Patient, Fannie B. 184
Patient, James 184
Patton, George 140
Payne, Janet 46, 114, 186
Pennington, Edward 31–32, 45
Pennington, Mary Jane 176–77

Penry, Elizabeth 103
Pershing, John 5, 20, 29–30, 43, 126, 132, 168
Piehler, Kurt 13, 40–41, 44, 60, 96
Pierce, Charles C. 34
Pilgrimage film 9, 195–97
Pilgrimage law 65–66; as amended 69–72
Pilgrimages: constitutionality 62–63; correspondence 98–101; diversions 23, 147; do-it-yourself 75–94, 145–46; eligibility 59–61, 69–72, 173–74, 181–82; finances 63–68; at the grave 151–52, 170, 174–77, 184, 190, 192–94; health 108–10, 175–76; legislation 17, 50–74; logistics 19, 95–101, 202–3; opposition 58–59, 73–74; as peace mission 72–73; prior pilgrimages 103–6; at sea 129, 135–36, 148–49, 155, 161–66; segregation 18, 116–38; statistics 11
Plant, Rebecca Jo 22, 60, 141
Platt, Anna 24, 175
Plattsburgh Academy 86
Ploisy Cemetery 34
Pope, Francis 113
Porter, Cole 128
Potter, Connie 97
President Harding, S.S. 103, 106, 148–49
President Roosevelt, S.S. 182
Preston, William 91
Prince, William Stevens 10, 28, 30, 64, 187
Public Law 70–952 65–66
Public Law 71–155 69
Public Law 71–227 69

Quartermaster Corps, U.S. Army 9, 18, 68–71, 95–115
Quentin Roosevelt: A Sketch with Letters 88–93
Quiesser, Robert L. 5, 14

Railroad travel 68
Ramsey, Margaret 179
Ransby, Barbara 121, 135
Raymond, Illinois 32
Red Cloud, Nebraska 159, 163, 170
Red Cross 56–57, 61, 65, 75–76, 78, 107
Reid, Howell L. 103–4
Reid, Nina 103–5, 115
Reinhardt, Django 128
Repatriation of bodies 33–41
Republic, S.S. 105
Restaurant Laurent 20, 176, 180
Return of the dead 33–41
Reynolds, Mary 175

Robinson, Mrs. E.H.I. 110
Robinson, Grace 162–63, 166
Rochelle, Illinois 39
Rock, William 76–77
Rock, Mr. and Mrs. William D. 76–77
Rockford Morning Star 139
Rockwell, Loula 62
Rogers, J.A. 127
Romagne-sous-Montfaucon 46–47
Roosevelt, Archibald 87
Roosevelt, Edith 6, 17, 86–87, 92
Roosevelt, Ethel 87
Roosevelt, Franklin D. 9, 10
Roosevelt, Kermit 87
Roosevelt, Quentin 5, 17, 29, 38, 69, 74, 81, 86–94, 172
Roosevelt, Theodore 6, 29, 38, 86–87, 90–92
Roosevelt, Theodore, Jr. 6, 94
Root, Waverley 133–34
"Rouge Bouquet" 82–83
Rulon, Blanche 67, 176

Sagamore Hill 87, 90
St. Mihiel American Cemetery 34, 42, 48, 122–23, 181
St. Quentin 47
Salvation Army 78
San Antonio, Texas 57
San Francisco, California 58
Savannah, Georgia 121
Schmitt, Katherine 173–74
Sealey, Marion 132
Second A.E.F. 6, 70, 78–81
Sehrt, Della 146
Sehrt, Sophia 146
Senate Committee on Military Affairs 57
77th Division 31
Shannon, R. E. 156
Shaw, Anna Howard 5, 12
Shellman, Georgia 181
Shuffle Along 128
Sissle, Noble 8, 127–28, 130–31, 134–35
Sladen, Fred 104
Slagle, Alfred 179
Slagle, Margaret 179
Smith, Ada Brick Top 127–35
Smith Centre, Kansas 109
Somme American Cemetery 21, 42, 47–48, 80, 184, 192–94
South, Eddie 128
South Fergus Falls, Minnesota 109
Specht, Paul L. 15
Spence, Mrs. Thomas G. 61

Spencer, Maurice W. 120
"The Star of Gold" 92
Stars of David markers 43–44
Stevens, Laura 7, 30, 187
Stevens, Percy 5, 30, 45, 67
Stevenson, Philip 10, 197–99
Stokes, Patrick 82
Streiber, Elizabeth 183
Streiber, William 183
Summerall, Charles P. 160–61
Sunnit, John 73
Suresnes American Cemetery 34, 48, 77, 170–71
Sutherland, Nebraska 160
Sweet, Emma Kessler 58

Tampa (ship) 61
Taylor, Edmond L. 172
Tender Is the Night 134–35, 181
"There's a Service Flag Flying at Our House" 14
Thiacourt Cemetery 76
3rd Division 32
32nd Division 32
33rd Division 141–45
37th Division 45
Thomas, Norman 127
Thompson, Hugh 164–66
Thompson, John Means 163–66
Thompson, Phil 90
Thompson, Sarah 24, 163–66, 168–69, 177
Thoren, Edward 146, 158
338th Infantry 170
370th Infantry 125
Throckmorton, John 164–66
Throckmorton, Minnie 24, 163–66, 177
Throckmorton, Wesley 164
Ticonderoga (ship) 29
"To My Boy Who Lies in France" 85
Toul, France 87
Trask, David F. 27
"Trees" 24, 47, 82
Trowbridge, Eva 19–20, 189–90
Tuscania (ship) 29–30, 45, 187
Tuskegee Airmen 138
27th Division 29, 37, 80, 82, 188
Tyrone, Pennsylvania 186

U-Boats 29–30
United States Army Quartermaster Corps 9, 18, 68–71, 95–115
United States Army War College 124
United States Lines 6, 18, 77–78, 95, 97
United States Marine Corps 33

University of Chicago 134
University of Illinois at Chicago 121, 135

Vedder, Effie 52–53
Vimy Ridge, France 10, 194
Von Gessler, Otto 172–73, 181
Von Hindenburg, Paul 27

Wagner, Robert 62–63, 73
Wainwright, J. Mayhew 54
Walker, Jimmy 147
Walsh, David 55
Walsh, Jennie 38, 53–54
Walter, Tony 185
War Department 18, 34–35, 55, 66
The War to End All Wars 143
Weeks, John 55
Weitmuller, Herman 182–83
West Mansfield, Ohio 107
Wevill, Duane 148
Wheeler, Mary 201
"When a Blue Star Turns to Gold" 15
White, Clarence Cameron 127, 132

WILL-TV 10, 200
Williams, A. E. 97
Williams, Don 180
Williams, Florence 175
Williams County Farmer Press 189
Williston, North Dakota 189
Wilson, Woodrow 5, 12, 26–27, 36–37
Wood, Alison Davis 201
Wooding, Sam 127
Woolley, J. Edward 15
Wooten, Brooks 181
The World Tomorrow 118
World War I casualties 32–33

Yockelson, Mitch 185

Ziegler, Fred M. 6, 24, 139, 141–45, 151–52
Ziegler, Gladys 146
Ziegler, Grace 9, 24, 139–58
Ziegler, Louise 9, 24, 139–58
Ziegler, Martin 146
Ziegler, Tressa 141–45

www.ingramcontent.com/pod-product-compliance
Ingram Content Group UK Ltd.
Pitfield, Milton Keynes, MK11 3LW, UK
UKHW041945140426
5217IPUK00014B/671